Linguistic Structures

Harry van der Hulst

University of Connecticut

KENDALL/HUNT PUBLISHING COMPANY
4050 Westmark Drive   Dubuque, Iowa 52002

Copyright © 2008 by Harry van der Hulst

ISBN 978-0-7575-4987-8

Printed in the United States of America
10 9 8 7 6 5 4 3 2 1

Contents

Preface

This is a somewhat unusual introduction to linguistics. My goal has been to explain the business of linguistics to readers with no prior background in this discipline. There are, of course, numerous books that claim to do the same thing using all sorts of different approaches, but this attempt is different from all of these taken together. Firstly, in Part I, I deal with many different aspects of the discipline that one will usually not find in other introductory texts. This part includes short essays that answer everything you always wanted to know about language (but were afraid to ask). It also provides a short and accessible overview of the history of linguistics and the various subfields of this discipline. Part I clears to way to the remainder of this book, which deals with more formal issues. However, to appreciate these issues it is often helpful to show novices the landscape of linguistics so that it is clear why it is important to focus on formal issues and to show that, while doing so, we are not downplaying or forgetting all sorts of other pursuits that are equally important for gaining understanding of such a multi-facetted phenomenon as human language.

Parts II and III contained a detailed introduction to the components of grammar, i.e., the system of units and rules that together make up the core of what language is and how it works. My mode of explanation is different from what we usually find in other introductions in that, firstly, I treat the various components of grammar as an integrated whole and, secondly, I emphasize the analogous design of all these components. This means that I iron away unnecessary differences (which otherwise would merely reflect that these components have their own traditionally grown notations and terminology) while trying to understand the true differences in relation to what these components do in the grammar. Thus, rather than dragging the reader into a battery of traditional assumptions and confusing (alleged) differences between the grammatical components, I depart from "first principles" and derive necessary distinctions and terminology from these. Meanwhile, I do explain and use the traditional terms so that the reader can easily connect what he learns here to what he learns in other places.

There is repetition in discussing the material in that basic distinctions that I introduce first are repeated and then built upon, adding more detail, in subsequent chapters. Finally, I have tried to discuss the material in a manner that is accessible to students who are trained in other disciplines, drawing attention to comparable goals and formalisms in different disciplines.

The reality is that not all linguists agree on some very important issues, and this is reflected in the fact that there exists a broad variety of different approaches that are divided on broad issues and points of detail. Where what I perceive as deep controversies exist between different approaches to language I will explain what the fundamental differences are without getting lost in detailed comparisons.

In Part IV I give an overview of the structure of sign languages.

Needless to say, the present introduction to the grammatical components cannot replace books that focus on individual components. It would, in fact, be disappointing if this were the case. The journey does not stop here. It my hope, however, that this book lays a foundation for further explorations into the components of grammar which no doubt would reveal many controversies and uncertainties but not, I would hope, significant divergence from the basic story with which the reader will become familiar in this book.

Finally, I wish to thank Diane Lillo-Martin for helpful comments on chapter 15.

Chapter 1

Everything You Always Wanted To Know About Linguistics
(But Were Afraid To Ask)

Introduction

In this chapter I provide a series of mini essays that explain a variety of general notions that are part of the enterprise called **linguistics** or that concern questions about the phenomenon of language. See this as the chapter in which you find 'everything you always wanted to know about languages and linguistics (but were afraid to ask)'. I have tried to order the pieces of information in a logical order so that they form a continuing story, but most of them stand on their own.

What is Linguistics?

When people ask me what I do, I sometimes say: "Well, the University of Connecticut gives me a modest salary to talk about anything I want; I give this money to my wife, and for the rest I fold the laundry and drive my children to and from various activities." Usually, however, I say that I'm a **linguist**. Unlike the first answer, this more serious answer almost always calls for additional explanation. Is it the case that I speak a lot of languages? No, that is not the case. (I only speak Dutch, English, some German, and even less French). However, it is true that this *is* one meaning of the word *linguist*. In the most general sense, the word refers to a person, *-ist*, who has something to do with *lingua*, which is a Latin word meaning "tongue" or "speech." However, the vague phrase *has something to do with* has been narrowed down in more than one way:

Linguist. A person who is skilled in many languages. Polyglot.

A different meaning (one that applies to me better) is:

Linguist. A specialist in linguistics.

Then we look up *linguistics* and find something like:

Linguistics. The science of language.

(In fact, linguistics is *what linguists do*. One thing they do is analyze words such as linguistics into their meaningful parts: *lingu(a) – ist – ics*.)

A linguist, like me and other people in linguistics or language departments, studies **language**, that is, *the phenomenon of language*. The primary goal is *not* to learn a specific language in order to communicate with foreigners (although that's always useful), but rather to understand how languages *in general* work.

There is nothing odd about studying the phenomenon of language, given that language is an extremely central aspect of human societies (sociology) and of people's mental life (psychology). It is actually quite strange that people come to college with an understanding of subjects like physics, chemistry, mathematics, and so on, whereas something as important as *language* has never been introduced to them as a fascinating subject for study. I think we should do something about that and introduce linguistics as a subject in primary, middle and high school.

Linguists are interested in describing and analyzing languages, hoping, like any scientist, to come up with *general laws* that will allow us to understand how languages work. There are innumerable ways in which languages can be studied. A linguist can ask how children acquire language, or how languages change over time, why there are so many different languages (about 7,000 in use today), when humans first started using language, and so on. You can also ask more technical questions relating to how people articulate the **speech sounds** that make up words, how people combine words into sentences, or how languages come to have new words. These are all valid and sensible questions, and none of them has simple answers. Accordingly, there are many subdisciplines within the field of linguistics, each addressing specific questions regarding the phenomenon of language. In fact, I don't think anyone could come up with any question regarding language that has not inspired a subdiscipline of linguistics.

Because language is so central, many different disciplines have dealings with it (psychology, anthropology etc.) and this leads to many areas where linguistics overlaps with these disciplines.

Linguistics is Science

Like all scientists, linguists are simply curious people who have decided to focus their curiosity on language. It stands to reason that in order to study any aspect of language, you must first be occupied with *collecting, describing and analyzing the facts*. This work can be very time consuming; some people devote their entire career (and life) to describing everything there is to know about a single language. This kind of work often first results in **descriptions** (of languages) in terms of what we call **the grammar of a language**. We have all seen or studied grammar books, usually with the aim of learning a particular language that we like or need to speak for some purpose. Some grammar books have been written with the specific goal of making learning as easy as possible (**teaching grammars**), whereas other, more scientific grammars aim at describing the language in technical terms, going for complete coverage (which, by the way, has not been reached for any language); these grammars we call **reference grammars**. These latter works are foremost meant for other linguists who study an aspect of language (let us say, how words are strung together to form sentences, a subsystem of the grammar called **syntax**), hoping to discover general syntactic laws, that is, statements that are valid for the structure of sentences in all languages. A linguist trying to find law-like generalizations that might be valid for all languages needs to consider the facts from as many languages as he can lay his hands on. One could not possibly study each and every language firsthand, so, even though a linguist will always rely on what he knows of his native language, or language(s) that he has studied firsthand, he will also use the grammar books that his colleagues have written.

The laws that a linguist tries to formulate make up a **theory** for that aspect of the grammar to which the laws apply (e.g., sentence structure, or the sounds of language). Any such theory is technically a **hypothesis** (or collection of hypotheses) because it remains to be seen whether the proposed laws really hold for *all* languages. Hence proposed laws need to be tested using other languages than those that led to the laws in the fist place. Because in principle it is impossible to study all languages (there are too many and only a fraction have been described in detail), any system of proposed laws, applicable to an open or infinite domain, will always have the status of a hypothesis. This is nothing to be depressed about. This is the normal situation in sciences that study an aspect of the observable world that we live in. Such sciences are called **empirical** sciences (in addition to linguistics, for example, physics, biology, psychology).

What keeps linguists busy, then, is formulating, testing, and refining their hypothetical laws by taking into consideration as many languages as possible from all corners of the planet. This type of inquiry constantly calls for the description and analysis of languages that have not yet been described, as well as further studies of languages, like English and many others, that have already received a lot of attention. Linguistics, like other empirical sciences, involves an endless upward spiral in which we go back and forth between data gathering, description, theory formation, and testing. (This collection of activities follows what is often called *the scientific method*.) In this process, linguists gain more and more knowledge of individual language and also of Language-with-a-capital-L, which is a system of hypothetical laws that is claimed to be valid for all human languages:

Study of languages   ↔   Formulation of a Theory of Language

Linguists who try to formulate general laws of language (also known as **language universals**) are often called **theoretical linguists**, whereas those who focus more on the precise description of languages are called **descriptive linguists**. So-called descriptive linguistics is also sometimes referred to as **field linguistics** because the description of a language that is not the linguist's own can lead him into the field, i.e., into remote areas of our planet where people speak languages that have not or that have hardly been described. However, the "field" can also be a linguist's backyard when he aims at making a detailed description of his own language.

In practice, as we have just seen, theorizing and description go hand in hand, and most linguists are involved in both kinds of activities. (At the same time it is an undeniable fact that, due to people's characters, some scientists are more inclined to theory whereas others like to get their hands dirty.)

All this cannot be taken to mean that there is only one theory in linguistics that all linguists work on to refine. There are, again as in all other healthy sciences, different theories whose proponents disagree on what counts as a proper explanation, or even on what it is exactly that needs to be explained.

Functions of Language

There are, indeed, different views on what language *is* and what it *is for*. With respect to the second question one can take a *psychological* point of view and see language as a mental trait of individuals, a **cognitive faculty** or **module**, i.e., a unit of (subconscious) knowledge of words and sentence structure. In line with this psychological view, it seems reasonable to say that the functions of language are:

(a) to organize thought;

(b) to express emotions (irrespective of whether such expression is meant to be informative to others, e.g., cursing, frustration, anger, happiness);

(c) the effect that its sounds may have in rhyming, chanting, or singing, which leads to the esthetic function of language as in poetry and other forms of verbal art.

Another perspective on what language is can be called *sociological*. Now we say that language is the property of a speech community, a system shared by a number of individuals who tacitly have agreed on sticking to a set of grammatical norms. The sociological perspective invites a focus on different functions of language, namely:

(a) the need or possibility to *externalize* thoughts, i.e. **communicate** (correct or incorrect) information in order to influence the behavior of others. Related to communicating information is **preserving information**. This role of language was much enhanced after the invention of writing. Libraries, courthouses, and government buildings are all packed with information that has been recorded (in books, documents, and databases) for the purpose of being available at later times. Today, the Internet is *the* ultimate language-based databank of human knowledge.

(b) the need to establish a **social bonds** and **social structure.** One might say that language is the glue that holds people together. Closely related to this function is the function of **identification with the group**. Being group animals, people like to emphasize their membership to specific groups. Language serves an important function in this respect. Consider the fact that people have an extremely good ear for detecting accents. Why would this be? Some say that it serves the purpose of being able to detect whether another human being belongs to your group. It is certainly true that we "place" people in boxes on the basis of fine details of their speech. We identify varieties of speech with social class and cultural groups.

(c) the use of language in religious/magical rituals, but also in other non-secular rituals or ceremonies. In this latter case the function of language is to **control** or even **constitute reality**.

Summarizing, we have identified the following functions of language:

Functions of language

Psychological perspective:

a. Organizing thought
b. Expression of emotions
c. Esthetic expression

Sociological perspective:

a. Information exchange and preservation
b. Social bonding and group identification
c. Control and constitution of reality

Some linguists such as **Robin Dunbar** like to stress the social bonding function, which he compares to "grooming," which enables Chimpanzees to maintain a **social hierarchy and interaction**. According to Dunbar people spend most of their talking time on **gossip,** and he in fact explains the emergence of human language from the need to establish and maintain social relationships among humans who also always lived in groups. Other linguists, like **Noam Chomsky**, focus on the function of language in facilitating thought. (This viewpoint, by the way, does not necessarily mean that thought is controlled by language, a view that I will discuss later on.) However, most ordinary people when asked what the function of language is will say "communication," by which they usually mean information exchange. There is no denying that language does have that function, but it is good to bear in mind that language may have other functions, even more than the ones that I have mentioned here. In the end we will not understand the phenomenon of language in all its complexity by exclusively focusing on one perspective and one function. However, it is common and in fact productive for scientists to focus on one particular one perspective of the phenomenon that they investigate just to make some headway.

The two perspectives (psychological and sociological), as well as the six functions, cannot always be strictly separated. Take for example the expressive and esthetic functions, both called psychological. People write poetry or even novels to both express emotions and enjoy the esthetic side of language. In addition, they enter into a communicative relation with an audience or readership, which makes their activity sociological.

The psychological perspective stands a greater chance of characterizing language, or rather its grammar, as a fairly homogeneous system because we focus, in principle, on a mental system of an individual (although even within the individual there is variability relating to matters of style), whereas the sociological perspective cannot get around the fact that within speech communities there is lots of variation.

Behavior and Knowledge

Language is often seen as a form of human **behavior**. Language is something that people "do" with some specific intention in mind such as exchanging information, making someone else do or think something, expressing feelings, or breaking the unbearable silence in a waiting room or elevator. There is nothing wrong with seeing language as a form of behavior, but there is more to it, as, in fact, we have already learned. Language is also system of words and rules, a grammar that underlies the behavior.

Important linguists have invented separate terms for linguistic behavior and linguistic system. **Ferdinand de Saussure** spoke of *parole* and *langue*, whereas Noam Chomsky uses the terms *performance* and *competence*.

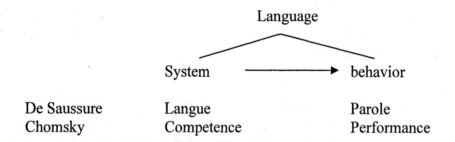

	Language	
	System ⟶ behavior	
De Saussure	Langue	Parole
Chomsky	Competence	Performance

In making this distinction Chomsky has taken a definite psychological viewpoint, seeing competence as the knowledge of language as located in the mind of an individual. De Saussure took a more sociological perspective and regarded language as a system that was shared by the members of a speech community, although he was certainly aware of the necessity for each individual to know this system. (It is, in fact, unclear where such a shared system would exist other than in the minds of people.)

The psychological perspective is also called the **cognitive approach** toward human behavior. Not everyone has recognized the dual nature of language. People like B.F. Skinner promoted a strict focus and limitation to the behavioral side, an approach (now outdated) that is called **behaviorism**. In fact, it might be argued that Chomsky, whose starting point was to criticize behaviorism. has swung in the other direction by disregarding the behavioral side of language and focusing on language as a mental system; this explains his emphasis on the function of language to facilitate thought and his lack of interest in the communicative function of language.

More recently, Chomsky has replaced his usage of the terms competence and performance with the terms **Internal language (I-language)** and **External language (E-language)**. Another, perhaps more obvious, term for I-language is simply **grammar**, i.e., a **mental grammar**. Often people equate grammar with sentence structure (syntax), but linguists use this term to cover all units and rules of language, including those that govern the speech side of language, the structure of words, etc. Henceforth I will use terms like I-language or mental grammar instead of system or competence, and I will continue using the term language when the distinction between internal and external aspect of language is not in focus.

It is important to bear in mind that the language knowledge that people have is hidden in the subconscious areas of the mind. People are not aware of the units and rules that they put to use when they organize their thoughts or communicate these thoughts to others.

Looking back at the preceding diagram I need to add one further remark. There is an arrow going from *system* to *behavior*, but this should not be taken to mean that linguistic behavior is exclusively determined by or solely dependent on the knowledge of language (however we flesh out this notion, something we will do later on in this book). Actual linguistic behavior is also dependent on other factors such as what people happen to be thinking about, whether they are tired, drunk, angry, or have a cold, even whether they are speaking to someone who constantly interrupts them. Fine details of linguistic performance are also dependent on purely physical factors such as the size or gender of the speaker.

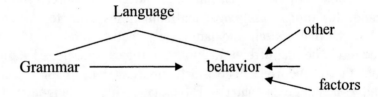

In short, there are a multitude of physical, psychological, cultural and interpersonal factors that put their stamp on language behavior. This does not mean that we always know where to draw the line between aspects of language behavior that do and those that do not depend on I-language.

Language Processing

There's something else we need to say about the arrow. In order to display actual linguistic behavior, even only that part of it that depends on I-language, we need to relate the abstract knowledge of language to processes in the mind that transform thought processes and emotions into utterances up to the motor commands to muscles that drive the speech organs. The process is called *language production* and it mediates between (preverbal) thoughts, knowledge of language, and linguistic behavior. And then we also have processing in the opposite direction. After all, linguistic behavior is not only produced (by the speaker) but also perceived (by the hearer). There is a way from the ear to the brain that can be seen as the arrow going in the other direction:

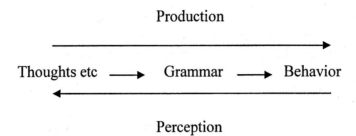

Both language production and language perception are referred to as **language processing**. Language processing happens in real time as people produce and perceive language.

When we describe the mental grammar we try to abstract away language processing issues, although it is by no means always easy to maintain that separation clearly or to know in all cases where to draw the line. In any event, mental grammar (or I-language) is meant to be neutral with respect to the production and perception of language.

Speech and Sign

Outside the context of weddings, funerals, and graduation ceremonies, the term **speech** simply stands for *spoken language*, and sometimes even for *language*. However, it is important to see that speech and language (whether internal or external) are different things. One might be inclined, at this point, to regard speech as E-language (performance, parole), but that is incorrect. The most important reason for rejecting the equation of speech and E-language is that the E-language side of language does not have to be spoken. Firstly, one might say that language can also be written, but in that case it is fair to say that written language is essentially a visual (or tactile in the case of **Braille**) manifestation of speech. A more principled reason for rejecting the equation is that we also have **sign languages**, i.e., the languages that are used in communities formed by deaf people and the hearing people that they communicate with. We will learn below and more extensively in chapter 19 of this book that sign languages are in all respects equal to spoken languages and thus not just primitive systems of pantomimic gestures. In short, languages can be spoken out load, spoken in the form of silent speech, or signed. E-language, then, can be spoken or signed.

I wish to add that we should not come away from this section thinking that either speech or sign is a matter of E-language alone. If a language is spoken, the mental grammar that underlies it must comprise knowledge of the speech forms that the language has, whereas knowledge of the way signs are formed must be part of the I-language of a sign language.

How Many Languages?

All *6.4 billion* people that live on this planet today speak (or sign) *at least* one language, unless certain mental or anatomical defects stand in the way. But, as everyone knows, they do not all speak the same language. An extreme but not necessarily incorrect claim would be that each person speaks a different language, which would bring the total number of languages to 6.4 billion. The fact is that no two individuals ever speak exactly the same way. There always seem to be little differences in pronunciation, differences in the words that two people know, or even differences in sentence structure. (One might think that the strictly individual nature of language is witnessed by the possibility of voice identification systems, but the differences that are measured by such systems regard properties of speech behavior that are not dependent on the grammar but instead on physical properties of the speaker.)

We refer to the individual language of one person as an **idiolect**. We do not, of course, think of languages as idiolects. Rather we think of languages as the collection of all idiolects that are mutually understandable (mutually intelligible). Before we make that more precise, let us consider another extreme view.

On the other extreme end, an extraterrestrial being studying earthlings might come up with the claim that there is just one language, **Human Language**, arguing that all the differences among human languages are superficial when you compare them to the languages of other animal species. From this viewpoint humans would be just one of the primitive creatures that inhabit planet Earth, and the differences that exist within species, in appearance and behavior, would be hardly noticeable to our extraterrestrial friend.

In between these two extremes lay the estimates that linguists make, namely that the number of languages in the world ranges from 5,000 to 7,000 (and beyond). There are various reasons for why it is difficult if not impossible to come up with a precise number even after the two extreme views (6.4 billion, 1) have been rejected.

For starters, it might be that new research in certain remote or less accessible areas may lead to the discovery of a couple of more languages (especially in South America, Central Africa, Asia, and New Guinea). And even in areas that are less remote it may also happen that linguistic surveys lead to the conclusion that there are more languages than believed today. Secondly, there is a lot of confusion about the names of languages in areas that have not been surveyed too well. For example, in certain areas one name that is now in use may cover more than one language, or vice versa, meaning two names may be in use for the same language. But all these factors are not going to influence the numbers very much.

A more important reason for the different counts is that it is not so easy to define the concept of a language as opposed to a **dialect**. Both a language and a dialect can be understood as a collection of **mutually intelligible** idiolects. The truth is that there is no way of making a linguistic distinction between the notion of dialect and the notion of language. Often people say that dialects are varieties of one language that are restricted to a certain geographical area of a country, but the same *can* be true of languages. Different language labels are used (or proposed) for speech varieties *within* one country wherever different groups of speakers want to form an independent country (sometimes because in the past they used to form an independent country or at least a political unit of some sort). Often such communities form a separate ethnic and cultural group. For example, in a certain region of Spain people speak *Catalan*, which is generally regarded as a separate language by the Catalans, while others might call it a dialect of Spanish. In the Netherlands one province uses *Frisian*, which is regarded as a separate language by its speakers but not necessarily by all Dutch people. In both cases some inhabitants of these areas feel that they should form a separate nation. I suggest that the use of the term language here is appropriate when the speech varieties are mutually unintelligible to speakers of Spanish or Dutch, respectively. (The truth is that Frisian is almost as distinct from Dutch as English is.)

However, the use of the term language for different speech varieties within one country, even when the varieties are associated with strong political and cultural separation, is not always justifiable in this way. Consider the example of former Yugoslavia, which was split up into countries like Serbia and Croatia (among others). Serbs and Croats now say they speak different languages (*Serbian* and *Croatian*), whereas earlier they spoke varieties of one language (*Serbo-Croatian*). In this case ethnic and religious factors play a big role. Religious factors alone can also impose a language division on speech varieties that, again, really do not differ that much (e.g., *Hindi* and *Urdu* in India). In both examples, the different varieties are mutually intelligible and should thus be called dialects, as I will argue below.

The situation in which what are really dialects are called languages also extends to cases in which mutually intelligible varieties are used in different countries. Examples are *Swedish* and *Norwegian*, languages that are perfectly mutually comprehensible. Not too long ago both countries formed one nation.

In many cases, then, it would seem that the term language is used where we should really speak of different dialects because the varieties are mutually intelligible.

There are also cases in which one speaks of one language for several speech varieties within a nation that are mutually unintelligible and thus really should be called different languages. A striking case involves *Chinese*, which according to popular believe covers a great many dialects, whereas most linguists regard Chinese as a collection of languages. In this case, since all these languages share the same writing system that is based on the meaning rather than on the sound form of words, the idea of all of them being one language is very strong.

We can conclude that the use of terms like language and dialect is often based on and defended on **non-linguistic criteria**. To clarify matters I propose that we regard any collection of mutually intelligible idiolects as a language. We then recognize that all the idiolects that form a language in this sense can cluster into regional, sociological, ethnic, or cultural varieties (or combinations of these) that have certain distinctive combinations of properties (without being unintelligible to other such clusters), and we could refer to these clusters as dialects; thus, we can have regional dialects, dialects that are associated with a city (Boston dialect) or a part of a city, where part can be defined in terms of neighborhood and/or social class.

If we would apply the above definitions of language and dialect, we would still encounter many unclear cases:

	Called	*Should be called*
Catalan	dialect (of Spanish)	separate language
Frisian	dialect (of Dutch)	separate language
Swedish/Norwegian	different languages	(dialects of) one language
Hindi/Urdu	different languages	(dialects) of one language
Chinese	one language	group of languages

The question arises, of course, how we define *mutual intelligibility*. In practice, it may often seem that many other speech varieties than your own are pretty inaccessible, but often this is merely due to rather shallow differences in pronunciation and the use of words that you don't know. It seems somewhat counterintuitive to regard such varieties as different languages if the only differences between them lie in the superficial pronunciation of words and choice of words. So let's say that mutual intelligibility becomes the decisive factor after allowing for a few days of "getting used to." (I suspect dialects that are hard to understand could actually be pronounced more understandably, since for whatever speech variety we deal with there is always a *careful version* of it that would be pretty accessible to all speakers of the language that the dialect falls under.)

Another question is whether different dialects of one language involve different I-languages, or rather just one I-language with some internal options. This is a hard question to answer. No one really knows.

The nice aspect of taking (un)intelligibility as a criterion for separating significant linguistic units like languages is that it seems to parallel to how we define *biological species*—in terms of the possibility for interbreeding. In this analogy we can call dialects *sub*species. Indeed, the ability to mate successfully (i.e., such that viable offspring are produced) seems intuitively close to the ability to communicate successfully. In the former case the interaction leads to transfer of **genes** (units of genetic information) while in the latter case it leads to the transfer of thoughts, in this context often called **memes** (units of cultural information).

Leaving (or rather ignoring) the definitional issue of language and dialect, let us see how many languages linguists say there are. According to the **Ethnologue** (1996), we have, at this moment in time 6,703 languages spoken in 228 countries. According to the **Wycliff** organization (an organization that translates the Bible into as many languages as possible), we have 6,858 languages. Several other numbers are around, ranging from 5,000 to 10,000. A project called **Linguasphere** recognizes around 10,000 languages, for example.

Dialects are Not Inferior

In most nations one of the dialects has come to prevail as the norm, the standard version of the language. This is the variety that is used in the media, education, law, and government. The official spelling system is also based on this variety. The reason why this particular variety has acquired a special status usually correlates with its speakers and region playing (or in the past having played) a dominant political, economic, and cultural role.

Some people will speak the norm variety as their daily variety (if they grew up in the general area where this variety originates), while others will speak a different dialect at home and among friends while perhaps using the norm at work, in school, etc. Such people, then, speak more than one dialect.

Among ordinary people there is a strong inclination to regard the standard variety as superior to the (other) dialects, but this is misguided in the sense that, from a linguistic point of view, all varieties of whatever language are considered fundamentally equal. Each speech variety, no matter who speaks it, is the outer form of an internal language that is complete, self-contained, and systematic. I cannot prove this statement, but the point is that the burden of proof lies with those who believe otherwise. Disqualifications of other speech varieties than ones own (everyone speaks with an accent, except me) are unfounded and usually based on discriminatory views of other people and, in addition, on a prescriptive attitude toward language.

Prescription Versus Description

In college or earlier we learn that there is such a thing as grammar, which is understood as a system of prescriptive rules (such as: *don't end a sentence with a preposition*) that you need to apply to pass a writing course. We also find a prescriptive attitude in popular works on language, newspaper columns, etc., in which writers proclaim to know how language should properly be used, what must be avoided, etc. Such claims are usually made in the context of complaints about the misuse of language, especially among the younger generations.

But linguists are not interested at all in *prescriptive* grammar rules, in spelling or even in matters of style. If you want to use the word *like* in every sentence (four times), that is just fine with us (although we reserve the right not to read you or listen to you). What we do is different. We study how you use the word like, we ask whether there are hidden rules in how this little word is used and what it means. And then we write articles about what we find, which are published in respectable journals. In other words, we don't tell you how to use your language; we assume that you know what you are doing and we carefully describe your linguistic behavior, which we subsequently analyze, trying to establish which rules guide that behavior. This is what it means to say that linguistics is an *empirical science*. This means that linguists form hypotheses about how language works on the basis of observation, *description*, and analysis. What would you say to a field biologist who jumps out of his hiding place to tell the Bonobos that he is observing that they ought to eat with a fork and a knife or that they should adopt certain positions in sexual intercourse? In linguistics the descriptive approach started in the nineteenth century.

Earlier I made a (somewhat artificial) distinction between theoretical and descriptive linguistics, but we should realize that *all* of linguistics, whether theoretical or descriptive, rejects the prescriptive attitude. A theory is, after all, really a description constructed in the form of a system of testable hypothetical laws (a theory) from which the observed phenomena can de derived.

All spontaneous language behavior is based on mental grammars, and it is simply preposterous to think that the relevant rules have been invented and dictated by human beings who somehow had the wisdom to know or decide that certain ways of speaking are better than others. The rules are present in the minds of speakers and comprise what we have called knowledge of language, or I-language. This knowledge is hidden or tacit, and even though we use it we do have direct access to it. (If we had, linguistics would be easy.)

Styles of Speech

I have said that each person has his own idiolect. In fact even *within* individuals there seem to be a number of idiolects, which are often called **styles of speech** or **registers**, each of them being appropriate for certain circumstances. One style of speech is, for example, the earlier mentioned careful pronunciation style (used in official settings, or settings where the speaker is reprimanded to speak clearly). Registers from a continuum from highly informal to formal, or whatever labels one wishes to attach to the large, perhaps infinite variety of communicative circumstances. As in the case of different dialects used by one person, it remains to be seen to what extent this stylistic intrapersonal variation is due to the presence of more than one I-language or rather to differences resulting from how a single I-language is put to use in actual performance (E-language). Perhaps both possibilities must be deemed possible.

Language Families

Earlier I mentioned an analogy between languages and species. There are more such analogies. For example, the diversification of languages shares all kinds of properties with the diversification of the species. Languages can be grouped in classes (called *language families*) just like species. When looking at the languages in the world, it is quite easy to see that some are more alike than others and the reason for why this is so is that languages, like species, evolve (change over time) and sometime split into two different languages because a certain speech community for whatever reasons decided to split up and move in different regions. Because languages evolve in erratic and unpredictable ways (see below), the speech of the two resulting communities will come to differ over time and in due course will differ so much that mutual intelligibility has disappeared. We now have two languages, a form of speciation. Biologists decide that two groups of animals cease to form one species if members of these groups no longer can interbreed.

Linguists have managed to group the languages of the world into several sometimes very large families, but it has so far not been possible to show that all languages stem from the same source. It is nonetheless likely that this is so, and one day it may be possible to show this.

Language Change

What does it mean to say that language change is erratic and unpredictable? First let us be clear about the fact that language change "happens." It is not planned or controlled by the government and it cannot be stopped. Language change finds its roots in variability. Different variants of the same language compete for survival, and when one variety starts to predominate the others will perish.

How do varieties come about? One view is that new variations may come about as random mutations, and that may be true to some extent. When children learn language they may get things slightly differently for no particular reason at all. Or, in some cases they might simplify something (see *foots* instead of *feet*). But the source of variation can also lie with adult speakers, who also have a tendency to simplify things, for example, the way they articulate words; they cut corners and say "he's" instead of "he is." That creates variation between those two ways of saying the same thing. There are millions of ways to simplify utterances, and different speakers of different languages do different things at different times. And then it remains to be seen whether an innovation will prevail. That usually depends on who is doing the innovating. If that is a person with prestige the variant may spread within his community; from there it may spread to other speech communities or stay confined to a smaller group.

Now you might think that languages will get simpler and simpler over time, but that is not the case. A simplification here may create a complication somewhere else in the language. *He's* is shorter, simpler to articulate, but perhaps more difficult to understand. Language is not just production, it is also perception. Hence, not only will *the need to be clear* control excessive simplification urges, sometimes a new variant actively serves **ease of perception** rather than **ease of production**, and so the endless process continues.

Some people speak of **languages evolution**, meaning that they *change*, a term that is mostly used. It is certainly true that language change is a form of evolution. One can say that any system or phenomenon that is subject to change over time evolves. However, two things must be borne in mind when using the term evolution for language change. Firstly, whereas in the evolution of biological species we do see a continuum of complexity going from single celled organisms and multi-celled organisms, all languages, as mentioned earlier, are of equal complexity. Secondly, when talking about language evolution many people specifically refer to the way that human language came about as a property of our species; we'll talk about that below.

Why Are There So Many Languages?

To answer this question we have to return to the sociological function of **social bonding** and **group identity**. The instinct to form, belong to, and defend a tribe is deeply rooted in humans, as it is in many other animal species. For humans, language is probably the most important way of expressing group identity. Having your own language is therefore essential, and we are prepared to go to war over it and kill or die for it. Touching or threatening someone's language is equal to invading and questioning his or her cultural identity. The function of bonding and identity provides the glue that connects the members of a group together, but is also keeps non-group individuals out. Both aspects motivate the multitude of languages. Having your own language gives you your own identity and it shuts individuals outside your group out.

If this is so, language *must* be much more than just a means of **exchanging packages of (true or false) information**, which I mentioned as another function of language. If its only function were to exchange information one would expect that all people would use the same language. But even though the world is, in some sense, getting smaller (due to human mobility and the Internet), it is simply a fact that the global village houses many different social and cultural groups of people that dislike each other enough to do terrible things to each other. Therefore, we still have many different languages that arose in days when the world was nowhere near to being a global village.

Multilingualism

A person growing up in a rural area might easily come to think that it is normal to speak just one language. If this area happens to be in the U.S., and the person in question later on moves to another place, like New York City, or happens to travel a lot to other countries he might come to think that this single language is sufficient even when you have to communicate with people who grew up speaking different languages. After all, most people speak some English. But it is not normal to grow up and old with just a single language (although it is OK).

With 7,000 languages and around 228 nations, it must be the case that there are many nations within which we find the use of several or many different languages. And within such nations we find many people who grow up with and in their daily lives use more than one language, sometimes three or four of them. This phenomenon, referred to earlier, is called *multilingualism*. People who speak more than one language are multilingual, and countries where more than one language is in use can be called multilingual.

In this case it seems reasonable to believe that each language comes with its own mental grammar. It is more than likely that a multilingual person's choice of using a given language is dependent on the circumstances within which the person is communicating. He might use one language at home and another one at work. In some sense, the different languages (although each can, in principle, be used in different styles) function themselves as the style registers of a person who speaks just one language. One language may be only used in formal circumstances, while another only in informal circumstances.

How Many Languages Still?

Many of the 7,000 languages are spoken by small groups of people, and most of these languages are endangered in that they will probably go extinct very soon. Some experts say that by the end of the 21st century the number of 7,000 may have gone down by as much as 75%.

Why do languages die? The simple explanation is that there are other languages (sometimes called *killer languages*) that claim more and more speakers by controlling the media and education in a country or even on a more global scale. English is, as we all know, one of the most strongly expanding languages due in no small amount to globalization of American culture, economy, and, of late, the Internet and the World Wide Web. Globalization of cultures entails globalization of the languages of those cultures. English is not the only global language. In certain regions of the world we find other widespread languages such as Spanish, Arabic, Russian, Indonesian, and so on. With the rise of China as a world power it is likely that in the future Mandarin Chinese will become a world language.

In the past, presumably, many languages have gone extinct due to a variety of factors: populations may be been absorbed into other populations (voluntarily or by force), populations may have died out because of starvation or genocide. However, as long as the hunter-and-gatherer lifestyle was dominant, populations would continue to split up and go different ways, and over time their speech would come to differ because, as we have learned, languages are always subject to processes of change. This, as we have seen, leads to the emergence of language families, sets of language that go back to a common ancestor. But in this day and age such diversification (speciation) no longer happens. Thus, today languages go, but none come (with a few exceptions).

It is true that the many "Englishes" that are used in different parts of the world differ in all sorts of ways, like dialects do, but global communication networks assure that the varieties stay mutually intelligible. Thus it is unlikely that from those Englishes a new language family will arise.

Languages that are on the verge of extinction or sometimes beyond that point (when there is no living native speaker) can sometimes be revitalized. This happens when the groups whose ancestors spoke these languages have a strong sense of cultural identity. Often revitalized languages are merely used on special occasions, but in some cases they have made a complete comeback. This happened to Hebrew, a language that had no native speakers for centuries until it was introduced as the official language of the state of Israel, a development that was preceded by a considerable period, going back to the 19th century, of raising interest for the language among the Jews that lived in various places in the world and who took an interest in reclaiming their original homeland.

Languages form a central part of cultures and a primary factor in people sense of group (and thus cultural) identity. Thus when languages die, people feel that their culture dies. This is not only because of the role of language as a marker of cultural identity. Languages are the medium of information transmission from one generation to the next and even though one might think that the relevant information can also be passed on using some other languages (after all, translation is possible), languages differ considerably in their vocabularies which mirror the word view and environment of its speakers in specific ways that are felt to get lost in translation.

The topic of extinction brings us to another analogue between linguistics and biology. The diversity of animal species is also under severe threat, and it is noteworthy that the parts of the world with the greatest variety of species are also the parts with the greatest linguistic variety. This suggests that the loss of diversity in both domains may be due to the same kinds of factors.

The Emergence of Language

Most people that I come across are interested in the question of where language comes from in the first place. How and when and where and why did it emerge in our species? This issue is also often referred to as *language evolution*, but that term, as mentioned, is also used for the fact that languages change over time. This being so, it is nonetheless the case that for most people the expression *the evolution of language* refers to the emergence of language in (or with) our species.

There is no direct information on the way that language developed from scratch. Writing was not invented for the first time until 5,000 to 6,000 years ago, and the languages that were written then did not look primitive. They could have been spoken today. So since then, and presumably before that time, languages changed and split up, but all those changes, as argued earlier, did not alter the fundamental nature of languages. It just produced variations on one general theme.

It is likely that all languages that are now or were once spoken outside Africa have develop from one ancestor language that was spoken by the people who left Africa some 100,000 years ago and then populated the whole planet, but it is very difficult, some say impossible, to prove this point because the languages have had so much time to change and become different in all sorts of ways.

This alleged ancestor language would then have to be seen as one of the languages that were spoken in Africa to begin, with and this raises the question whether all languages (including the African ones) go back to one language that a certain group of humans started to use. When was this? How did they get to that point? Does human language go back further to a different and perhaps simpler kind of communication system, perhaps comparable to communication systems that we find in other animal species? We know that many species use specific *calls* (isolated screams) that are triggered by the presence of specific predators. Different predators trigger different calls. Are those calls the first words, and did the ability to combine words into sentences arise only in our species (perhaps as the result of a mutation that caused the necessary cognitive means to combine things into bigger wholes)?

A persistent idea is that a call-like one-word stage transitioned into the sentence stage via a two-word stage that only allowed simpler combinations of two "words." It has been claimed that nonhuman nonhumanprimates can actually grasp such a two-word type of system (if you teach it to them), but cannot go beyond it. Humans can. Was this the result of a genetic mutation that caused a specifically human capacity for elaborate combinations of words, or was the elaboration of a hypothetical (or rather speculative) two-word language to language as we know it a cultural development that could happen because there was a more general genetic change toward a mind that allowed complex reasoning, invention, and culture.

And why did language emerge? Was it to facilitate thinking (Chomsky), was it to support social organization (Dunbar), or was it to allow more sophisticated communities (most others)?

These are all interesting ideas, and in recent times we have witnessed a large-scale interdisciplinary effort to piece together a story that is compatible with evidence from different sectors. The most direct evidence (data from these or other evolutionary stages) is lacking because the spoken word does not fossilize.

All Language Are Equal

I made reference to the fact that the oldest written languages do not appear to be primitive in any way. This brings me to a more general point (also made in reference to dialects). All languages that we have records of (living or dead) are equal in complexity. There is no reason that any linguist can think of for regarding some languages as more structured, more logical, easier to learn, etc., than others. Yet it is a persistent belief that such differences do exist. In all cases people transfer their (misguided and discriminatory) opinions about cultures (in which the languages are used) or people (who use the languages) to the languages themselves.

Language, Culture, and Thought

Although I just denied it, it was long believed that there is an intimate connection between the structure of a language and the organization of a culture within which the language is used. However, it must be said that no linguist or anthropologist has ever demonstrated that such a connection truly exists, except in the sense that cultural practices (which may in part depend on the environment, climate, geography, etc.), rituals, and belief systems usually are reflected in the vocabulary of languages. In turn, it has been claimed that the vocabulary of a language, or even its grammatical organization, may determine or constrain the way that its speakers "see" the world. This latter idea is sometimes called the **Sapir-Whorf Hypothesis**, because it was articulated, in a variety of ways, by **Edward Sapir** and **Benjamin Lee Whorf**.

Yes, languages and cultures are correlated, either as parallel systems or as one being part of the other. This connection, as mentioned before, leaves traces in the vocabularies of languages, not in the size of vocabularies, but in the things that languages have words for. However, the nature of technology of a culture is not correlated with the complexity of the grammar or they way in which languages differ.

Languages differ and there is no external reason for the possible properties that grammars have. In addition, languages also share characteristics (universals), and for most linguists the main task of linguistics is to establish these universals and the extent of variation. This important goal leaves no room for unsubstantiated ideas about "superior" or "primitive" languages.

The Broader Concept of Communication

I will now briefly discuss the relationship between terms like *language* and *communication*. These terms are used in many different ways, sometimes to mean the same things, sometimes in such a manner that communication is a broader concept than language.

Consider **art**, which according to many is a form of communication. The painter wishes to express an idea of some kind and, in some sense, he enters into a (one-way) dialogue with people who look at his artwork. But we don't have to be artists in order to communicate through colors and shapes: clothing, hairstyle, all sorts of visual body ornaments including make-up, tattoos, piercing, as well as scents (both natural and artificial) are forms of communication. All these things can be very informative with respect to who or what we are. Consciously or subconsciously, we are sending a message by all the **artifacts** that we use to give a personal touch to our appearance. Thus, each artifact potentially is a **sign** in the sense that it stands for something (an idea, a mood, a rank, a group identity, and so on). The total set of artifacts makes up an important part of what we call **culture**. Hence, culture is, in part, a system of communication. (It is more than that. It is also our behavioral patterns, belief systems, utilitarian artifacts, etc.)

So this is how communication works: the one who wishes to transfer information produces or somehow displays something that the intended receiver can perceive, for example a sound or a gesture. Sender and receiver are in agreement on the fact that a certain sound or gesture *stands for* a certain piece of information. In the picture below, the little blob inside the head of A is information and the text balloon is the sound that is produced by the sender in an attempt to transfer information to B. The receiver is capable of hearing the sound and knows that the producer intends to transfer the blob by producing this particular sound.

(A) Production

(B) Perception

Thus, what we see in A is a capability to *produce* signs (in this case spoken words) and in B a capability to *perceive* and interpret such signs.

Since we are dealing with signs, it follows that the act of production and perception involves much more than the abilities to produce and perceive forms (sequences of speech sounds or manual gestures). Those abilities are certainly necessary, but they merely constitute peripheral systems. It is crucial that the participants in the communicative events know the **meaning** that is carried by the (perceivable) **form** of the sign.

In this book I limit the focus to communicative interactions between ordinary individuals in ordinary life that do not depend on artifacts (including hairstyles). This leaves us with our **body** and our **voice**. I limit our attention further to things that we do more or less **intentionally**. Blushing, sweating, or gasping for breath are non-intentional (or **symptomatic**) indicators of how we feel. These symptoms can provide information to others who notice them. However, I will exclude them from the domain of communication because it is not the case that people in those circumstances **intend** to send a message to others.

When thinking about human communication (now excluding art, etc.), the first thing that comes to mind is the voice, or spoken language. However, we have learned that we must also include sign(ed) languages. I propose that we restrict the use of the term language to human communication that is based on speech or sign.

Definition: Language is a system of communication that uses auditory or visual (combinations of) signs to intentionally externalize information (thoughts, feelings, etc.) so that it becomes available for others to decode and activate internally the same or highly comparable information. Language also plays a central role in organizing the internal information (i.e., thought) before it is externalized.

Note how I have made both communicating and facilitating thoughts part of my definition of human language.

We often use the term **verbal communication** for language in this sense. (The Latin word for *word* is *verbum*, a word that is also used as a technical grammatical term for specific kinds of words, namely *verb*.)

Verbal and Non-verbal Communication

Most of the time when humans communicate verbally (using speech), they also use their **hands, face,** and even their whole **body** to bring across messages. According to some, we extract more information from the hands, face, and body than from the spoken language when we communicate with another person.

The part of communication that makes use of hands, face, and body is often called **nonverbal communication**. The study of nonverbal communication is a field in its own right that has revealed that especially hand and face activity is highly structured (and coordinated with speech). We call the hand or face movements that accompany our speech *gesturing*. We call hand or face gestures that can *replace* words or phrases (thumbs up, the finger, OK, etc.) *emblems*. Finally, we call the posture of our whole body *body language*.

Rightly or wrongly, most linguists construct their theories of the mental grammar only with reference to verbal communication, but some propose mental grammars that integrate verbal and nonverbal communication. Observe that some words are pretty useless unless they are accompanied by a pointing gesture of some sort. I'm thinking of words like *this, that, here, there*, etc., called **deictic words**.

Sign Languages

Let me briefly place sign languages in this context. Sign languages do not use the voice, but we now know that these languages are based on words and sentences. Thus, they are in that sense **verbal** languages.

For a long time people (including linguists) did not think that sign languages were equal to or the same kinds of communication systems as spoken languages. But they are. Unfortunately, there are many persistent myths about sign languages. Many people believe that all deaf people across the world use the same sign language. But there is no innate sign language. and there is no reason to suppose that all deaf people would spontaneously come up with the same system. Not all deaf people are taught the same system. Sign languages differ from community to community, and they are no more taught to deaf children than hearing parents teach language to their children. Like spoken languages, sign languages have not been invented by people; they have emerged, and we don't know when or how.

You might think that signers cannot use their hands and face to gesture or to make emblems because those body parts are already in use for the language itself. However, detailed study of actual sign utterance reveals that even in that channel, verbal language and non-verbal communicative acts can be intermixed.

We might finally ask whether sign languages are included in the estimates of how many languages there are. Asking this question implies that there is more than one sign language. We do find that signers living in the same country usually use the same language (although there can be different dialects). The Ethnologue now has information about more than 100 sign languages, but it is possible if not likely that there are more given that there are about 200 nations. Not much is known about the scope of the differences between different sign languages. Are they all mutually unintelligible? How different are they? In any event, deaf communities in different nations regard their own sign languages as autonomous languages and not as dialects of one world sign language. So perhaps there are indeed at least as many sign languages as there are nations.

It is interesting that a few sign languages have only come into existence very recently in cases where the right circumstances happen to occur. Thus, it does sometimes happen that new languages come about.

Natural and Artificial Languages

Languages, whether spoken or signed, were not invented; they emerged as a trait of our species, presumably because this trait had an adaptive value of some sort. Views on what this adaptive value was, if there was once a crucial one, depend on what people take to be the fundamental or first function of language.

There are languages that have been consciously constructed and those we call *artificial,* but there are many names for them (auxiliary, constructed, model, fictional, etc.). Since artificial has a somewhat negative connotation, I will call these languages *constructed.* Constructed languages have been designed for many different reasons, ranging from:

- Ideals of providing the human species with one common language (Esperanto)
- Bridging the communicative gap between deaf and hearing people, between people and other animal species, aliens or computers
- The desire to construct the perfect logical language
- Needing a language in works of fiction (Tolkien's many languages and Star Trek's Klingon)
- Hobby-ism (Some people build model ships; other build model languages.)

Natural languages are acquired by children and used within language communities, sometimes as the only language in that community. Constructed languages are used only on special occasions that are often devoted to promoting the language. A famous constructed language is **Esperanto**. In this case, interestingly, Esperanto has become the native language of those people who acquired it in childhood, being raised in Esperanto loving families who would use the language in the household (often next to another language or languages). It might be argued that the Esperanto of those people has transgressed the boundary between constructed and natural languages.

Human Language and Animal Communication Systems

By limiting ourselves to human languages we exclude systems that animals use for communication, leaving it open whether animals have communication systems that have words *and* sentences. Some say that animals are incapable of using such systems. This does not mean that the communication systems that nonhumannonhuman animals use cannot be sophisticated; they certainly can. The language of the bees is famous for its sophistication, and one of its famous investigators, **Karl von Frisch**, received the Nobel Prize for his important work.

Different species, so it seems, have their own communication systems, and all these systems differ in many ways. We are probably the only species that studies the communication systems of other species. However, it is important to bear in mind that while we can *study* them, we cannot really learn them or use them. It is therefore not surprising that nonhuman animal species cannot be taught to learn a human language. You may say that your dog can understand you, and that you know what he means when he barks, but I doubt that in these cases each of you completely masters the communicative means of the other.

Animal communication systems come in a wide variety and some can be said to have a small number of isolated word-like expressions (referred to earlier as *calls*). Other species (like song birds or whales) can make complex combinations of pitches, but it is uncertain or even unlikely that the individual notes or clusters of notes that occur in a broader pattern can be seen as pieces that are meaningful in their own right such that the song is a combination of these meanings and thus a complex message. It is more likely that the notes all together form a message, like the sounds of a word in human languages together form a message, being meaningless individually.

Semiotics

Even though linguistics focuses on human languages, there is a science that studies communication in the broadest sense, the science of semiotics (also sometimes called semiology), a social science that studies all communicative systems, in man and other animals, whether natural or artificial. This field is based on the pioneering work of **Charles Sanders Pierce** (1839-1914), an American philosopher, and the work of the Swiss linguist **Ferdinand de Saussure** (1857-1913), whose work was foundational for the idea of **structuralism** that deeply influenced fields such as linguistics and anthropology. The well-known Italian author **Umberto Eco** is a present-day semioticist.
The fundamental unit in semiotics is the notion of **sign** that I have already started using as a general term. Here I will define a sign as a **perceptible form** (a sound, a visual image,

an odor, and so on) **and** a **meaning**, i.e., whatever that form refers to or stands for. These two sides or dimensions of a sign are sometimes called *signifier* and *signified.*

While the use of the term *form* (for signifier) is not problematic, the use of the term *meaning* (for signified) can cause confusion because the signified can be something that one might be inclined to called meaningless. For example, a letter (say "k") is a form that stands for a sound. Together the graphic form and the sound constitute a sign that in this case belongs to a system of signs called a spelling or writing system.

There are many types of sign systems such as the system of traffic signs, Morse code, the system of emblems used in a culture, a system of smells (where different smells are meant to send different messages to the receiver), and, of course, human languages in which the signs are called words if the language is spoken and signs if the language is visual (i.e., a sign language). But, as mentioned, the English writing system is also a sign system in the sense that the graphic units (called **letters**) stand for the sounds that make up words.

A sign system can only exist by virtue of the fact that its users *know* the relationship between certain forms and certain meanings.

In some cases, as mentioned, we actually use the word *sign* for the signs of a particular sign system. So, don't confuse the general semiotic notion of sign that we talk about here with the specific use of this term in "traffic sign" or "sign language" (as used by Deaf communities). Apparently the term *sign* has a general use and more specific uses:

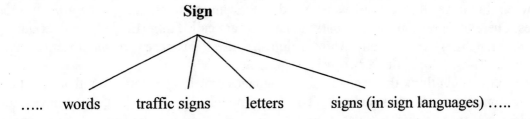

Hence, signs in spoken language are called words by linguists, but when we talk about sign languages we call the basic units signs. As linguists, we might just as well call them words.

I want to emphasize again that we also have a general and specific use of the term *meaning*. In a semiotic sense the side of a sign that is not the form (i.e., the signified) is often called the meaning of the sign. If the sign is a letter, the meaning is a sound, but if the sign is a word, the form is the sound and the meaning is called… well, the meaning. When we say that the graphic symbol "k" has a meaning we speak in a semiotic sense and we do not wish to say that it has the same kind of meaning that complete words have. To avoid all this confusion we might try to get used to referring to the meaning of a word as a **concept.**

Form	**Meaning**
Letter	sound
Word	concept

Any more or less coherent collection of signs forms a **sign system**. Clothing, tattoos, or body piercing can be studied as a sign system. As mentioned, many material (artifacts) and behavioral aspects of human culture can be studied as sign systems, and this is what makes semiotics such a broad field.

Signs (in whatever kind of system) can be classified in various types depending on the nature of the relationship between the form and the meaning:

- arbitrary signs (called **symbols**)
- motivated signs (called **icons**)
- deictic signs (called **indexes**)

In a motivated or iconic sign the form is (partly) motivated by the meaning. Most of the icons on your computer screen are indeed iconic because they visually mimic an aspect of their meaning so that you can reasonably guess (and more easily remember) what they stand for.

Here's an example from spoken language. If we would refer to a cat by using the word *meow* (as some languages do) that word would be an iconic sign. The word *cat*, on the other hand, is an arbitrary sign. There is nothing in the sound properties of the word *cat* that resembles or mimics properties of a cat. In many languages animal names are iconic.

Although all languages have iconic words (called **onomatopoeia**), most words in spoken human languages are arbitrary signs (hence symbols). In short, the relationship between the noise (the form of words) and the meaning is essentially *arbitrary* in most cases. There is no reason for why barking animals are called *dog* (English), *hond* (Dutch), *chien* (French), *gos* (Catalan), *koira* (Finnish), *asu* (Javanese), *beana* (Sami), *perro* (Spanish), *kutya* (Hungarian), *txakur* (Basque), etc.

You might think that signs in sign languages are always iconic, but that is just one of the common misunderstandings. It is true, though, that sign languages have more iconic words than spoken languages, and this is simply because the form of words in sign language is visual and many things in our world have a visual appearance that can thus be mimicked.

Deictic signs are special in that their meaning does not involve an autonomous referent. Indexes refer indirectly. The interpretation of an index is based on the interpretation of another sign. Words like *he* or *she* are indexes in that they refer to another word that does have a direct referent: *a man came in; he started screaming*. In this utterance *he* refers to *a man*. Words like *there* and *here* are indexes in that they only refer to something if they come along with a pointing gesture. In other words, they receive their interpretation via the interpretation of the pointing gesture.

Signs are thus packages of a form and a meaning. Besides a meaning and form, a sign will need a *combinatorial directive* if the sign system has a way of combining signs. This can be a directive about which other signs the sign combines with or where in the complex expression it must occur (first, last, etc.). In language, these directives are labels like *noun* and *verb*.

We can classify sign systems in terms of the perceptual channel (or the sense) that is involved:

- hearing (auditory)
- vision (visual)
- touch (tactile)
- smell (olfactory)
- taste (gustatory)

Human spoken verbal language is an auditory sign system. Human signed verbal language is a visual sign system. People who are deaf and blind sometimes use a tactile language. A famous person who communicated in this way with her governess, Annie Sullivan (who taught her the system), was **Helen Keller**.

Semiotics can be directed at humans' sign systems, in which case it is sometimes called **anthroposemiotics**. This includes language, gesture, and all other sign systems (such as drumming or whistle languages), but also, more broadly, all forms of art and culture. **Zoosemiotics** studies animal communication.

Concept and Referent

Words, as signs, have a meaning (a concept) in addition to their form. However, we also often say that words **refer to** (or **denote**) things or events in the surrounding reality. Is the referent of a word the same as its concept? And, if not, what exactly do we take to be the meaning in the sense of the signified side of words, the concept or the **referent**? This question could be the beginning of a beautiful debate among linguists and among philosophers. We will not go there. But I do suggest that we observe a clear distinction between a referent and a concept. Referents are things in the world; they are mind-external. Concepts are in the mind; they are mind-internal.

We can think of the triplet word form, concept and referent as two interlocking signs. The form and the concept form a sign, but in a way the concept and the referent also constitute the sign in as far as the concept can be said to stand for or refer to the referent; the problem is that it is unclear in what sense a concept can be said to be a form, since we can't perceive it. At best, we could say that the concept is a form because it is a set of neural (physical and thus in principle perceivable) connections in the brain. It is perhaps better to see the relationship between concepts and referents in a different way:

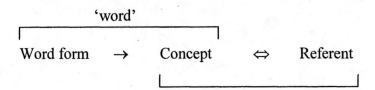

Where '→' can be read as 'stands for' and '⇔' as 'correlates with'

Referents, then, are not a part of words. In fact, words do not need to have referents at all, at least not in the sense of things or events that actually exist in the world as we know it. Think of the word *unicorn*. If, however, we acknowledge possible (imaginary) worlds we could say that even the word *unicorn* has a referent, namely in a world that happens to be not ours. However, now think of words like *and* and *or* or *the*. What do these words refer to? Things get more complicated here, although it is possible to maintain that even in these cases there are referents (see chapter 15).

The inclusion of possible worlds suggests that referents are not necessarily "out there," i.e., mind-external, but can be part of our mental life. In fact, it has been argued that even referents in the real world are really only known to us in terms of a mental perceptual representation, i.e. a percept that is created by our perceptual systems and our brain:

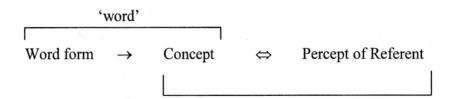

It is often speculated that only humans have the ability to use signs, that is, packages of form and meaning (and a category label if the signs can be combined). But this seems untrue if animals can have calls, which also strike one as packages of form and meaning. But what is the meaning of the form (of the call)? Is it a concept or a referent? Surely form, concept, and referent are all part of animal communication. If an animal can recognize a predator as belonging to a certain kind, it must have a concept of that animal species. However, it would seem that this concept is activated only in the presence of the actual predator. At the same time the referent (not the concept) triggers the call response. Finally, the percept of the call form triggers the same behavior as the percept of the predator. I believe that perceiving a call, as does perceiving the predator, may trigger both making the call and hiding in the appropriate way:

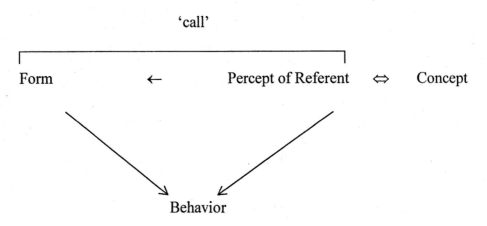

(Here all mono-directional arrows should be read as "activates")

We could say that the call forms a sign with the referent, while the concept (of the predator) is itself not part of any sign. The concept plays a role (as in humans) in identifying the referent, but it is not connected to the call form.

Nonhuman animal communication, in this view, would have all three aspects (form, concept, and referent), but, crucially, there would be no mental link between the concept and the form. If an animal emits a warning call it would do so because it perceives a referent and this perceptual experience, which presupposes that the animal can link the referent to a concept (which explains why it recognizes the referent as an instantiation of that concept or category), would then trigger the production of the call.

Another difference between human and nonhuman animals is that the production of the sign is mandatory and only possible if the referent presents itself to the call maker. Words in human languages are never mandatory. We can activate a concept in the absence or presence of a referent, but either way we do not have to then utter the relevant word. Also note that words can be used in the absence of (percepts of) referents. Concepts can trigger forms on their own. Using a word, or language in general, is not bound to the here and now.

A third difference is that both the perception of the call and of the predator trigger the automatic response of going in hiding. The perception of words in (human) language, however, does not necessarily entail a fixed response or any response at all.

Writing Systems

Many but by no means all languages have a writing system. Writing is non-essential to language and, in fact, a fairly recent invention. Writing systems consist of graphic units that represent either the form of words (individual sounds or sound combinations called syllables), or the concepts of words (or words' parts called morphemes). The former are called **phonographic** systems, the latter **logographic** systems. Phonographic systems that use letters (graphs for sounds) are called **alphabetic**, those that use graphs for syllables are called **syllabaries**.

Either way, the graphic units can be regarded as signs whose meaning is a certain property of words. Thus the letter "k" is a sign that has a certain graphic form and a meaning which is the sound /k/.

A signs, units of writing systems can be arbitrary or iconic. Logographs that are iconic are like little drawings of the (referent of the) concept. The iconicity of early logographic systems has usually faded away over time or become irrelevant. Phonographs could be called iconic if they try to represent the way in which a sound is articulation (for example the tongue and lip position).

Logograhic systems have sometimes developed into phonographic systems when the graphs gradually came to represent the sound of the word rather than its meaning, in which case it could be used for other words that contain similar sounds.

Human Language as a Creative System

It is commonly stated that on top of the differences between human language and communicative systems in the rest of the animal kingdom that were discussed earlier there is another important difference. Not only do human languages allow the combination of words into sentences, the combinatorial systems allow for an infinite array of sentences, given that any sentence can always be made longer. Later we will characterize the property of infinity in more precise terms. What matters now is that the possibility to create an infinite number of expressions with finite means (finite set of words, finite set of combination rules) is unique to human language. If we tie this trait with the above-mentioned trait that words are not tied to referents, but can be used in the absence of referents, we arrive at a system that is so creative that everything that can be imaged or thought can be expressed in language anywhere and at any time. Animal communication systems (while in some cases allowing an infinite number of expressions) lack this particular kind of creativity because of the fact that the number of expressions is both fixed and in any event tied to the immediate context, to the here and now.

Conclusions

In this chapter we have learned about a variety of distinctions, notions, terms, etc., that form an important part of the science called linguistics. Even though the primary purpose of this book is to discuss the more technical aspects of I-language, I felt that potential readers might be unable to digest the technical matters while wondering about these various aspects of language that frequently are on people's minds when they reflect on this wonderful human trait.

Chapter 2

The History of Linguistics

Introduction

In this chapter we will focus on the history of linguistics. Numerous articles and books have been written about this subject and it is therefore inevitable that the following is very sketchy. Nonetheless, I have tried to highlight important distinctions that will make it easier to understand our present activities.

The History of Linguistics

Judging from the earliest written texts that humankind has produced (some 5,000 years ago), we can say that linguistics, or at least reflection on language, is as old as religion and philosophy. We see attention to language and grammar in all the ancient cultures (e.g., of India, Greece, China, and the Middle East). Often such endeavors arose from the need to analyze sacred texts so that they could be understood properly and pronounced correctly long after they had been written down. This, over time, lead to descriptions of the languages of these cultures in the form of grammars. The more down to earth Greeks had different motives and were interested in describing their language so that foreigners could learn this noble language. Another kind of linguistic interest was triggered by curiosity about the origin of human language, or more often, by the question of which language was the oldest and most original language. **Plato** (427-347 BC), for example, already wrote about the origin of language in this sense. He was particularly interested in the origin of words, as well as the nature of the relationship between the form and meaning of words. We also find such interest in religious texts such as, for example, the Bible. In short, both religious and secular philosophical treatises on the subject of language are numerous. These various religious and non-religions incentives to think and write about language all became part of the linguistic tradition that modern linguistics is based on. However, as with many other aspects of Western thought, we must realize that these Western traditions have not profited from sophisticated traditions in all parts of the world. In some cases, as with China, there also was an early and rich linguistic tradition, which, however, was (and is) largely unknown outside China. Detailed and important work in India, dating just as far back as the Greek and Latin contributions, remained unnoticed in the west until the 19th century.

The western tradition in grammar writing is entirely based on the practices developed by the Greek and, after them, Latin scholars. A landmark is the grammar of Greek of the Dionysius Thrax, written around 100 BC. This work was translated into Latin and continued to be a model for grammar writing for a long time. Modern western terminology is largely based on the Latin tradition, which continued the Greek tradition. Arabic and Hebrew works (coming available due to the crusades) enters this western line of thought. First, throughout Europe, this traditional mixture continued to focus on the classical languages themselves which were widely used in religion, administration, law, education, and science. During the Renaissance, more attention arises for the vernacular languages of Europe (i.e. the languages spoken in the various countries and regions by ordinary people), and we see the emergence of grammars of the languages that were spoken throughout this continent.

As a result of the colonial enterprises of western states starting in the 16th century, and due to world explorers who perhaps had less commercial drives, gradually information started coming in about languages in other parts of the world, often in the form of word lists, brief notes and so on.

Beside grammar writing, mostly for practical, educational purposes, and some work that stemmed from a curiosity into languages as such, we see that the history of linguistics before the 19th century is dominated by speculative thinking and writing (often in the form of enormous multi-volume works) about the origin of language. Why, where, and how did language emerge, and what did the original language look like? In the absence of any empirical evidence about the existence or nature of language before the era of the written classical languages there was, of course, a lot of room for imaginative, and purely speculative stories, often interwoven with deep philosophical excursions about the nature or true meaning of words.

The earliest interest in the study of languages as such, involving comparing languages and even trying to develop general principles, can be seen in the 17th and 18th century, but linguistics as a science (in the modern sense) dates back to the late 18th and especially 19th century when important progress was made in showing that the languages that we know constitute families and subfamilies. Very important was the discovery of **Sir William Jones** (1746-1794) that Greek, Latin, and Sanskrit, and perhaps Gothic, Celtic, and old Persian are related languages, meaning that they all have derived from a common ancestor language, a **proto-language** that was later baptized Proto-Indo-European (PIE). After it had been noted that several languages displayed such striking resemblances that they probably had developed from a common ancestor language that was once spoken, linguists started reconstructing this ancestor language and thus, at the same time, tracing the changes that had taken place from this ancestor to the languages that were thought to have derived from it. Jones' insight was further developed by a group of Danish and largely German linguists in the 19th century. One of them, **August Schleicher** (1821-1868), being familiar with Darwin's *Origin of Species* (1859), compared language to an organism whose changes through time could be studied in truly scientific terms and along similar lines as the sciences of physics and (evolutionary) biology. Scholars believed that the historical development of languages was governed by rigid laws (comparable to physical laws), while at the same time seeing language as a living organism that developed and evolved over time like biological organisms.

Through comparison of the oldest (written) phases of languages that look similar, linguists tried to reconstruct the ancestor language; this was called comparative reconstruction. This method was, as said, first applied to languages in Europe, India, and the Middle East that were noted by Sir William Jones to form a language family. Subsequently, and throughout the 20th century as information on more and more languages became available, more and more language families were proposed. The reconstruction of proto-languages did not share the speculative aspects of thinking about the emergence of the first language, but it did not shed much light on this issue either. The reconstructive method has not been able to scientifically show that *all* human languages form one family and thus derive from one proto-language, although some scholars are more daring (some say reckless) in this respect than others.

With the discovery of the comparative method and the family relationships between languages, the attention of Western scholars almost exclusively focused on the study of language change and linguists developed many ideas about the reasons for and mechanism of change. Many of them mixed their work on the history of language with ideas characteristic of Romanticism, a cultural movement that involved the search for the authentic cultural roots of the German people. Among them was **Jacob Grimm** (1785-1863), the famous collector of fairy tales. But the historical study of languages was by no means an exclusive German undertaking. These were the also days in which linguists started ambitious dictionary projects which aimed at collecting the entire treasure of words (and their **etymology,** i.e., development from their earliest, reconstructed forms), hoping to uncover and preserve the (roots of) the cultural heritage of the people. Such projects were initiated in many European countries.

Throughout the 19th century, linguistics was synonymous with historical and comparative linguistics, together often called *historical linguistics*; we also see the term *philology*, mostly in connection with the linguistic analysis of old texts. This does not mean that linguists in those days all agreed on the kind of object that they were studying. I mentioned the comparison that linguists made between biological organisms and languages. A shift in perspective took place during the last quarter of the 19th century when a group of linguists known as the **neogrammarians** combined the idea of the law-like development of languages with the belief that languages exist in the individual, thus making language more like a psychological object. A further point of disagreement regarded the details of the analogies between biological evolution and the evolution of languages. Biological evolution inevitably reveals a development from simple organisms to complex organisms. Although the simple organisms have never ceased to exist, we see that over time more and more complex organisms have entered the arena of life, with humans perhaps being the most complex (as far as the development of their brain is concerned). No such trends can be noticed in the way that languages change. This, somewhat disappointingly to some, lead to the conclusion that one could do no more than register random (albeit it law-like) fluctuations. One could not make predictions on the direction that languages are taking.

Factors like these perhaps contributed to an important shift in attention that took place around the year 1900 away from the **diachronic** interest and toward an approach that looks at languages as communicative systems from a **synchronic** point of view, ignoring their development. Such study can be carried out with respect to language of the past (say the Latin of the classical writers) and would still be historical in this sense, but in practice attention focused more on the synchronic state of modern languages that could be studied more directly (given that actual speakers are around).

The linguist who changed the perspective of linguistics or at least added this new perspective, namely the study of languages at a given point in time, was **Ferdinand de Saussure** (1857-1913). The book in which De Saussure's ideas are stated (*Cours de linguistique générale*) appeared in 1916 and was (thus) not written by himself. Rather two of his colleagues reconstructed the ideas on the basis of the notes that he left behind of the classes that he had taught during the last 4 or 5 years of his life.

In "his" writings, De Saussure placed the *synchronic* approach in opposition to the *diachronic* approach. In a way this was not so new because the synchronic approach shows a resemblance to the old tradition of grammar writing. The difference was that De Saussure's interest was not to write practical grammars, but rather to study the structure of language scientifically as a system in which all the elements crucially function together. This line of thinking founded **structuralism**, a movement that extended far beyond linguistics, and heavily influenced researchers in other fields of inquiry, notably **Claude Levi-Strauss** (1908-1990) in his structural approach to **anthropology**.

De Saussure saw language neither as a biological organism nor as a psychological phenomenon. Rather he saw language primarily as a social phenomenon. This understanding agreed with the emergence of the field of sociology which indeed recognized **social facts** as legitimate objects of study. The founder of sociology, **Emile Durkheim** (1858-1917) suggested in his *Rules of Sociological Method* (1905) that there ought to be room for the study of a class of phenomena (social phenomena) which are neither biological nor psychological in nature, for example: legal systems, conventions for dressing, how to behave publicly, and so on. De Saussure took it that language was such a phenomenon.

De Saussure referred to language as a social fact as **langue**, which he contrasted with the actual utterances that individual people produce, which he called **parole**. The langue was primarily seen as a system of words where each word covered a niche in the domain of speech sound (the form) and conceptual space (the meaning). Both the form and the meaning of words could therefore only be understood by placing them in contrast with the forms and meanings of all other words. De Saussure regarded words as a particular type of signs, thus placing linguistics within the context of a broader science that was later called semiotics.

Of course, there is more to language than words. When we speak we combine words into sentences and this cannot be done at random. Languages have rules of syntax that regulate the arrangement of words and **inflection** that regulates the connections between words. De Saussure regarded such rules as belonging to the parole, and as such they received much less attention by him and his followers.

Meanwhile, in the U.S. another linguistic trend had set in, one coming from the broader study of human behavior in different cultures, **cultural anthropology**, with anthropologist and linguist **Franz Boas** (1858-1942) as an important founding father. He worked on Native American cultures and languages were naturally regarded as a crucial if not central aspect of cultures, apart from the practical fact that in order to study such cultures knowledge of their languages was necessary. This work naturally entailed a focus on synchrony because for the American Indian languages there simply was no diachronic record. Boas was born in Germany and his original training was in physics and geography. On a field trip to the west coast of the U.S. he came to realize that people's way of living, people's culture, is not simply determined by the geographical circumstances that surround them. Thus he recognized that there was a need for a special science of human behavior. Anthropology was already an existing term for the study of human cultures, but with Boas it acquired autonomy and method. Boas believed that language was a central component of culture. Hence his interest in language description. He and his followers were not interested in *theories* about language as a social, psychological, or biological phenomenon. The closest thing to theory was the development of precise method of description. What kept the Boasians away from theorizing about language as a general phenomenon was the belief that all languages are unique, that the variations between languages are without limits, that, in other words, nothing more can be done than cataloging the endless varieties as precisely as possible and trying to match these findings with the equally unlimited variety of culture at large. Boas laid the foundation for a tradition in American linguistics that dominated the field until the 1950s.

This descriptive tradition mixed with the structuralist approach that had been imported from Europe. It then also adopted a view on the study of language that was due to a dominant paradigm in American Psychology, namely **behaviorism**. According to this view it was unscientific to study anything else than *observable* behavior. To speak of language as a form of knowledge became a definite no-no.

Great American linguists that were heavily influenced by Boas are **Edward Sapir** (1884-1939), **Leonard Bloomfield** (1887-1949), **Charles Hockett** (1916-2000), and **Zellig Harris** (1909-1992). All of them performed descriptive work of Native American languages, but all of them also had a much stronger theoretical interest than Boas.

Sapir is often associated with certain ideas about the relation between language and thought, further developed by his student Benjamin Lee Whorf (and consequently called the Sapir-Whorf hypothesis), and his writing reflected a broad interest in language not just as a formal system of rules but also as a cultural phenomenon. Bloomfield was mostly influenced by behaviorism. Thus language had to be studied in terms of observable events, i.e., utterances. Bloomfield was even reluctant to ponder on the aspect of word meaning.

The next important phase, one that we are still in, started in the 1950s when **Noam Chomsky** (1929-) entered the scene of linguistics. Maintaining a synchronic perspective, Chomsky reinforced the idea of recognizing the distinction between language as a system (competence) and language behavior (performance). Chomsky added several powerful ideas to the study of competence on which he proposed to focus all the attention. Firstly, by shifting the attention to competence Chomsky departed sharply from the behaviorist claim that one cannot say anything sensible about mental capacities which are unobservable as such. Secondly, Chomsky developed specific and explicit (mathematical) formalism for expressing the rules of grammar. Thirdly, he proposed that humans have an **innate capacity** for language, or, to put it differently, that aspects of the structure of all languages are innate and thus universal. This claim is called the **Innateness Hypothesis**. In this view, differences between languages are largely due to the fact that the innate capacity allows options (in using or not using certain units or rules), as well as to the fact that the innate capacity leaves the pairing of form and meaning of words completely open. Because this pairing is largely arbitrary and wildly different from language to language it cannot be innate.

In the early 1950s many psychologists had already moved away from behaviorism, shifting their attention to the mental processes that underlie human actions. The rise of computers installed the belief that the human mind could perhaps be seen as a "program" specifying the units and rules that underlie human action. Noam Chomsky added to this shift in attention. In a fierce attack on behaviorist accounts of language, specifically language acquisition, Chomsky defended the idea that the real object of study on linguistics is a mental ability.

Chomsky, taking for granted that a language has a set of words, focused his attention on the system that allows speakers to form sentences, which he, unlike de Saussure, regarded as the central aspect of human language. Chomsky showed that the vast, yes infinite number of sentences can be described with finite means and he developed explicit, mathematical ways to characterize those means.

The so-called **cognitive revolution** that started in the 1950s due to the factors just mentioned, including Chomsky's turn to mentalism, is still ongoing, but linguistics today is still also very much a product of everything that preceded it in the 19th and 20th centuries (and even before). Chomsky's views are not the only ones that are considered valid today and they are not uncontroversial. Many of his former students or, more generally, followers are now his fiercest opponents. His views have also not remained the same over the last 50 years and he has gradually come to express ideas that are not that different from the ideas of his opponents.

Conclusions

In this chapter we have taken a quick tour through the history of linguistics. This tour has made it evident that linguists can take a variety of approaches, raise different types of questions, and adopt different methodologies.

Chapter 3

Fields of Linguistics

Introduction

In this chapter I enumerate the various subfields of linguistics. Because language has so many aspects, linguistics is a rich and complex science. Given that language can be studied from different perspectives, linguistics can be seen as belonging to or overlapping with several other fields. Within the psychological perspective, linguistics overlaps with (cognitive) psychology. As an individual property language is part of the human mind and thus also encoded in the neural circuitry of the brain. This brings linguistics within the realm of biology, more specifically neuroscience where the biophysical and biochemical aspects the brain are studied. If, then, the claim is made that some of the circuitry for language is genetically determined, the study of language can be said to be even more firmly rooted in biology (genetics and developmental biology).

The sociological perspective places linguistics within the social sciences, firstly one might think within sociology where relationships between language variation and social stratification as well as the role of language in social institutions are studied. However, anthropology has always had an even bigger claim on linguistics, especially in the U.S. This is simply because the study of other cultures naturally starts out with not only learning the relevant language, but also studying its structure for what it may reveal about the way people think.

Another umbrella for linguistics is the new field of **Cognitive Science**, which is not really a unified field at this point but rather an interdisciplinary endeavor of all scientists that study the mind. This involves psychologists, philosophers, computer scientists, evolutionary psychologists, linguists, and more.

Finally, linguistics, as we have seen, can be thought of as being included in the broad science of semiotics.

Depending on what one take linguistics to be, one will group it in the social sciences, the humanities, or the life sciences. With its links to "hard sciences" such as physics, chemistry, biology, genetics, neuroscience, and mathematics, it is perhaps the "hardest" of the "soft" sciences.

In any event, all these different overlaps produce a wide variety of linguistic subfields. In addition, even within linguistics proper, we see the need for subfields that deal with different aspects of language such as the sound structure or the sentence structure.

The Major Fields of Linguistics Proper

I will first mention distinctions in the study of language by itself, i.e., without taking overlap with other sciences into consideration:

a. **Descriptive linguistics**: focusing on the description of languages in the form of grammars and dictionaries. This is especially important in areas of the world where languages are dying out rapidly. In the United States, descriptive linguistics, focusing on the Native American languages, is identified with linguistic anthropology. Descriptive linguistics is also often regarded as **field linguistics** in as far as the description takes place in the natural setting where the languages are being used.

b. **Theoretical or General linguistics**: focusing on making law-like generalizations about the structures that languages have in common, aiming at an inventory and theory of linguistic universals.

c. **Typological linguistics**: classifying languages into types in accordance with their differences, aiming at registering the array of variation between languages (e.g., looking at word order and grouping language into Subject-Object-Verb, SVO, VSO, etc.). In practice, typologists also do theoretical linguistics, but they try to strike a different balance between descriptive work and theory formation, staying close to the facts and away from sweeping generalizations based on only a handful of languages.

d. **Contrastive linguistics**: comparing the grammars of two different languages to establish how exactly they differ, often with the practical purpose in mind of teaching one of them to speakers of the other one.

Descriptive linguistics logically precedes all further activities. Theoretical (General) and Typological linguistics should really be taken together in as far as they share the goal of understanding the *unity and diversity of human languages*. Typological linguistics falls in between descriptive and theoretical linguistics in pursuing less abstract and more functional theories of languages based on close description of data from many different languages. As such, it aims at being an alternative to the kind of general linguistics that has emerged from Noam Chomsky's ideas, where it sometimes seems that only those language facts that fit the theory are taken into consideration. There are clear reasons for the more abstract pursuit (to put it politely) of Chomskyan linguists that I will discuss below, but it is also true that a consideration of a wide variety of languages is of crucial importance if the method of linguistics is to be considered scientific.

The study of language in whatever form (descriptive, general, or typological) can focus on the specific state of a language or languages at a given point in time:

e. **Synchronic linguistics**: studying the structure of languages at a fixed moment in time (e.g. Modern English, Classical Latin)

Or trace a language through time:

f. **Diachronic linguistics**: studying the development or change of language through time.

We also find the term **historical linguistics,** which is either synonymous with diachronic linguistics or meant to include both diachronic linguistics and synchronic linguistics in as far as it studies older phases (often literary) of existing languages or languages that are now extinct (such as Gothic, Hittite, etc.). In this latter sense we also find the older term **philology**.

In the 18th and 19th century diachronic linguistics would go hand-in-hand with the desire to group languages into families and to reconstruct ancestor languages for these families, if this ancestor was not preserved itself in the written record:

g. **Comparative linguistics**: classifying languages into language families and trying to reconstruct their common ancestor

We also find the term **genetic linguistics** for this activity. There is, of course, a comparative aspect to general and typological linguistics in as far as the latter compares and classifies languages, and the former often compares languages to deepen understanding of the universal properties of languages and their possible differences. As a result, one may find a use of the term comparative linguistics that does not refer to the genetic classification and reconstruction. The general and typological approaches go hand-in-hand with the synchronic angle in that the pool of languages that is investigated is the set of (known) synchronic states of all languages. Comparative linguistics makes use of the diachronic angle, because reconstruction involves reversing the changes that have led to a group of daughter languages from a common ancestor. It also, however, uses the synchronic method because reconstruction always starts with taking the oldest synchronic states of these languages that are compared for their "genetic" (or "genealogical") relationship.

The study of language change, genetic classification, and reconstruction excludes the issue of **language origin**, which is sometimes included in anthropological linguistics. For one thing, it does not seem possible to group all the known languages into one big super-family. Hence, even if it were true that all existing languages derive from a common source (sometimes called *proto-world*), we cannot get to that language through comparative reconstruction. Secondly, the question of language origin is about how human language got there in the first place and about potential predecessors of human language in our ancestor species. These are evolutionary issues because they involve the evolution of our species *including its cognitive capacities*. This has not stopped people from using the term *language evolution* for *language change*, since, after all, the term *evolution* means *change* in a general way. But this causes a potential terminological confusion that we must be aware of since language evolution in the sense of language change does not address the (biological) evolutionary question of how language as a human faculty has arisen. When this question is addressed we speak of **evolutionary linguistics**.

h.   **Evolutionary linguistics.** The study of the emergence of language.

All above-mentioned linguistic activities may be and often are focused on only specific aspects of grammar such as **syntax** (sentence structure), **morphology** (word structure), **semantics** (meaning structure), **phonology** (sound structure), or even more specific topics within these areas. Units larger than the sentence also form a subdiscipline referred to as **text linguistics**. **Pragmatics** is the study of sentences in context or, more generally, the study of the relationship between sentences and situations in which they are used. Both text linguistics and pragmatics relate to or are included in **discourse analysis** (see below). We also have **phonetics**, which focuses on a particular aspect of language processing, namely the production and perception of speech (or sign), as well as on the physical property of the signal itself.

The Notion Theory

One might argue that the ultimate goal of all the different activities mentioned so far is to arrive at the fullest possible understanding of the phenomenon of human language. The methods of investigation involve the construction of a *model* (or *theory*), i.e., *a coherent set of hypotheses*, that is subsequently tested in terms of data that is collected from languages (written or spoken) or in terms of various sorts of experiments. Linguistics is thus foremost an *empirical* science. An *inductive phase* of collecting data and making relevant generalizations leads to the construction of a model or theory, which is then tested against new observations (from spontaneous language use, or the result of experiments) that may or may not mesh with the **predictions** that can be derived from the model. The only subdiscipline that faces problems in this respect is evolutionary linguistics, which tries to shed light on phases of language for which we have no direct evidence. For this reason, this approach must rely heavily on results from other disciplines such as archeology and human paleontology, as well as indirect reasoning based on the study of communication in other species, computer modeling, and so on.

Another remark on the notion theory is in order. I already mentioned that the term *theoretical* instead of *general* linguistics is somewhat misleading in that all the approaches mentioned also involve constructing a theory, for example, a theory of how languages change. More to the point, one might say that all linguistic work is theoretical in as far as it always involves a network of categories.

With specific reference to general linguistics we might furthermore ask what the theory or model is about? Is the model about the set of utterances from a given language, language as an interpersonal social phenomenon, or is it about the mental capacity that underlies all these utterances. Are we satisfied with a model that concerns the mental grammar (a system of primitives and rules), or do we wish to include how language is used in daily life?

We have seen that since the beginning of the 20th century, when the synchronic study of language became as focus of attention, opinions have differed on what exactly constitutes the topic of inquiry. No one excludes the study of grammar as a system of primitives and rules, which is seen by all as the core of human language. In the view of Chomsky, this grammar is a private mental property of individuals. In most cases, even a Chomskyan linguist will not limit his attention to one individual, however. Rather most linguists, in practice, base their theory of the grammar on the study of a group of individuals whose mental grammars are assumed to be (more or less) the same. Thus, interpersonal variation that always exists, but that apparently does not stand in the way of judging these people's language as the same, is usually ignored.

Interdisciplinary Fields

With its focus on the innateness of a capacity for this specific communication system that we call language, Chomskyan linguistics has come to overlap with the field of genetics in as far as the presumed language instinct must somehow be encoded in the genes. In addition, it is assumed that the genetic information leads to the development of a specialized area of the brain (the language organ), which again brings linguistics within the domain of biology (anatomy, physiology). Accordingly, some linguists have come to use the term *biolinguistics* for this approach:

i.   **Biolinguistics**. The study of language as a physical organ of the body, developed on the basis of information encoded in the human genome.

The Chomskyan approach has inspired a lot of research into the way languages (in the sense of mental grammars) are acquired. This is not surprising. In Chomsky's view humans are endowed with an innate capacity for language that grows into adult mental grammars. It is not unreasonable to expect that an investigation of the process of first language acquisition, which is by no means an exclusive interest of Chomskyan linguists, may shed light on the structure of the innate capacity:

j.   **First Language acquisition**: how do children acquire language and which phases do they pass through on their way to grammatical adulthood.

The study of acquisition may focus on the so-called **logical problem of language acquisition.** (How is it possible that children acquire their mental grammar with infinite capacity based on exposure to a finite set of only positive data, i.e., sentences actually uttered, both grammatical and ungrammatical.) Another aspect of acquisition deals with the stages of development, which is sometimes separately referred to as **developmental linguistics**.

A question that is relevant when children grow up in a bilingual or **multilingual** environment is how they acquire more than one language; are they kept separate or is there **interference**? The study of multilingualism is a subfield in its own right.

In view of the so-called *critical period hypothesis* (which says that humans must be exposed to their first language within a certain period of their life, from birth to around puberty) it is then also reasonable to investigate how languages are acquired later in life to see whether, as is expected, differences can be found in how the actual learning process unfolds. Indeed, one might say that, when it comes to second languages that people learn later in life, "learning" is the more appropriate term:

k. **Second Language acquisition**: how do people acquire language later in life?

In focusing on acquisition and learning these forms of linguistics are clearly quite close to the field of psychology, especially developmental psychology. Language acquisition is just one facet of cognitive development, and as such it makes sense to study language development in the context of **cognitive development**. Second language acquisition fits in with areas of psychology that focus on the cognitive processes that are involved in learning and education in general. Where psychology and linguistics overlap, people often speak of psycholinguistics as an interdisciplinary field that then not only looks at acquisition and learning under normal circumstances but also under special circumstances in which difficulties or delays occur that are due to a variety of mental or physical factors. Psycholinguistics also studies how people process language, i.e., how the act of speaking relies on sequences of mental processes from the most abstract (planning of what one wishes to say) to the motor commands that allow articulation, and how hearing and understanding do the reverse (**language processing**).

l. **Psycholinguistics**: The study of normal or deviant language acquisition/learning and language use in the context of cognitive development and cognitive processing.

The study of language acquisition is and long has been an area of linguistic research in its own right, and not just an area that helps exploring the innateness hypothesis. The same can be said of other areas of research that involve language. In particular, this regards the study of how the mental grammar (and other cognitive modules) is represented in the brain in both healthy subjects and subjects that have suffered brain damage. Thus, an interdisciplinary field has emerged that combines insight from *neurology* or *neuroscience* (brain science) and linguistics.

m. **Neurolinguistics**. Knowledge of language is physically located in the brain. Language processing involves physical processes. Damage to the brain influences the perception and production of language.

Psycho- and neurolinguistics, when focused on language disorders (pathologies), often takes place in a clinical environment and is thus also called:

n. **Clinical linguistics**: The study of language disorders and the development of methods for diagnosis and therapy.

Another area that involves research on language focuses on the formal properties of the mental grammar as a rule system. In his earlier work, Chomsky himself put great emphasis on this aspect of linguistics and in doing so he established a field of study known as *algebraic linguistics* that has formed the basis for the study of formal languages in general, especially those used in computer programming. Here linguistics forms an interdisciplinary area with *mathematics, logic, and computer science*.

o. **Algebraic linguistics**: Language as a formal system can be compared to artificial languages, the properties of which have been extensively studied in sciences that operate with precisely defined formal languages: *mathematical or computational linguistics.*

In more recent times this field has focused on ways to use computers in the analysis of human language, aiming in particular at developing programs that would allow computers to understand and produce human language. This field, which can be seen as a branch of **artificial intelligence,** is now called *computational linguistics.*

p. **Computational linguistics**: The use of computers in language analysis as well as the development of computer programs that allow computers to understand and produce human language.

The Chomskyan approach, including the interdisciplinary areas just mentioned, has been and still is fruitful in its focus on the mental grammar, but many linguists have found the scope of Chomskyan linguistics too narrow. Two linguists in particular have been responsible for initiating new, or reviving old ways of looking at language.

William Labov (1927-) played an essential role in founding a field that is known as sociolinguistics. Labov rejected three aspects that are quite fundamental to the Chomskyan (as well as in general structuralist approaches following the lead of de Saussure). Firstly, he rejected the idea of treating language as an invariant system, i.e., abstracting away from differences between speakers of the same language. Secondly, he rejected the strict separation of synchronic and diachronic linguistics (introduced by de Saussure). Both points are related because variation causes and results from change (which is always ongoing). Thirdly, Labov insisted that the study of language be based on observational data, i.e., records of actual speech performance. In other words, he rejected the sole reliance (or perhaps even relevance) on elicited or introspective grammaticality judgments.

q. **Sociolinguistics** concerns the relation between language and social variables such as age, gender, or social class of the speakers and contextual factors that determine the formality or informality of speech (which involves the status of the addressee, the rate of speech, and so on). Subsequently, Labov then also tried to determine how change starts and who is responsible for initiating variants (**the actuation problem**), and how the change is spread in a speech community (**the diffusion problem**). This kind of work forms a link between sociolinguistics and historical linguistics. In looking at variants of languages, sociolinguistics includes a new approach to the study of dialects (**dialectolology**), traditionally understood as regional, geographic variants of languages, and in doing so extends the concept of dialects to include variants that are used by rural populations, called city dialects.

There is a broad range of activities that have come to fall under the rubric of sociolinguistics. Some activities that started out under that umbrella have developed into recognized separate disciplines. For example, the study of language and gender is considered to be a separate subfield of linguistics:

r. **Language and gender** studies the correlations between gender and language use.

Labov's emphasis on the study of language use entailed an interest in the communicative interaction and stimulated research in *discourse* (*conversational* analysis) and *texts*. Thus, Labov rejected a fourth characteristic of Chomskyan linguistics, namely its focus on the sentence as the maximal unit of analysis.

s. **Discourse analysis** studies the structure of linguistic discourse or conversation, focusing on the structures and rules underlying larger linguistic units and processes that underlie such phenomena as turn-taking.

Another name for this approach to language is **pragmatics,** although this term is also in use for the study of the relationship between language utterances (especially their meaning properties) and the specific situation in which the utterances take place. Here, there is also an influence from philosophy, especially the concern with so-called **speech acts theory**.

Another linguist who revolted against the Chomskyan paradigm was **Dell Hymes** (1927-) who in 1962 initiated a field of study that he called *Ethnography of Speaking* (which is now often called *Ethnography of Communication*). This field shares with sociolinguistics a focus on language use and discourse. It looks at how and why people speak or enter into communicative interaction; it investigates speaking and communication as a cultural phenomenon, thus focusing on cultural differences in communicative behavior.

n. **Ethnography of Communication** examines how and why language is used and how these things vary from culture to culture.

This kind of work is sometimes subsumed under fields such as sociolinguistics or anthropological linguistics.

o. **Anthropological linguistics/Linguistic anthropology.** Linguistics was once seen as a branch of anthropology, the study of humankind in the most general sense. Today this interdisciplinary field focuses on the relationships between language (its grammar, specifically its vocabulary) and people's conceptualization of the world that they live in, including their worldview, beliefs systems, as well as rituals and social structures that they have created in a particular culture. The so-called **Sapir-Whorf Hypothesis** (which focuses on how a language determines or influences people's conceptual systems) is often of central concern.

Another field that acquired autonomous status investigates the use of language in establishing or maintaining relations of power. This line includes language interaction between individuals or groups of unequal rank. Some also include the use of language by government officials and advertisers to mislead people (**doubletalk**).

p. **Language and power**.

Once we allow attention on language use in a broader context, several other important subfields of linguistics come into focus that all share an interest into the impact of the fact that in most places and for most speakers different languages are used side by side. Although perhaps unusual for English speaking people in the U.S. or England, for most people elsewhere in the world being **bilingual** or **multilingual** is the norm. In many cases more than one language is acquired from birth, while in others second or third languages are learned later in life. Henceforth, I will use multilingualism as the general term. A subfield of linguistics studies this phenomenon:

q. **Bi/Multilingualism** is a field that specifically studies how speakers manage more than one language, how they switch between different languages (code switching) and how the languages/grammars of multilingual speakers influence each other.

When different languages meet within the minds of speakers it is likely that interference will happen, and this interference may be asymmetrical when the different languages have a different status. Thus, bilingualism may induce linguistic change. The same is true when contact between languages arises because people speaking different languages live in the same or neighboring areas. In that case the different languages may borrow vocabulary and grammatical properties. This may lead to so-called *areal* properties of languages.

r. **Areal linguistics** studies processes of borrowing and convergence.

In special circumstances of language, contact-mixed languages may arise that are used as an interlanguage between groups that share no common language. Such interlanguages may start out as being very restricted in vocabulary and grammar and are often called pidgin languages. Over time a pidgin may become the mother tongue of a new generation, in which case they are called creole languages.

s. **Creole and pidgin linguistics**. The study of pidgin and creole languages, the processes that give rise to their emergence and their grammatical properties.

A more intimate contact situation arises when a country has been conquered by a foreign power. In that case speakers may pick up sporadic knowledge of the other languages that may have consequences for their mother tongue. The language of the conquerors may acquire the status of a dominant language that starts pushing the local language (sometimes called the substrate language) away. Languages can also become dominant in an area that houses other languages on economical grounds. In situations like this, substrate or non-dominant languages may become endangered and eventually disappear **(language death)**. In recent years a field has emerged that studies the relationships between languages among each other, and the relationship between languages and the biological, political, and economical environment:

t. **Ecolinguistics.** Studies the ecology of languages, i.e., their cohabitation in the same areas, their expansion and shrinking, also in relation to changes in the biological, economic, and political sphere. An important observation is the relation between the loss of biological and cultural diversity.

The various subdisciplines and phenomena that involve or result from language contact are sometimes jointly referred to as **contact linguistics**.

All the subfields of linguistics also belong to the realm of theoretical linguistics. There is in addition **applied linguistics,** which specifically aims at translating theoretical insight into practical applications, which could involve the development of educational or therapy methods, or even commercial products such as spelling checkers or other language-related software.

u. **Applied linguistics.** Any activity that uses findings within linguistics to some practical use, often in the context of education or therapy.

A Cognitive Revolution Within a Cognitive Revolution

I have mentioned how linguistics can be grouped within the so-called cognitive sciences, which together try to understand the nature and workings of minds, human or otherwise. In fact, the kind of perspective on linguistics that Chomsky brought about is often seen as one of the most important incentives toward the emergence of the area of cognitive science, and in this context people speak of **the cognitive revolution**. But the Chomskyan approach, despite its important role within cognitive science, should not be confused with **cognitive linguistics,** which is an approach that sees categorization and conceptual systems resulting from that as fundamental to the structure and functioning of language and, in fact, the whole of human cognition. This approach breaks in fundamental ways with the Chomskyan approach in that it does not place syntax in the center of grammar. Nor does it see language as the result of an innate system (in which syntax is central) that is specifically specialized in the acquisition of mental grammars. Cognitive linguistics is part of a different take on human cognition, namely one that regards categorization as the basis of everything, including language.

Conclusion

One can undoubtedly make or find more distinctions within linguistics. It should not surprise us that a phenomenon that is so complex and so central to all aspects of the human experience has lead, and is still leading, to numerous types of inquiry.

Chapter 4

The Generative Enterprise

Introduction

Chomsky's approach is or used to be called "generative – transformational grammar." *Generative* refers to the fact that the grammar is seen as an explicit system that generates or characterizes the wellformedness of linguistic expressions. *Transformational* refers to an aspect of the theory (namely the use of so-called transformational rules) that I will discuss later in some detail. People often leave out Transformational and simply speak of Generative Grammar.

Focus on I-Language

Generative grammar studies language, or rather the underlying mental grammar (competence, I-language), as a property of an individual. There is no guarantee that any two I-languages will ever be identical, not even of people who are said to speak the same language. The only aspect of grammars that is identical, in all people, is the part that is innate, although since innate can only mean genetic we must perhaps reckon with *language mutants*, or, to put it more friendly, with genetically determined variations in mental grammars. Little is known about such genetic variation.

Generative grammarians foremost see linguistics as a branch of biology, more properly genetics, since, ultimately, the primary interest lies in developing theories of the innate, thus genetic, aspects of language. In addition, of course, there is an interest in maturation and development of human organisms, especially with regard to the development of their *language organ* to be physically located somewhere in the brain. With its emphasis on these issues linguistics *is* biolinguistics for Chomskyan hard-liners.

One might wonder whether linguistics then is a branch of **behavior genetics** (a branch of science that studies the genetic and environmental basis of *differences* in human behavior) or perhaps of **evolutionary psychology**, an approach that seeks to establish *universals* of human behavior, trying to explain their existence as instincts that from an evolutionary perspective can be explained as adaptation to the challenges that our distant ancestors were exposed to. From what I've said so far it could go both ways. It is fair to say that Chomskyan linguists do not care much for behavior genetics, and thus for genetic variation, believing, for no reasons that I've ever seen spelled out, that the genetic basis of the language organ is largely invariant. As for evolutionary aspects, we note that for a long time Chomsky was not inclined to consider the evolutionary development of the language organ, largely because we know nothing about the origin and development of human language on a time scale that is relevant for evolution. Strictly speaking, evidence for language does not extend any further back in time than the oldest record of writing, at best some 6,000 years old. Around this time, the human species with all its genes was well established, and little if any genetic change bearing on cognitive capacities has been claimed to have occurred since then.

Within linguistics, as we have seen in Chapter 3, there are different approaches and not everybody is, like Chomsky, so focused on universals. Other schools of linguistics are more into cataloging all the differences between languages. In the end, both schools of thought recognize unity (universals, or at least tendencies) and diversity (differences). Chomsky and his followers try to control the extent of the differences which they see as the manifestations of a finite number of *universal options* (called **parameters**) that are built into the innate language faculty; universal are called **principles**. Crucially, these parameters are not to be seen as reflexes of differences in the innate capacity of the speakers of the relevant languages. Chomsky's idea is, as mentioned, that all members of the human species have the same genetic endowment for language, and this endowment comes with built-in options. From this perspective, rather than mentally establishing what is present in a language the learner needs to erase or suppress from his or her built-in system what is not present in or supported by the environment.

Linguists who focus on language differences (**typologists**) usually have less of an interest in postulating an innate language component with principles and parameters. In fact, many of them question that any true universals exist.

Focus on Language Acquisition

While linguists labor throughout their whole careers to discover tiny details of the structure of language, all children display behavior when they are two years or so that seems to suggest the presence of a full-blown mental grammar. Even at the age of one most children start forming their first sentences, and long before that they understand a lot of what their parents say to them. How is that possible? Why are children such fast learners? Do parents instruct them so well, do they listen so much better than they do when they get older?

The truth is that children build up this mental grammar upon exposure to the language utterances that they hear from their caretakers, siblings, friends, and so on. They do not receive formal instruction. Presented with this puzzle, Chomsky thought it was obvious that the human species must be equipped with a specific innate ability that allows children to form their mental grammars so quickly.

Chomksy's most famous argument for the Innateness Hypothesis is **the Poverty of the Stimulus Argument,** which is based on the claim that the input that children are exposed to vastly under-determines the knowledge that is required to use a language. In addition, he argues that children do not learn language; rather language grows or develops spontaneously as long as there is some input. All children, barring medical conditions, are equally good at the task, just like all children are good at growing hair or walking. Language acquisition has all the traits of biologically controlled development, according to Chomsky.

With his focus on the mental grammar and its innate basis, Chomsky thus framed the central problem of linguistics as the (logical) problem of language acquisition. How is it logically possible that children being exposed to unsystematic and random input quickly come forward with a rich output? This cannot, Chomsky argues tirelessly, be explained in terms of learning mechanisms based on memorization and analogy. It must be the case that children are born with all the properties that all languages share (universals, principles), as well as the options in those areas where languages show variations (parameters).

The Term Grammar

Thus far we've been seeing the term *grammar* a lot. Let me summarize the different ways in which the term has been used.

When people use the term grammar the first thing that usually comes to mind is the rules that underlie the formation of sentences. In line with this popular view, the grammar of a language is seen as a collection of **words** and a collection of **rules** to put the words into sentences. This makes the term grammar almost equivalent to the notion of syntax (sentence structure), which, as we will see, is only a part of grammar. One other use of this term is to refer to a book that contains "the grammar of English," for example. As we have learned, such a book can be prescriptive or descriptive. A prescriptive grammar tells you how to use your language, how to make proper sentences and what things you should avoid doing. Descriptive grammars are usually meant as pedagogical or teaching grammars and they come in all sorts and varieties, ranging from popular books that claim that you can learn the language in "just three hours" to serious school grammars or textbooks with exercises. A descriptive grammar (or *reference grammar*) on the other hand registers how people actually use their language. It aims to provide a description of the grammar that is based on firsthand fieldwork and analysis. No descriptive grammar can ever be complete, but there is a certain standard that prescribes the various parts of a descriptive grammar. These are the parts that I will discuss below.

A descriptive grammar can be taken to be a description of the systematic patterns in a collection of sentences that someone has recorded. Another interpretation of a descriptive grammar is to see it as a description of the grammar that people who speak these sentences have in their heads. After all, you must realize by now that every speaker of every language must know a bunch of words and a bunch of rules. These two approaches focus on E-language (utterances) and I-language (internal grammar), respectively. Therefore we have introduced another way of referring to I-language (next to *competence*), namely **mental grammar**. The mental grammar is a body of knowledge (largely unconscious) that allows a person to speak and understand a language. When I use the term grammar henceforth, I take it to be the mental grammar. General or theoretical linguists see it as their main task to design a model of people's mental grammars. Then they write books about what they think this model (or a part of it) is.

Such books are not called grammar books, they are not grammars; they are books about mental grammars.

How Do We Study the Mental Grammar?

What keeps linguists busy and off the street is trying to find the hidden units and rules of language. People use them, but except in a very superficial sense they are not aware of them. The rules of grammar are hidden in the subconscious territories of our minds. Yet we know that the rules exist because it is obvious that there are regularities in people's spontaneous speech.

A first step in trying to formulate the rules of grammar is to collect a database (on paper, or, today, in digital form) of words and utterances. Linguists call such a database a **language corpus** (a "body" of language data). To make a good database can be a time- and money-consuming activity. In this day and age it is fortunately the case that large amounts of language data are available digitally because of the way that newspapers and so on are printed. The Internet is also, of course, a large (very large) set of language data. The drawback is, of course, that all this regards written language as opposed to spontaneously spoken language, although there is also digital data that is meant to be a faithful transcription of actual speech.

Digital data usually requires a lot of prepping and coding to be able to get the right linguistic information to the surface. Part of this coding can be done by writing smart computer programs that identify nouns, verbs, etc. (word classes), and even do a bit of sentence analysis, but a lot of manual labor always remains. An interesting more recent development is to actually use the Internet, that is, all the text that is available through browsers such as Google. Say you want to know whether a certain construction that you are interested in as a linguist really occurs, and with what frequency. You can now type a specific sentence into Google, and in seconds you will know whether that particular sentence has actually been used, and if it has been used, how often. So these days you sometimes hear linguists saying: "Well, I Googled it and it turned out that …." The future will tell whether this remarkable use of the Internet (a form of **data mining**) will reach a sophisticated level. Again, though, we must remember that this language corpus is also almost entirely based on written language. In addition, the data comes from an uncontrolled multitude of sources, so it can hardly be regarded as the output of a mental grammar as located in an individual.

A second method that is used by linguists is rather different in nature. If a linguist wishes to know whether a certain array of words (or morphemes or phonemes) is possible in a given language, it is possible to fabricate the relevant expression and then present it to a native speaker of that language and ask: Is this sentence grammatical (possible, acceptable)? Thus, the linguist elicits what is called **grammaticality judgments**. Producing grammaticality judgments is a form of **meta-linguistic behavior**. It is linguistic behavior that is *about* linguistic behavior.

Let us say that the initial description made by some linguist contains sentences like the following.

Who did you see John kick? (answer: I saw John kick *Bill*.)

The rule is apparently that we can formulate a question by placing a question word *who* at the beginning of a sentence. Formulated in that way, the rule doesn't tell you whether the following sentence would be grammatical or not.

Who did you seen John and? (corresponding to: I saw John and *Bill*.)

Now, instead of waiting until someone spontaneously produces that sentence, which in this case will never happen, a linguist can also ask a speaker whether the sentence is acceptable (i.e., grammatical). This method (which is much quicker) is, in fact, crucial because a sentence that does not occur in a large collection of sentences could still be grammatical because every collection, no matter how extensive, can only contain a tiny portion of all the possible sentences.

Even checking data that you have found in reference grammars with speakers is useful because utterances that occur in a descriptive grammar *can* be ungrammatical. It is also possible after all that the grammar-book writer simply made a mistake.

For these reasons linguists rely a lot on meta-linguistic grammaticality judgments. Grammaticality judgments are also called **acceptability judgments**. (One could make a distinction between these terms, because when a speaker says that a certain sentence is OK, he could be mistaken in that he finds it acceptable because he kind of knows what the intended meaning is, even though when pressed he'll admit that the sentence is ungrammatical.)

When soliciting grammaticality judgments, a linguist should foremost rely on so-called **native speakers**, that is, speakers who have acquired a certain language in childhood. This is important because people who learn languages later in life often fail to fully grasp the workings of the grammatical rules of the language that they try to learn.

The method of using grammaticality judgments forms a major yet very simple (and cheap) experimental tool of modern linguistics. It gets even simpler (and cheaper) when the linguist uses himself as the provider of the judgments. Here he needs to be careful, however. After all, the linguist may want to show that his theory is right and thus be biased toward accepting a sentence that his theory predicts. Thus, linguists should be very careful with using grammaticality judgments as evidence. On the one hand they must use such evidence; on the other hand the evidence should not be purely introspective (i.e., based on the linguist's intuitions only).

The use of grammaticality judgments has been criticized as being unreliable if not carried out with care. As already said, if a linguist uses himself as the source of judgments, chances are that he will subconsciously approve examples that support his theory. But even if other people are used, it might be argued that it is simply not reliable to walk over to a colleague or student and say: "Hey, can you say such and such?" and take that one answer as sufficient.

Despite these serious methodological issues, Chomskyan linguists are generally not the kind of people to work with extensive questionnaires and careful statistical analysis. In practice they rely a lot on introspective data and casual judgments made by others. This practice has, however, not been devastating because, while using this imperfect method, linguists have made enormous progress in analyzing languages and coming up with insight in general properties.

Writing again needs special mentioning. It is a general belief that, whereas one can speak in various ways, writing must follow the prescriptive rules. However, although the relationship between written language and prescriptive rules *is* strong (due to the origin of the prescriptive tradition which lies in a phase of language study which exclusively deals with written forms of language), both speech and writing occur in formal settings (more sensitive to prescriptive rules) and informal settings (less sensitive to prescriptive rules). A very informal kind of written language occurs in e-mail messages, for example. (Clearly, some of the informal e-mail language is more and more often used in papers that students write.)

In any event, in writing we tend to be more sensitive to the prescriptive rules that are around. (In fact, the original meaning of the word *grammar* is "the art of writing.") Therefore descriptive grammars are best based on spoken language.

A third way of getting data is to elicit sentences from people in test situations, e.g., by showing them a picture and asking them to describe what they see. A fourth method for studying the hidden rules is to subject people to clever psycholinguistic experiments in which we use reaction time measurements and a myriad of other tricks to find out how the mind processes language. Finally, and fifthly, one might say that since the hidden rules are somehow represented in the brain it is perhaps possible to shed some light on these rules by directly investigating the brain. However, neuroscience (neurolinguistics) has not yet progressed to this point.

As a separate source of information we should perhaps mention descriptive grammars, or, more generally, the body of linguistic literature. Descriptive grammars and so on are indeed a vital source of information, not only because such works contain many examples of words and utterances of the language being described, but also because the linguists who wrote them have made attempts to formulate rules. These rules may be meant to be nothing more than generalizations about the language data that have been recorded, but it seems obvious that we can also regard them as approximations of the rules that people have internalized in their mental grammar. However, we must bear in mind that descriptive and theoretical work is itself based on the five types of method just discussed.

It is through the systematic empirical study of spontaneous linguistic behavior, meta-linguistic behavior, elicitation, laboratory-induced behavior, brain studies, and the linguistic literature that linguists and psychologists and, more generally, cognitive scientists study people's capacity for language. And the work is nowhere near done! It is fair to say that the grammar of no single language, not even of English, has been fully described, analyzed, and dissected into all the relevant rules. Thousands and thousands of linguists, anthropologists, and psychologists have spent decades on this matter and the complexity of even a single language is too elusive to have been brought to the surface. Not even philosophers interested in human language have been able to change that fact. If all the rules of let us say English were known, computer giants would be selling computers that speak to you and understand what you mutter to them. Our kids would be talking to their toys and the toys would talk back to them.

Finally, let us notice a specific methodological problem inherent in the goal of describing mental grammars. Given that there is variety all around (in speech communities and even within every person), any description that aims to be a true model of a mental grammar should be based on the utterances and judgments of a single person, while using or tapping into a single register of that person. In practice, as noticed above, linguists seldom use a single speaker, pretending that even though all speakers differ somewhat there is still such a thing as a **homogenous speech community**, that is, a group of speakers who all use and share a solid core of grammatical units and rules. Even if they do use a single speaker (usually themselves), they believe that the resulting model is representative of the speech community that they consider themselves a part of.

Nature and Nurture

The Chomskyan perspective on language has stirred an ancient philosophical debate, a debate that Aristotle already had with his predecessor Plato, the debate that once it had started never stopped, the never-ending debate about the roles of **nurture** and **nature**, the debate about how we come to know what we know, the debate about the origin and nature of human knowledge and behavior, the debate that fuels the branch of philosophy that we know as *epistemology*. In modern day discussions the points of reference are the British **empiricists George Berkeley** (1685-1753), **David Hume** (1711-1776), and **John Locke** (1632-1704), and **John Stuart Mill** (1806-1873) who thought of the mind of a newborn as a **blank slate** (*an empty hard drive*) which is filled by sensory experience (*scanners, microphones, people touching the screen, fondling the mouse, or hitting the keys on the keyboard*), guided only by very (and presumably *a priori*) general principles of categorization and association (*a simple operating system*), and whose formulation traced back to the work of Aristotle. On the other side of the camp we find continental philosophers such as **René Descartes** (Cartesius) (1596-1650), **Gottfried Wilhelm von Leibniz** (1646-1716), and **Emmanuel Kant** (1724-1804) who do not think of the newborn's mind as quite so empty, thus taking a **rationalist** stance which makes far more room for so-called innate ideas, a position that dates back to Plato's view of the origin of human knowledge. While Descartes and Plato attributed the innate ideas to either a divine source or a prior life, today the most likely ultimate place where these ideas would have to be located is the human genome. And it does not seem to be the case that this debate is going to be over any time soon. Each year we see many new books and articles appearing that discuss the nature/nurture debate in all its glory and then claim to present yet another perspective on this issue.

Human language is a perfect playground for the nature/nurture debate, and it is clear that one the modern players on the rationalist team is Noam Chomsky. Chomsky's answer to the question as to how children manage to master their mental grammar is clearly rationalistic: children are born with most of their grammars already in place. We have to take note of the fact that Chomsky has been advocating his position for 50 years now, and we'll see later on that the claim for innateness knowledge has undergone substantial change and, some would say, considerable reduction.

Now, clearly, it is not the case, and not even the most radical rationalist would claim this, that all of language is innate, that children are born with complete mental grammars. The reason seems obvious: there are 7,000 different languages today (many of which will go extinct very soon), and since extinction is not a new phenomenon it is probably the case that hundreds of thousands of languages have gone extinct in the past. And new languages, or at least dialects, arise as, for example, English fractures into a myriad of regional varieties across the world. Thus, unless one is willing to defend the idea that children are born with hundreds of thousands of mental grammars and a mechanism to select the correct ones for the languages that they are exposed to, something else must be postulated. In addition, it is a well-known fact that children will not start speaking any language unless exposed to utterances belonging to some language. In short, there must be some kind of interaction between nature (innate aspect of grammar) and nurture (exposure to language utterances).

One could write the history of generative grammar by reviewing the evolution of how this interaction has been characterized. I will not do that here (for this see van der Hulst 2007), but toward the end of this chapter I will have a few things to say about the most recent developments of this evolution.

A Note on the Terms Empirical and Empiricism

The terms empirical (as in empirical science) and empiricism (as a view on the nature of the human mind that is opposed to rationalism; see below) are not just coincidentally similar: in both cases the central idea is that knowledge arises on the basis of sensory-based experience. In the empirical sciences this experience involves conscious and voluntary **observation** (of the indeed observable world); in the case of empiricism we refer to the sensory-based experience that individuals have in their daily life. Indeed, language acquisition (by children or adults) or the development of knowledge in general can be seen as a kind of hypothesis formation and testing process, much as we see it in the empirical sciences, the difference being that children (at least to Chomsky) have the advantage that the relevant (and in fact correct) theory is already installed in their minds; they just need make it specific to the language that they are exposed to. Scientists, on the other hand, are not born with the right theory in their mind (and even if they were it would presumably be locked away in their subconscious). They have to formulate the theory from scratch. (This does not deny that scientists, as all humans, may have an innate theory-formation capacity, as well as innate folk theories of their surrounding environments. The value of the latter, by the way, as a starting point for forming scientific theories of that same environment is questionable.)

Some linguists, like, for example, **Geoffrey Sampson** (1944-), a modern day hardcore empiricist who therefore does not believe in an innate language capacity, do compare the acquisition of knowledge by children (of language, or other abilities) to scientific theory formation, a viewpoint that has led people to characterize babies as "scientists in the crib." Sampson's emphasis on empirical observation has led him to not only deny the innateness hypothesis, but also to reject introspection and sloppy data collection as appropriate methods in linguistics. He pleads for an **empirical linguistics**, i.e., a linguistics that is based on solid corpus-based data collection and careful analysis using computers and statistics.

The Minimalist Program

Chomsky's proposals have gone though several phases, which is understandable given that he has been leading the generative camp for 50 years. From the start (in the mid-1950s) Chomsky has taken the mental grammar to be the development of an innate system, at some point called **UG** (**universal grammar**). Always, the mental grammar was assumed to be a modular system consisting of various subparts dealing with syntax, phonology, and meaning (morphology being included in syntax). UG would thus itself be modular and specify innately the design of each module and aspects of its content up to the part where whatever was specified could be said to be shared by all languages. Chomsky proposed specific formalism for the units and rules present in each module as well as a specific interaction between the modules in which the syntactic module was held to be the central engine, which would generate syntactic structure which would then be provided with words from the lexicon. The syntactic module contained two types of rules to generate syntactic structures: structure building rules (**phrase structure rules**), and structure changing rules (**transformations**). The phonological and semantic component would then interpret the syntactic structure-plus-words in terms of their pronunciation and meaning. Extensive work in the 1970s and 1980s discussed technical details of the workings of the modules and provided applications, case studies, of fragments of languages.

In the 1980s Chomsky proposed the so-called **principles-and-parameters model**, in which the principles captured the invariant universals and the parameters were universal with a variable that the language learner was supposed to replace with a value (choosing from a finite set of values for these variables). Thus, the parameters would account for the differences between languages. Over the years linguists proposed various universals (none of which went undisputed) and many parameters, whose number grew uncomfortably fast.

In the 1990s Chomsky introduced a new approach that he termed **the Minimalist Program (MP)**, which is rather difficult to pin down. Firstly, the MP involves some technical changes in how the mental grammar generates syntactic structures based on a conflation of the structure building and the structure changing rules into a structure building operation called **merge** (essentially meaning: combine two things, thus forming one bigger thing). Secondly, at a meta-theoretical level the normal scientific rule of thumb to minimize the complexity of a theory as much as possible (called **Ockam's Razor**) was now declared to be a specific property of the MP which promoted the reduction of unnecessary apparatus. The development of merge can be seen as an example of this rule, but in addition Chomsky recommended getting rid of practically everything that had been proposed in the preceding decades. That this overzealous application of Ockam's Razor led to difficulties in accounting for many of the facts was seen as problematic by many generative linguists, but not by all. Accordingly, we now see that the MP is in such extreme forms not adopted in most sectors of the generative camp. A third, and also meta-theoretical aspect of the MP lies in the conjecture that the innate universal grammar is a perfect system. What this means is not so easy to grasp because it is not explained clearly (or I fail to understand what is being said). I take the claim to mean that its design is not the result of numerous evolutionary steps, which, as evolutionists always say, would produce a system with older and newer layers, along with allowing ever more complex forms of language. Rather, the design of UG is as it would be if one had the opportunity to choose the most economical solution for the kind of system that is needed for human languages as we know them (and have had them for tens of thousands of years). In this view, then, language as we know it sprung into being as the result of perhaps one mutation of some sort. Obviously, one mutation could not bring about a system of great complexity, which is why Chomsky now believes that the content of UG is a mechanism lying at the heart of the syntactic module, namely its **recursivity**, a mathematical notion that allows a finite system to generate an infinite number of structures.

Many linguists have protested against the narrowing down of language to this notion of recursion, a view which entails that everything else about language (phonology, lexicon, and so on) is either nonessential to the nature of language or results from the intersection of UG proper (syntactic recursion) and non-linguistic cognitive systems.

Nonetheless, there is interest in Chomsky's speculations because it is possible that the innate capacity for language as a natural object (i.e., a part of nature) depends not only on genes and environment but also on laws of form such as the laws that mathematicians try to understand when they study the seemingly perfect shapes and structures of natural objects like air bubbles, cells, etc.

Conclusions

In this and the preceding three chapters I have explained a large number of linguistic notions, facts about linguistics as a science and linguistic issues. Many of these deserve a broader treatment, but it is my hope that the reader now, at least, has a general sense of the most important linguistic matters.

There are many aspects to language that go far beyond the facts and rules of grammar (such as language acquisition, language change, language disorders, etc.). Many of these topics can only be sensibly studied, however, if we first have a basic understanding of how languages work in terms of their grammars. It must also be understood that the mental grammar is embedded in, or interacts with, a host of other mental systems that are relevant, or perhaps even specific, to language (such as language processing systems).

The next chapter will make a beginning with explaining the structure of the mental grammar, the subject of linguistics proper.

Chapter 5

The Parts of Grammar

Introduction

In this chapter, I will discuss the overall organization of the mental grammar. I will start with information that might be familiar to the average reader, namely what it is that we find in a grammar *books*. Then I will present the structure of the grammar in more schematic terms, meant as a model of the grammar that speakers have in their heads, the mental grammar.

What Do We Find in a Grammar Book?

Although our goal is to study the structure of the mental grammar, that is the system that speakers of languages have in their heads, I will start by asking what kind of information is usually contained in a grammar (whether prescriptive or descriptive) book. I do this because most readers must have seen or used grammar books, so they know a fair amount about the structure of grammars already. It is reasonable to expect that there are resemblances between grammar books and mental grammars, although the two are quite different things as well.

Pronunciation

Grammar books (for whatever purposes they have been written) often describe the facts of languages by first introducing the reader to the **pronunciation**. This is usually done by listing the sounds of the relevant language, each sound followed by an English word that has that sound or something close to it.

a as *a* in *father*	carta = paper
e as *a* in *mate*	mele = apples
o as *o* in *rope*	colore = color
o as *o* in *soft*	toro = bull

Some grammars use a specific way of indicating the pronunciation of foreign words such as for the following Italian words:

carta	cárr-tah
mele	máy-lay
colore	coh-lóh-ray
toro	táw-rroh

Sometimes the grammar will even describe the sounds in terms of the articulatory movements needed to produce them and/or in terms of impressionistic descriptions of the sounds:

p	lip sound, hard
b	lip sound, soft

A linguist calls the sounds of languages (not the letters to write them!) **PHONemes,** and the study of these units falls under the heading **PHONology.** Phonemes are divided into various subclasses, notably **consonants** and **vowels** (but further subdivisions can be made). Different languages have different sets of phonemes. *English*, for example, has 14 vowels and 24 consonants. The language *Haida* (an American-Indian language) has 3 vowels and 46 consonants.

The words of each language are made up of sequences of consonants and vowels, but it is not the case that any sequence of phonemes will be a **well-formed** word (which means grammatical, or in accordance with the grammar) in any given language. In *English*, for example, the sequence *pr* can occur at the beginning of a word, whereas the same combination is not allowed in many other languages that have a *p* and *r* phoneme, such as, for example, *Hawaiian*. General statements about which combinations of consonants and vowels are permitted in a given language make reference to the notion of **syllable**, assuming that any combination of wellformed syllables will make a wellformed word. A more accurate statement about the phoneme sequence *pr* in English is, then, that it can occur at the beginning of a syllable, for example, *prince, com-pre-.hend, a-pron* (where the dashes indicate syllable divisions). Once we know which syllable types are allowed in a given language, we can say that sequences of wellformed syllables make up wellformed words. Only very detailed grammars will be explicit on the ways that phonemes can be combined into syllables. In most teaching grammars this is left implicit. After having learned many words, you get a sense of what the words of a language generally sound like and you might recognize certain sequences of phonemes as being foreign to the language, just like the sequence *kbom* sounds foreign to, or impossible in English.

Phonemes and Letters

Do not confuse letters and phonemes! Letters belong to the **writing** or **spelling system**, a graphic system for writing down words. Writing is not a part of language in the strict sense. Writing was invented long after languages had come about, and a large number, perhaps the majority, of languages do not even have a writing system today. This observation does not imply that these languages are in any sense incomplete. Teaching grammars will often be concerned with the spelling system and will tell you what the relation is between letters and phonemes.

In many writing systems there is no one-to-one correspondence between letter and phoneme. English spelling is notorious in this respect. Such discrepancies arise for all sorts of reasons, an important one being that the phoneme system of a language may change over time while the spelling system remains as it is.

The Phonotactic Structure

By describing the phonemes, the rules that specify their combinations into syllables and of syllables into words, we say that we capture the **phonotactic structure** of the language. Discovering what the phonotactic structure is of a language is an important task of a **phonological analysis** of the language (which, as we will learn later, comprises *more* than only the phonotactic analysis).

The term **phonology** is used both for the sound side of language and the study of it. So you can say: we know a lot about the phonology of English; and, my field of specialization is phonology (which, in fact, it is for me).

Morphology

When we look at words we encounter cases like *cat, table, alligator, father,* and so on, as well as words like *friend-ship, un-fair, table-cloth, warm-th* (usually without the "dashes" that I put in here). The second group contains words that consist of **meaningful parts**, whereas the first group contains words that cannot be divided into meaningful parts; the words are meaningful wholes.

Any meaningful unit that cannot be divided into smaller meaningful parts is called a **morpheme**. Some morphemes can occur as words by themselves; they are called **free** morphemes (*cat, friend*, etc.), whereas others cannot (like *–th, un-*, etc.); these "word pieces" are called **bound** morphemes, and a technical term for them is **affix**. Affixes need a "base" to attach to. This base must minimally be a free morpheme (*child – hood*, where *child* is the base and *–hood* the affix), but the base can also be a word that already contains an affix (*read – able – ity*) where *-ity* is attached to the base *readable*. When an **affix** is placed *before* its **base**, it is called a **prefix** (like *un-* in *unwise*), otherwise it is called a **suffix** (*-th* in *warm-th*).

The existence of words like *childhood* (which are called **complex words**, as opposed to **simplex words** like *cat*) suggests that there is a procedure according to which complex words can be formed by combining morphemes. This procedure (as well as the study of it) is called **word formation** or **morphology**. Attaching affixes (like *un-* and *-th*) are called **derivation**. Another way in which complex words can be formed is by combining two independently occurring words (as in *table* and *cloth*). This is called **compounding**. (In the spelling systems, compounds sometimes are written with a space, sometimes with a dash, and sometimes connected.)

Note that morphemes typically consist of several phonemes, and, more importantly, note that phonemes, contrary to morphemes, are *not* in themselves meaningful. Morphemes *can* consist of just one phoneme, like *-th*, which is one phoneme despite the fact that in the English spelling system we use two letters for it. A word like *crocodile* consists of eight phonemes.

Grammar books may or may not be explicit about the system of word formation. When you know a language really well you get the hang of making new words through derivation or compounding. Some languages are very rich in morphology, others use it much less. Whatever can be expressed using an affix can usually also be expressed in a sentence (e.g., by adding an extra word), sometimes even within the same language. Compare: *This shirt looks greenish* and *This shirt looks **somewhat** green.*

The Lexicon

In addition to describing the phonotactic structure of words, grammar books usually contain a **list** of common words at the end. Each entry in the list specifies the phonotactic shape of a word (i.e., its pronunciation) and its meaning(s), usually given in the form of one or more English equivalents (if the grammar is meant for speakers of English). This list is often called a **glossary**. Of course, we can also have a separate book that lists the words, called a **dictionary**. The linguist's technical term for the component of the grammar that *contains* the inventory of words (and affixes) of a language is **lexicon,** which, like dictionaries, also might deal with fixed expressions (called **idioms**). Word lists, however we call them, usually also specify for each word a third type of information (next to pronunciation and meaning), namely whether it is a noun, verb, adjective, or preposition, and so on. This is called a **word class or category** (or **part of speech**) **label**.

Thus, words, as **lexical entries** (i.e., as units in a lexicon) contain besides the spelling form at least three pieces of information: the pronunciation (phonemes), one or more meanings, and a category label.

If the pronunciation is given separately rather then being implied in the spelled form of the word, it either uses the system that I referred to earlier (colore [coh-lóh-ray]) or a another type of system of symbols is used that look like letters but as referred to as **phonetic symbols** (colore [kolóre]). I will explain this special symbol system later. Note that either way there usually is an indication of the location of the **accent** or **stress**, i.e., an indication of which syllable must be pronounced with more force).

The lexicon must contain all free and bound morphemes. After all, from the standpoint of a language learner these must all be memorized. (Recall that the notion *free morpheme* is identical to *simplex word.*) For the moment we will assume that complex words, once formed, will also enter the lexicon. This means, among others, that the lexicon is not a fixed component. On the one hand it grows due to morphology and also due to the fact that languages frequently **borrow** words from other languages. It also shrinks because words may disappear when people stop using them for a variety of reasons.

Syntax

At this point we have words (both simplex and complex) with all their properties (phonotactic form, meaning, and word category label). But language is more than words. Memorizing a dictionary is a good first step, but is it not considered learning a language. One of the most eye-catching properties of human language is that words can be combined into sentences. We must thus have a system of rules that regulates how such combinations can be made. This subsystem of the grammar is called **syntax**. Clearly, words (like morphemes) cannot be combined randomly (ungrammaticality is signaled by putting a star in front of the utterance):

> *man the boy sees a
> the man sees a boy

In English, little words like *the* and *a* occur before the word that they go with, and combinations like *the man* occur before the verb if they refer to the subject of the sentence; objects like *a boy* occur after the verb. A combination of words that go together is called a **phrase**, named after the most important word in the combination. Hence we call *the man* a **noun phrase**. A phrase like *very beautiful* would be called an **adjective phrase** because beautiful is an adjective.

The rules for combining words into phrases and sentences (together called **phrase structure rules**) differ from language to language and are thus not universal. Languages differ quite a bit in this respect. In English we say: *I ate apples*, whereas a Japanese speaker would say (with the appropriate Japanese words): *I apples ate*. Phrase structure rules, then, specify the **grouping** of words *including* the **linear order** in which the words occur. The phrase structure rule that specifies that a verb forms a verb phrase with a noun phrase next to it specifies in addition what the order is of these two units.

Inflection

However, in some languages, like Latin or the aboriginal languages of Australia, word order can vary a lot without apparent differences in meaning (*apples I ate, apples ate I, ate I apples.* and so on). You might say that the phrase structure rules leave the order open or undecided so that the speaker can freely choose any order he likes. But how do we know who is eating whom? This may be obvious with people and apples, but now suppose I have *the boy hits the girl, the girl the boy hits, hits the girl the boy*. To keep track of who is doing what to whom such languages rely on rich systems of **inflection**, affixes that tell you who is the **subject** and who is the **object**. The term subject refers to the noun phrase that is the hitter (in semantic terms the **agent**) and the term subject refers to the noun phrase that expresses the one being hit (the **theme**).

Let me give a simple example of inflection. In *Latin* the word for *girl* occurs in different forms, among others *puella* and *puellam*. A similar difference exists for the word for *boy*. Consider the following two sentences:

> *Puella amat puerim*   the girl loves the boy
> *Puer amat puelllam*   the boy loves the girl

In the first sentence we find the form *puella*. The choice of this form indicates that it is the girl who loves the boy; *puella* is the subject form. In the second sentence the form *puellam* indicates that the girl is the one who is being loved; this is the object form. In English we make it clear who is doing what to who by **word order**. In Latin, however, we use inflection endings (suffixes) like *–m*, to do that, which implies that the following sentence still means that the girl is doing the loving:

> *Puerim amat puella*   the girl loves the boy

English doesn't have much inflection and thus relies heavily on fixed word order. We see a remnant of the Latin system in cases like this:

> he loves them
> they love him

Note that there are separate forms for the **pronouns** when occurring as subjects or objects. (That the object form has an *–m* like in Latin is not a coincidence but relates to the fact that English and Latin once were the same language.) In English this kind of inflection no longer occurs for regular nouns, which is why English has a fixed order even in the case of sentences with pronouns. The inverse relationship between inflection and fixed word order is more a tendency than a law. *German* has much more inflection than English (more like Latin), but its word order is not free as it was in Latin.

The inflectional system is best seen as a part of the syntax module of the grammar coming into action, especially when linear order is not fixed.

The question arises, though, whether inflection isn't part of morphology rather than of syntax, and there is debate about that. Inflection, after all, makes use of affixes and this makes it look like derivation. For the moment let us observe that inflectional endings do not really create *new* words, like word formation rules do (derivation and compounding). Rather, they "mark" words (with affixes) for use in specific **syntactic functions** (i.e., subject or object).

A set of inflectional forms for any given base word is called a **paradigm**. English has very simple paradigms. The paradigm for nouns consists of just two forms, the singular form (*table*) and the plural form (*tables*). In many other languages paradigms can be much more complex.

Grammar books need to inform the reader on matters of word order and inflection. Word orders that differ from the native language of the learner are not so difficult to master, while using inflection properly can be extremely demanding.

Conclusions

We have now discussed four subsystems of the grammar:

Phonology	(phonotactics)
Morphology	(derivation and compounding)
Syntax	(phrase structure and inflection)
Lexicon	(phonemic form, meaning, and category of lexical entries)

These are the parts of grammar that can usually be found in a grammar books, either explicitly or implicitly.

Chapter 6

The Organization of Grammar

Introduction

There is, as we have learned, another use of the term grammar and this concerns the grammar as an engine, i.e., as a mental system that underlies the *processing* of language utterances (production and perception). We assume that a grammar-as-engine, the mental grammar (or I-language), is encoded in your brain and it allows you to produce and perceive utterances (or, put differently, it allows you to evaluate potential utterances as being good or bad). In this chapter I offer a model of the mental grammar in the form of a schematic diagram that contains modules much like the grammar parts that we have discussed in the previous chapter.

Mental Grammars

When linguists talk about mental grammars they are especially concerned with the precise way in which the various parts of grammar (which, in your mental grammar, are more or less those that we also find in descriptive grammars) *interact*. Proposals for interaction are usually graphically depicted in the form of diagrams or flow charts with many arrows.

As a first attempt we can combine the subsystems that we have learned about in terms of a diagram that shows how they are interrelated. Perhaps the simplest way is to line them up in the following way:

The Organization of the Grammar (take 1)

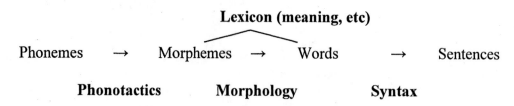

(Instead of the label *phonotactics* I could also use *phonology*, although phonology comprises more than phonotactics. We'll make that distinction precise later on.) In each case the arrow represents a set of combinations.

However, this diagram is not entirely accurate in two ways. Firstly, the phonotactic rules of phonology do not only indicate how phonemes combine into morphemes. Rather, they indicate, as I hope to have made clear already, how phonemes combine to form wellformed *words*. This is a subtle difference, because it is, after all, the case that morphemes *are* made up by sequences of phonemes. The crucial point is that morphemes are not units that are necessarily complete or pronounceable units; we pronounce words, not morphemes. A morpheme like *cat* forms a complete word by itself, so here it looks as if we are splitting hairs, but the morpheme *–th* (*warm-th*) is a word piece that we never need to pronounce as such, i.e., on its own. If we equate completeness or pronounceability with phonotactic wellformedness, we can say that the wellformedness of phoneme combinations need not be decided until we reach the level of words (simplex or complex). We can account for this point by slightly changing the diagram (for simplicity's sake I leave out the word *lexicon*, which I will put back later).

The Organization of the Grammar (take 2)

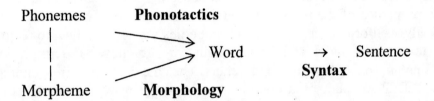

I want to be precise about the notion that the phonotactic rules specify how phonemes are combined to make up words. I do not intend to say that there literally is a procedure to build words from phonemes. Rather, when we speak of rules we mean statements that characterize which sequences of phonemes are wellformed and which are not. As we will point out below, the role of these statements is not *to make* but rather *to check what is there*. Some would call such rules or statements **constraints**.

This brings us to the second inadequacy of Take 1 that is not yet properly remedied in Take 2. If phonemes are an *aspect* or *property of* morphemes rather than exhaustively defining morphemes, what, then, are *morphemes* other than phonemes? Returning to our earlier definition we can say that morphemes are units that include form (phonemes) *and* meaning. Thus we must include the aspect of meaning in our diagram:

The Organization of the Grammar (take 3)

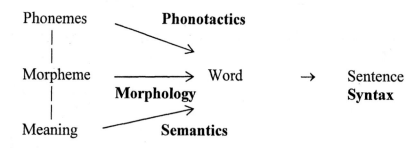

The study of meaning is called **semantics**. In descriptive grammars, as we have seen, meaning is usually only included in the glossary, where entries are provided with, well, a "meaning" (in the form of an English gloss, if they grammar is written in English). Just like phonology deals with the wellformedness of words in terms of their phonotactic structure, so will semantics deal with the semantic wellformedness of words: the combination of the meanings of morphemes must make sense for the word to be semantically wellformed. It is easier to give examples of phonological illformedness (e.g., the string *rpatn* is illformed in English) than to illustrate semantic illformedness, and I will come back to this below. For the moment consider that whereas a complex word like *reread* is fine, *resleep* is, at best, odd. This is probably due to the fact that the semantic properties of the prefix *re-* and those of the base *sleep* do not combine into a semantically wellformed unit. Semantic properties are often called **concepts**, but I also like the term **seme,** and I will later explain why; for now the term *concept* will do. Linguists notate concepts with capital letters. Thus the concept corresponding to the verb sleep is SLEEP, or perhaps a combination of more **basic concepts** like ACTIVITY, DURATIONAL, etc., while the concept corresponding to *re-* can be indicated as AGAIN. (What is and what is not a basic concept remains an important question that I will come back to later on.)

Now that we have peeled away **the phoneme dimension** and **the meaning dimension**, what then remains the content of the label morpheme in Take 3? What other properties do morphemes have beside their form and meaning? Well, earlier I stated that morphemes and words belong to *a part of speech*, also called a **word class** or **word category**. Morphemes need to have a category because they are the building blocks of a combinatorial system and thus they need to have an indication of how they can be combined; this indication is encoded in the **category label**. This categorial label enters into a combination with the categorial labels of other morphemes and words and this combination must be checked for its wellformedness. For example, the prefix *re-* requires its base to be a verb; **re-chair*, **re-happy* are no good. Semantically, **re-happy* could mean *again happy*, thus the problem with this word is not its semantics; nor is there anything obviously wrong with its phonology. Also, category labels (like prefix) indicate that this kind of affix comes *before* its base and not after it. (The difference that you might feel between labels like *verb* and labels like *prefix* will be addressed later.) By definition morphemes have one (simplex) category label. However, when morphemes are combined into complex words we see combinations of categorial class labels.

Accordingly we can revise the diagram as follows:

The Organization of the Grammar (take 4)

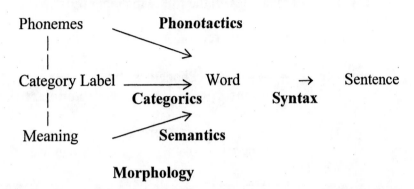

The term *categorics* for the system that accounts for the wellformedness of label combinations is not commonly used. However, we need a term and I want to reserve the term **morphology** for the combination of three-dimensional units (packages of form, category, and meaning) into complex words. Viewed this way there is nothing more to morphology than a single rule: combine two units. The implicit claim that morphology each time combines two units rather the three or four is here taken for granted, but will eventually be supported with arguments. Let us call the combination of such units **merge**.

The view of word formation advocated here is, straightforwardly, that complex words are formed by combining morphemes. However, since morphemes are three-dimensional objects, the result of combining them leads to structure in three dimensions. In fact, we can improve Take 4 by bringing to the surface that words, just like morphemes, have three dimensions that they inherit from the morphemes out of which they are formed.

The Organization of the Grammar (take 5)

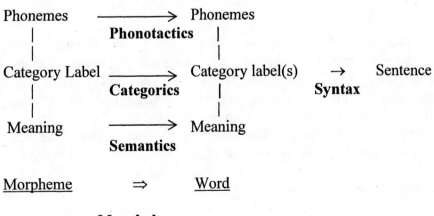

Are we done now? No. Take 5 has lead us to a detailed and accurate depiction of word formation or morphology. We now have the following question: if we clearly separate the three dimensions in morphemes and words, shouldn't we then also tease these layers apart in sentences? After all, sentences consist of sequences of words *with* all their properties. Thus, a sentence is a complex expression that results from merging words into larger wholes (phrases), each having a phonological, categorical, and semantic dimension. Hence, we should operate with the following diagram:

The Organization of the Grammar (take 6)

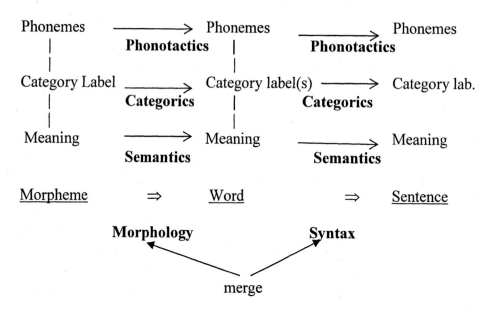

Both morphology and syntax are *generators*, i.e., dumb systems that merge units into large combinations. The intelligent part of the grammar lies in the three systems (phonotactics, categorics, and semantics) that check whether the combinations are wellformed in all relevant respects.

Where is the Lexicon and What's In It?

Where does the lexicon fit into our final diagram (Take 6)? There are different views. If we see the lexicon as the collection of expressions that we *must* commit to memory it might be enough to only store the morphemes. The linking between form and meaning for each morpheme is arbitrary and thus must be memorized. We certainly cannot predict the form from the meaning or vice versa. Likewise there is an arbitrary relation between form and category. The only relationship that is to some extent systematic is that between category and meaning. The meaning of nouns is often a THING and the meaning of verbs is often an ACTIVITY. (Here, recall, I use capital letter words as representing elements of meaning.) But most linguists agree that there is no complete generality in such relationships, so I will assume here that both the meaning and the category must be independently stated for any given morpheme.

We do *not* have to list complex words in the lexicon if we say that these can always be formed by the rules of morphology, and the same applies to sentences. However, there are tendencies in all languages due to which complex words develop unpredictable properties at one or more dimensions. Take the word *length*. It consists of two morphemes, *long* and *–th*. But combining these should give *longth*. This might be considered a reason for listing *length* in the lexicon. The change from *o* to *e* is unpredictable. But we see the same change in *strength* (from *strong* and *–th*), and this might suggest that there is some regularity in the change from *o* to *e* when you add *–th*. Linguists do not always agree about what is and what isn't a general rule. So what is unpredictable and what is predictable is not carved in stone.

Unpredictable properties may also arise in the meaning dimension, and perhaps also at the level of category structure. When complex words develop unpredictabilities we call that *lexicalization* because now those words must be listed in the lexicon.

Even word combinations (phrases) may develop unpredictable properties, often at the meaning level or in terms of their categorial structure. Clearly, the meaning DIE cannot be derived from the meaning elements of the phrase *kick the bucket*. Minimally, then, all expressions that have unpredictable properties must be listed in the lexicon.

A more permissive view on the lexicon would have it that *all* expressions that we somehow know (which means that we are familiar with them, having the sensation that we have heard the expression before) are in the lexicon even when all their properties are technically fully predictable from the properties out of which they are composed. For the moment I will be more conservative and assume that only expressions that have unpredictable properties must be listed in the lexicon:

The Organization of the Grammar (take 7)

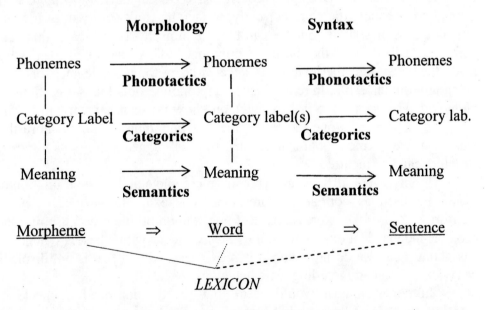

The dotted line indicates that only complex words and sentences with unpredictable properties are in the lexicon, while the closed line indicates that all morphemes must be listed there.

I conclude this chapter by repeating some important points.

The Wellformedness of Morphemes

As mentioned earlier, when we move from Take 1 to Take 2 it is not obvious that we need to check whether each of these three dimensions of morphemes are wellformed because we do not use morphemes as independent linguistic expressions. If certain morphemes, for whatever reason, have illformed phoneme combinations or illformed meanings those "errors" will be filtered out when we check the words that contain them.

As for the category label of morphemes, we said that by definition each morpheme has one category label, and never a categorial combination. Wellformedness in this dimension is thus not an issue unless we consider the option that a morpheme has a totally ungrammatical label, such as *proparticle* (which doesn't exist) or *Ford* (which is a brand label for cars).

So we don't really decide whether morphemes are illformed or not because it isn't relevant or necessary to do that. Meanwhile, free morphemes (i.e., morphemes that could also be words) will, in fact, always be complete and grammatical expressions unless we assume, theoretically, that the lexicon *could* contain words that are alien to the language in question. Or perhaps this isn't just a theoretical possibility. Words that do not fit in the phonotactic system of a language can be present in the lexicon of some language L if we consider the possibility of so-called unadapted **loan words**. For example, suppose a speaker of English hears a foreign word, *pdok*, for an object that he sees in the another country. He buys the object and has no other way to refer to it than by its original name *pdok*. The problem is that English doesn't have words that start with *pd*, so our friend has trouble pronouncing the word correctly; in fact, he can't get it out of his mouth. His ears tell him how it sounds, but he can't do it himself. This means that his lexicon has embraced a loan word that he can't pronounce. This unadapted loan word, however it made their way into the lexicon, is rejected at by the word level phonotactic system as being unpronounceable. In real life such unpronounceable loans are often changed by the phonological system (into *pok*, or *dok*), and how this can happen will be discussed later. That it *can* happen is one indication that the phonology is about more than specifying what the wellformed phonotactic structure is. Apparently, sometimes an illformed structure can be "repaired."

In any event, affixes are typically incomplete and as such ungrammatical if they would be used as complete expressions. For example *–th*, or even *–ness* are not wellformed word-like expressions. But this is not a problem because, in fact, they do not occur as independent expressions; they always occur with a base. (When, as linguists, we talk about them, we do pronounce them. However, doing that is not displaying linguistic behavior, it is called meta-linguistic behavior.)

In conclusion, it would seem that we do not need a checking system for morphemes, at least that is what we will assume from now on (until we see reasons to overthrow this decision).

The Difference Between Words and Sentences

I have been taking for granted that we must make a distinction between the constraint systems for words and the constraint system for sentences. This is a very traditional viewpoint (i.e., to assume that words and sentences are *different kinds* of linguistic units) that is not adopted in all theories of grammar. Indeed, it is not always completely clear whether a complex expression should be regarded as a word or a phrase. I recognize this as an important issue, but I will nonetheless maintain that a principled distinction between the word level and the sentence level is insightful, tenable, and necessary. You can call this a working hypothesis.

People have an amazing capacity for learning and memorizing words. On the average young children learn a dozen or so new words every day for many years of their lives, and learning new words appears to go on during our whole lives, a point of some significance. Sometimes a child needs to hear a word only once to adopt it in his lexicon.

Some would have it that the notion of *word* is quintessential to the nature of human language. Words are **symbols** (in the semiotic sense; see Chapter 1) in that they help in *externalizing* information, information that is otherwise locked up in the minds of individuals. In one way, words break through the barrier of subjective minds by linking a perceptible unit, a chunk of noise to a mental unit, a *concept* of some sort.

The Difference Between Phonology and Morphology

To avoid a common confusion let us clearly state how morphology is very different in nature from phonology. We can state the difference as follows:

- Phonology (rather phonotactics) deals with the combinations of meaningLESS units (phonemes, syllables)
- Morphology deals with the combinations of meaningFUL units (morphemes)

Phonology is a part of morphology, just like semantics and categorics.

Just like morphology deals with the combination of meaningful units below the word level, syntax deals with the combination of meaningful units (words) below the sentence level. In other words, as we have learned, morphology and syntax *are* very similar in nature. Both involve the merging of meaningful units (having a meaning, a phonological form, and belonging to a grammatical class such as verb, adjective, etc.). Just like morphology, syntax has three sides: phonology, semantics, and categorics.

Conclusions

We have now come to see the grammar as a "systems of systems" (grammatical modules), each one responsible for one dimension of either words or sentences. In total, then, we have 6 systems:

	Morpheme to Word (Morphology)	Word to Sentence (Syntax)
Phonotactics	word phonology	sentence phonology
Categorics	word categorics*	sentence categorics**
Semantics	word semantics***	sentence semantics

*I have to warn the reader that while it is common for linguists to use the term morphology as comprising all three dimensions there is sometimes a special emphasis on the categorial side of word formation and this is probably the reason that many use the term morphology as specifically referring to this dimension; as a consequence you will not find many linguists using the term categorics, which I made up to have a clear terminological distinction between morphology (the combination of morphemes) and categorics (the combination of category labels).

** The same issue arises here, but even stronger. Most linguists use the term syntax for what I have here called sentence categorics. This practice makes the term syntax ambiguous because it is then also used for the processes of combining words (with all their properties).

*** Here we also often find the term **lexical semantics**, a term based on the idea that words are the normal inhabitants of the lexicon. However, we have seen that regular complex words do not necessarily end up there, while on the other hand phrases with unpredictable properties must go into the lexicon.

Chapter 7

The Grammar as a Checking Device

Introduction

In this chapter I explain the workings of mental grammars in more detail, focusing more on the kinds of structures that are created when combinations of morphemes or words are made. This leads us to consider the notion of hierarchical structure.

Forming Words and Sentences

In essence, as we have seen, the grammar is a mechanism for characterizing wellformed words and sentences. At both levels,

- (a) we start with primitive units (P), morphemes and words respectively, and merge them into complex units (C), words and sentence respectively. Then,
- (b) we can merge the result of merging primitive units (C) with additional primitive units (P) or
- (c) with other combinations (C) of primitive units:

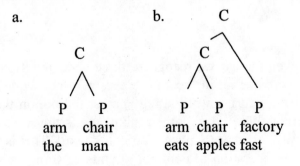

```
a.                    b.          C
                                 /\
        C                   C      \
       /\                  /\       \
      P   P               P   P      P
     arm chair           arm chair factory
     the  man            eats apples fast
```

c.

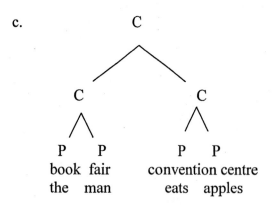

As mentioned, I will asume that any instance of merge simply groups two units (primitive or complex) into a larger unit:

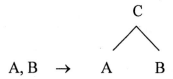

(where A and B are either primitive (P) or complex (C))

Obseve that the operation of merge produces **hierarchical structures**, often called **trees**, a notion that I will discuss in more detail later. The trees, as we draw them, are actually "hanging down" trees because the root is at the top and the leaves at the bottom.

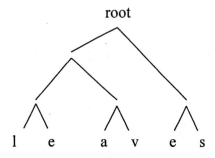

    I want to make it clear that even though we recognize three checking systems, I do not wish to deny that complex words arise, in the first place, as a consequence of merging morphemes. In making this explicit I am militating against the notion that our mental grammar combines, independently of each other, phoneme strings, category labels, and meaning, which are then put together to make a complex word. This is why I make a distinction between merge (the operation of combining units of form, meaning, and category) and checking systems.

    I have assumed so far that the structure that resuls from merge is itself an autonomous structure that is distinct from whatever structure is created in the phonological, categorial, and semantic dimensions. However, we will run into good reasons for deciding that the merge structure can be identified with the categorial structure, meaning that when we merge morphemes into words, or words into sentences, we assume that those units project their category labels into the merge structure, which then will reflect the categorial organization of the complex expression. The resulting structure still needs to be checked for its categorial wellformedness, but this checking would take priority over the checking of the phonological and semantic dimensions. The difference between these two points of view may now seem like splitting hairs, but we will learn that it lies at the heart of some major controversies in linguistics.

The Grammar as a Checking Device

We now need to worry about the following: what guarantees that every combination that results from a merge operation is a wellformed (i.e., grammatical) word or sentence? Nothing. In that sense, merge, which we already called *dumb*, can be said to be *blind* or *inconsiderate*. In order to guarantee that each combination is wellformed we need to check the resulting structures in each of their three dimensions, This checking is precisely the role of the three modules described so far.

- Phonotactics: check that the combination is a wellformed combination of phonemes and syllables.
- Categorics: check that the combination is a wellformed combination of category labels.
- Semantics: check the combination is a wellformed combination of semantic concepts (semes).

Given that morphemes, words, and sentences have three dimensions, a **linguistic expression** (i.e., a morpheme, a word, or a sentence) can be said to be wellformed *if and only if* it is wellformed **in all three dimensions**. Let's illustrate how things might go wrong with some (would be) words.

- A word *athe* is illformed because in English it is not allowable to form a complex word by combining just any two words. *Arm chair*, where we combine two words of the category Noun, is fine. However, *athe* is a combination of two determiners. That doesn't fly in English. Merge can bring this structure about, but it will not pass the categorial check.

- *Resleep* is illformed because of semantic incompatibility between the verb meaning SLEEP and the prefix meaning RE.

- *Importanter* is illformed because of a phonological reason that is too complicated to explain here. Essentially, stressless chunks like -er need to be "close" to a stressed syllable. (This example confirms that wellformedness in the phonological dimension involves more than just arrangements of phonemes; arrangements of syllables also matter.)

The following examples illustrate the three types of illformedness at the level of sentences:

- *Boy the ball a throws* is illformed at the level of categorial structure. Specifically, in English, determiners (the, a) come before nouns. Also, objects follow verbs.

- *Colorless green ideas sleep furiously* is illformed at the level of semantic structure. Specifically, *colorless* and *green* form a contradiction, *ideas* do not have colors, and *sleeping* is not an activity that can be done *furiously*.
  A simpler example of semantic illformedness is: *The boy sleeps and the boy doesn't sleep,* which is a straightforward contradiction.

- *That parrot is smarter than Bill's*
  Whereas we can say Bill's smart (with contraction of *Bill is* into *Bill's*), we cannot do the same thing in the illformed sentence. Hence, we would have to say *That parrot is smarter than Bill is*. Whatever the precise reason, the sentence is illformed because there's something wrong with the phonology of it.

In each case there is a grammatical statement that forbids a particular configuration, and I've referred to such statements as **constraints**. The main task of the mental grammar is to specify the sets of constraints for all three dimensions both at the word and the sentences level.

The claim that grammars are checking devices is sometimes seen as biased toward the perception of language, in view of the fact that when speakers utter complex words or sentences they are obviously "producing" structures rather than checking them. Checking, from this perspective, seems to be something that happens only on the listening end. But this is not true. The idea is simply that structures that are generated by the mental grammar (by the operation merge) must be checked before they are produced. Merge is not really meant as a psychological mechanism here, it is simply a way of allowing us to say that the grammar is a checking device. We need something that can be checked (and that's why we need merge), but truthfully it does not matter where the combinations of morphemes or words come from. The point is that they are not produced by the grammar because the grammar does not produce things; it checks things. If we were to build a model of language production and perception we would need something like merge (but not as dumb and blind) to construct words and sentences that match our preverbal thought that we wish to express. In such a model we would say that from a perception point of view linguistic expressions need to be checked so that only wellformed expressions would be "de-merged" by the listener to arrive at their meaning so that thought similar to that of the speaker can arise in the listener's mind. The bottom line is that the mental grammar as understood here is **neutral** with respect to production or perception of language, or rather, it forms just one part of the total chain of events that falls under speaking and listening (i.e., verbal communication). It would seem, then, that merge and de-merge (as psychological mechanisms) belong to the production and perception systems, respectively.

Constraints

How do we check the structure in each dimension? We need a set of statements that either expresses positively that a piece of structure is wellformed or negatively that it is illformed. Here I take a piece of structure to be each node and its immediate "daughters". In the following diagram we thus have three pieces of structure: a, b and c.

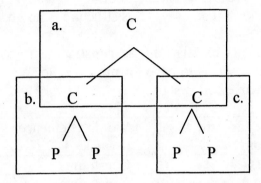

Let's take as a concrete example the word *pitcher*, formed by merging the free morpheme (word) *pitch* and the bound morpheme *–er*. This **binary branching** merge structure brings about a binary branching structure in all three dimensions:

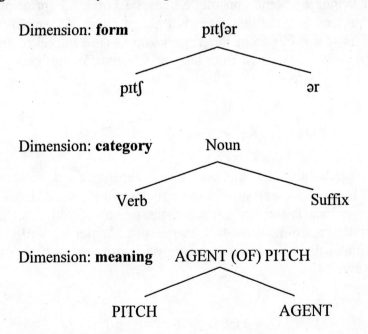

As for the phonological form, we seem to think of this as a sequential structure of speech sounds, here represented with special symbols, one for each phoneme (see below). We also see that even though the whole word is a noun it seems to contain a verb label and also a "word piece" label that, when added to a verb label turns the whole thing into a noun. Finally, it seems clear that the semantic structure of this word is complex, in fact, it probably is more complex than depicted here since PITCH is probably not a semantic primitive (or atom), i.e., a basic **seme**. If a word, simplex or complex, is no good at any of these levels it is illformed. However, our three checking systems find nothing wrong with *pitcher*; hence it passes.

As said, we can think of the checking statements as (positive) statements, but in some cases it is more straightforward to think of the statements in negative terms, i.e., a statement saying a structure of this kind is not a good structure. We can even have implicational statements saying if A is a good structure then B is also a good structure. In short, the statements can take a variety of forms (positive *allowing*, negative *prohibiting*, or if-then *conditional allowing*). In all cases the checker doesn't actually make the structure (that is done by merge), but looks at it and says "this structure is no good" or "I can find nothing wrong with it."

It is common to refer to statements of this kind as **constraints** to avoid the procedural interpretation that the term *rule* seems to have for most people. We can now build constraints into our grammar diagram as follows:

	Morpheme to Word (Morphology)	Word to Sentence (Syntax)
Phonotactics	Constraints	Constraints
Categorics	Constraints	Constraints
Semantics	Constraints	Constraints

In each box there is a system of constraints, and the task of the linguist is to state these constraints for any given language. Some constraints may be universal (principles of language), others will be present in some languages but not in others. It remains to be seen whether the constraints that differ from language to language are picked from a universal and finite pool of constraints, or whether languages can differ from each other in infinite ways.

The Issue of Isomorphism

As mentioned, it is to be expected that the structure in each dimension will be similar if not identical (isomorphic) because we expect that the structure in all three dimensions follows the merge structure which is the starting point, the default if you will, for the structure in each of the three dimensions. However, in the next chapter we will see that the structures in the three dimensions can differ in subtle yet interesting ways due to the specific properties of each dimension.

Compositionality

When complex expressions (words, sentences) are formed in the morphology or syntax (merge), we create, each time, a unit consisting of two subunits. Like its subunits, each complex unit will have three dimensions, a form, a meaning, and a category, and it seems rather obvious perhaps that those properties are the sum total of the properties of the subunits. In other words we are inclined to say that the properties of complex units can be *derived from* or *predicted from* the properties of their parts in each of their three dimensions.

This kind of predictability is usually called **compositionality**, and the rationale of this concept goes back to a formulation of the philosopher Gottlob Frege (1848-1925) who, while focusing on the meaning side of language, formulated the following principle:

Compositionality principle

The meaning of a complex expression is predictable from
      (a) the meaning of its parts and
      (b) the way these parts have been put together

The first clause seems obvious. Let me explain the relevance of the second clause. Consider the following two sentences:

the dog chases the cat - the cat chases the dog

Clearly the linear order is crucial here in determining who is chasing who. But the importance of the way that the parts have been put together goes beyond linear order. If we wish to compute the meaning of, for example, a sentence, we have to know the entire organization of the sentence, i.e., we need to make sure that we know how the words have been grouped. Consider the following sentence:

the dog chases the cat with the car

This string can mean two things, depending on who is using the car; the dog or the cat. The difference can exist because this string of words can have two different semantic structures that mirror two possible merge structures. In one (where the *cat* has the *car*), "with the car" is grouped together with "cat." In the other there is no such grouping, which means that we infer that it is the dog that is chasing the *cat* by means of a *car*:

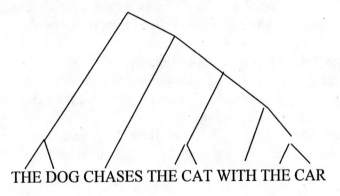

THE DOG CHASES THE CAT WITH THE CAR

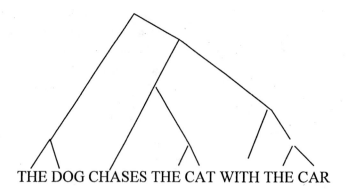

THE DOG CHASES THE CAT WITH THE CAR

These structures are meant to be semantic structures (hence the capitals which represent semantic concepts) which mirror the way that units (words and word groups) have been merged. Clearly, to derive the two different meanings we cannot just add up the meanings of words; we have to do this adding up while taking into account how words have been combined. In this case, the two merge structures show the same linear order of words; in other cases the linear organization of words is different:

The second clause of the compositionality principle is also important at the word level. For example, *boy lover* and *lover boy*, have two completely different meanings. The compound *spy book fair* is ambiguous depending on its structure. Can you figure out which two structures this string of words can have?

Thus, it is important not only to know the meaning of the words that are grouped together but also to know how the units have been put together.

The compositionality principle, while first formulated for the meaning dimension, can also be taken to apply to the two other dimensions.

The phonotactic form of a complex expression is predictable from the form of its parts and the way these parts have been put together.

The categorical structure of a complex expression is predictable from the categories of its parts and the way these parts have been put together.

It should not surprise us that the compositionality principles apply in all three dimensions. After all, language is not magic. Properties of complex units do not fall from the sky. They can only come, it would seem, from the part that they contain and, indeed, the structure into which these parts have entered.

In the next chapters I will show in detail how the principle of compositionality can be taken to apply to the categorial and phonological dimension of complex expressions.

Particulate Systems and Blending Systems

Compositionality exists by virtue of a specific characteristic that linguistic structures have. Among combinatorial systems a distinction is sometimes made between

particulate systems and **blending systems**. In a particulate system the primitives and higher units remain recognizable (or retrievable) at all times. Thus, in the case of chemical compounds one can decompose a complex unit into its constituent elements. Chemistry is thus a particulate system. Cooking may not be. Once you mix ingredients it will not be possible to retrieve them because they have blended. Mixing different colors of paint is another example of a blending system. (Perhaps you can decompose a cake or mixed paint at the molecular level, but that is beyond the domain of cooking or painting.) Morphology and syntax are also particulate systems, and it is obvious why this must be so. If you make a complex word or sentence, you want someone else to decompose (de-merge) it into its parts so that that person can reconstruct the meaning of your sentence. Hence, forming a complex word or sentence is not like cooking at all; it is more like forming a chemical compound. In fact, given this distinction one might argue that cooking doesn't produce wellformed structures from a checking point of view. How would we check whether your mother used the right ingredients to bake her cake? The best we can say is how things taste!

The Relationship Between Form and Meaning

Due to the compositionality principle complex expressions have predictable properties in all three dimensions, but this does not mean that the specific *co-occurrence* of these dimensions for any given word or sentence is predictable. A morpheme, recall, is simply an *arbitrary combination* of form and meaning and category. Thus, in principle, any form can have any meaning, and vice versa (compare English *dog*, Dutch *hond*, French *chien*). The relationship between category and meaning is somewhat predictable, but still not predictable enough to fully derive category labels from meanings or vice versa.

It is actually difficult to see what a non-arbitrary, i.e., motivated relation between form and meaning, could be since we don't know what meanings sound like; there could, however, be a non-arbitrary relation between the form and the referent (or rather some noise that is associated with the referent), although in natural languages this is mostly not the case. It does, of course, happen that the phonology of words seems to reflect an aspect of the referent. Such words are called **onomatopoeic words** or **onomatopoeia**. (Think of words like *buzz* or *sizzle*; names for animals are often onomatopoeic words: *cock-a-doodle-doo, pewit*) In a broad sense the phenomenon of such motivated relationships between form and meaning is called **iconicity**. Words like *buzz* are iconic (or partially iconic) signs, while most words (like *dog*) are symbols.

It is also said that in some cases certain aspects of the phonology (i.e., certain types of vowels or consonant combinations) are associated with a meaning that is intrinsically tied to the "character" of these sounds. This is called **sound symbolism**. A frequently cited example is that, in English, words that start with the consonant sequence *sl* refer to slimy things.

But even though relationships of this sort can exist and can even be quasi-regular in certain portions of the lexicon and morphology, they never seem to be absolute requirements that govern languages as a whole. There are deep reasons for why form and meaning are fundamentally unrelated, and you may want to think about this issue. Here, unfortunately, we cannot explore this issue any further.

This arbitrariness found at the morpheme level is inherited by complex expressions. Consider the following two examples:

Meaning units	Complex Meaning
TEACH - ER	SOMEONE WHO TEACHES
	*MUSEUM OF ART
THE DOG CHASES THE CAT	DOG (DEF) CHASES CAT (DEF)
	*RAINDROPS ARE FALLING ON MY HEAD

It is clear that the two expressions given here have a meaning that is, as per the compositionality principle, predictable. *However, the meaning is **not** predictable from the form as such*, or vice versa. The relationship between the form *teacher* and its meaning, "someone who teaches," is still arbitrary in that one could not guess what *teacher* means simply from its phonological form.

Repair Rules

So far we have assumed that complex words or sentences that apear to be illformed in one or more dimensions are rejected; they go into the waste basket! Returning to our brief discussion of loan words, we can now see that loan words that do not fit the phonotactic system of a language L would be rejected by the checking system. However, sometimes there is hope. It would appear that the boxes in our grammar diagram can contain more than constraints; it has been claimed that they can also contain *repair rules*. For example, a loan word that is illformed in the receiving language (although it is perfectly fine in the donor language) can be subjected to a repair rule that will modify the phonotactic structure of the word. For example, in English, syllables cannot start with the combination *kn*. At an earlier point in the history of English this combination was allowed and words like *knee* still reflect that in their spelling. Suppose now that you come across a brand name, *Knorr*. Many speakers of English will pronounce this brandname as "nor."

When we turn to a more detailed discussion of structures and constraints we will see that repair rules have been claimed to play a considerable role in generative grammar, especially in the phonological and categorial components. That repair rules are less known in semantics may reveal a true difference between this component and the other two, or it may be a result of approaching the apparent need of repair rules in a different way. It is certainly the case that the need for repair rules is controversial, and in some linguistic theories the alleged adjustments are taken care of differently.

Conclusions

We now have a general idea of the organization of mental grammars, as well as of what these grammars are supposed to do (namely check things). It is worth repeating that when combinations of units are formed, the crucial task of the mental grammar is:

> to guarantee that each combination is wellformed in all three dimensions (form, meaning, and category)

Wellformed is just another word for **grammatical,** which means "in accordance with the rules (or constraints) of the mental grammar."

Consider this chapter your *first* encounter with the notion of mental grammar *as a checking device*. In the following chapter we take our explanation to a deeper level and offer discussion of each of the three dimensions of linguistic expressions.

Chapter 8

Checking Three Dimensions and at Two Levels

Introduction

Having seen the general architecture of the grammar and the checking function of its modules, we will now descend deeper into this same material. I will start with a discussion of the word level (morphology), going though a discussion of each of the three dimensions. Then I'll do the same thing for sentences (syntax). I will repeat definitions of crucial terminology, just to give you an opportunity to become fluent in using the right terms.

Morphology

Morphemes are the smallest meaningful units, where smallest means that they cannot be further divided into form-meaning-category packages. The grammar has a procedure (merge) for making words that consist of more than one morpheme, called morphology. The following examples, once more, illustrate the important distinction between simplex and complex words:

Complex word	Morphemes
dog	arm - chair
house	employ - ee
father	play - er
crocodile	drink - able
enter	un - real
hippopotamus	enjoy - ment
structure	depart - ure

We could make both lists much, much longer. What is the difference between the words on the left and the words on the right? The difference is that the words on the right each consist of two parts that have their own meaning.

arm - chair
employ - ee
play - er
drink - able
un - real
enjoy - ment
depart - ure

Only a subset of the morphemes, namely those that are called "free" can stand on their own as linguistic expressions. By definition, then, these units are at the same time morphemes and (simplex) words. Another (self-evident) term for simplex words is **monomorphemic words**. Bound morphemes cannot stand on their own, such as the word pieces *un-* and *–able*, which we call affixes. An affix that is placed before a stem is called a **prefix** (e.g., *un*), one that comes after the stem is called a **suffix** (e.g., *able*). Some complex words (like *armchair*) do not contain an affix, but rather are formed from two free forms. Such complex words are called **compounds**, and the process for forming compounds is called **compounding**.

It would seem that all morphemes have a phonological form. Free morphemes also belong to a word category and with respect to the bound morphemes we will assume that they belong to the categories prefix and suffix. What about the meaning dimensions of morphemes? The meaning of all the free morphemes is easy enough to establish since they all occur as independent words. The meaning of the affixes (such as *-ee,- er, -able, un-, -ment,- ure*) is more difficult to grasp, but we can try:

ee	SOMEONE WHO IS X-ed (X = verb)
er	SOMEONE WHO X (X = verb)
able	CAN BE X (X = verb)
un	NOT X (X is adjective)
ment	FEELING OF X (X = verb)
ure	ACT OF X (X = verb)

Thus, it is clear that the words in question can be split up into two meaningful parts.

One might ask whether there are morphemes that lack one of the three dimensions. Are there meaningless, or formless (i.e., silent), or category-free morphemes? Maybe. This is not an unreasonable question, given that we have said that there are no wellformedness constraints for morphemes. You might want to think of some examples. I can only say at this point that such "degenerates" have been proposed in the linguistic literature. For now, we'll now take this possibility into account.

We cannot split up the words in the left column. (You can try.) Also, after we have split up the words in the right-hand column we end up with pieces that we cannot divide further into meaningful chunks. (Try it.)

You could say that *drink* can be divided into *dr* and *ink* and that *ink* has a meaning. True, but what is the meaning of *dr*, and, moreover, what does the meaning of *ink* have to do with the meaning of *drink*? You might then suggest that *employ* can be divided into *em* and *ploy*; *ploy* is a word but what is the meaning of *em* and how would the meaning of *ploy* fit into the meaning of *employ*? We have *em* in embark and other words, but it is simply hard to establish sets of words in which *em* has a recurrent meaning. It is reasonable to suppose (and, in fact, correct) that *employ* consists of two morphemes if we trace the origin of this word. From the view point of Modern English this ancient structure is no longer really detectable. It would seem that the chunks *ploy* and *ink* are only accidentally (or only historically) identical to independent words.

Complex (or **polymorphemic**) words can certainly consist of *more than two* meaningful chunks. Consider:

> un - friend - ly
> arm - chair - pillow - case
> re - read - able

In fact, English is rather modest in this respect, but there are languages where words can consist of more than a dozen meaningful chunks. Although English does have *antidisestablishmentarianism* and even longer words in specialized medical jargon.

Having established what linguists have in mind when they use the term morphology (which in addition to affixation also comprises compounding), we will now investigate morphological constructs, focusing on derivation, in terms of the constraints that exist at each of the three levels (phonology, category, and meaning).

The Phonotactic Structure of Words

Consider again the two columns of words that we have looked at above. A simplex word like *dog* consists of one morpheme. However, it seems clear that we can still divide up this word into smaller parts, like *d*, *o*, and *g*. We call these parts *speech sounds* or, with a technical term, **phonemes**. The crucial difference between morphemes and phonemes is that the latter have no meaning, they are pure building blocks of form. Thus, even simplex words have a structure. This is not, however, a morphological structure, but a **phonological structure**.

All languages have two major types of phonemes: **vowels** and **consonants**. Languages differ in terms of the vowels and consonants that they have. In marginal cases a morpheme can consist of one phoneme. Think of the English word *I* (as in, I play). Words that consist of one phoneme always have a vowel phoneme (at least in English). The number of such words is limited, since each language only has a small and in any event finite number of vowels. When we look at affixes, we see that they often can consist of just one phoneme, even consonants, such as the suffixes *–th* (*warm-th*) and *–ee* (*employ-ee*).

In the English spelling system phonemes are represented by letters taken from the Roman alphabet. The relationship between letters and phonemes is tricky, however. The phoneme /k/ is represented by the letter <c> (in *cat*) and <k> (*kiss*) or by the phoneme combination <ck> (*trick*). At the same time we also use the letter <c> for the phoneme /s/ (*trace*). The latter word ends in a letter <e> that does not correspond to any phoneme. (When we explicitly refer to spelling we place the letter between < and >.)

To avoid such complications linguists have agreed on using an **International Phonetic Alphabet (IPA)** that has exactly one letter symbol for each possible phoneme in whatever language. IPA uses all the letters from the English (or rather Roman) alphabet, but since there aren't enough Roman letters to have a unique symbol for every possible phoneme, many additional odd looking symbols have been invented, as well as so-called **diacritic** symbols that can be added to letters to make more distinctions. Below, I will start using IPA symbols and explain them as we go along. You'll be able to recognize an IPA symbol or string of symbols because we flank them by slant lines: /kæt/ is the IPA transcription of the English word *cat*. It has three symbols /k æ t/.

We might now ask:

(a) whether the phonological structure is simply a linear arrangement
(b) whether there are any rules that govern the way that phonemes are arranged

In previous chapters we have, in fact, already answered these questions. With respect to question (a) we have mentioned syllables as groupings of phonemes, and with respect to question (b) we have confirmed that not all combinations are wellformed.

To continue answering to the first question in more detail let us ask how we can detect any further phonotactic structure in words beyond the phonemes. Compare, for example, a word like *dog* with a word like *crocodile*. The latter word is longer, but is there more to it than that? It doesn't take much to convince people that the latter word consists of three **syllables** (*cro - co - dile*), whereas *dog* has just one syllable. Mind you, we are here considering the way that the words are pronounced rather than how they are written (in other words, we ignore the silent <e> at the end of *crocodile*).

What is a syllable? A syllable is a vowel with possibly one or two flanking consonants. Until further notice let us say that any given syllable could be a word by itself. Hence, the word *dog* consists of one syllable; it is **monosyllabic**. *Crocodile* is different, though. It has three vowels, thus a first good guess is that it contains three syllables; it is **trisyllabic**. The tricky part is to decide which consonants go with which vowel. In a word like *crocodile* it is not clear whether the consonant represented by the second letter <c> goes with the first or with the second syllable; some say it goes with both. Usually a single consonant flanked by two vowels goes with the second vowel. Thus, we can represent syllable grouping in terms of a hierarchical layer *in between* the phonemes and the whole word.

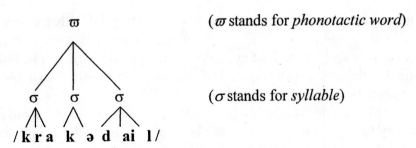

(ϖ stands for *phonotactic word*)

(σ stands for *syllable*)

(The vowel in the third syllable is represented by two symbols. However, we still treat /ai/ as one vowel, a so-called **diphthong**. Vowels that do not have this complexity are called **monophthongs**.)

In linguistics, as we have learned, we use tree diagrams to indicate grouping, and we assign a label to the group as a whole which indicates the type of group.

We now turn to the second question posed above. Are there any rules that govern the combinations of phonemes? In a sense we have already provided a partial answer by answering the first question. We can say that phonemes are grouped into syllables and that syllables are grouped into words.

We can furthermore note that there are specific phonotactic rules for both types of grouping. Consider syllables first. In English a syllable can start with the consonant sequences /kr/, but it cannot start with the reverse sequence. Thus the following sequence is ungrammatical, i.e., not in accordance with the phonological rules of the English grammar. We can express this in the form of a constraint:

* **r k** (at the beginning of a syllable)

It turns out that many sequences of phonemes do not constitute grammatical syllable beginnings or endings and that indeed we can come up with a finite set of constraints that defines what is a grammatical syllable in English. Just like languages differ in terms of their vowel and consonant sets, so they also differ in their syllable constraints. Even if they would have the same phonemes, they could still differ in allowing different combinations within the syllable.

There are also rules that govern how syllables can be combined into words. One such rule in English has to do with what kind of vowel the syllable contains. English has a vowel that is called the **schwa** (IPA /ə/). This is the second vowel in *father*, the first vowel in *balloon*, the second vowel in *crocodile*, and so on. Note that the schwa vowel is written in several different ways in the spelling system. A rule about syllable combinations is that a syllable with a schwa can never be in position where it is **stressed**.

This allows me to make a remark about the notion **word stress**. Every word in English can be said to have a stressed syllable. You can hear this best if the word has more than one syllable. The stressed syllable is the most prominent syllable.

f<u>a</u>ther	pe<u>cu</u>liar
<u>cro</u>codile	Missis<u>si</u>ppi
bal<u>loon</u>	pa<u>ren</u>tal
A<u>me</u>rica	<u>arm</u>chair

Languages have interesting rules for choosing the syllable that is stressed. In English the rule is not so obvious, but in other languages there is a clear rule. In Icelandic, for example, it is always the first syllable that is stressed, whereas in Polish it is always the pre-final syllable that is stressed. The specification of which syllable bears stress is part of the phonotactic analysis.

Another rule concerning the occurrence of syllables in a word is, for example, that certain syllables can only occur at the beginning of a word. In English, syllables that start with /spr/ tend to occur only at the beginning of simplex words (e.g., *spring*). If we find /spr/ in the middle of a word, this string is divided between two syllables: *as-prin*. In general, words seem to allow bigger consonant sequences at their beginning or end.

Now that we know that there is such a thing as phonotactic wellformedness we need to ask what happens when we make complex words. The phoneme strings of the parts of complex words need to be integrated into one π (phonotactic word). Consider the word *walker*. When the word *walk* occurs on its own it already has a structure, which has one syllable in it that all the phonemes belong to:

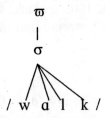

What happens when we add the string -/ər/? We can't just add it as a separate syllable:

a.

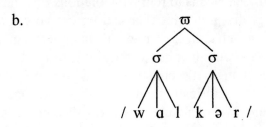

This perhaps would be strictly compositional, but unfortunately this phonotactic structure is illformed because in English (and this is true in all languages) consonants that occur in between vowels group as much as possible to the right. The correct structure is thus:

b.

We can accomplish this result in either of two ways. (a) We can erase all syllable grouping when affixes are added and construct the correct structure or (b) we can assume that the structure of the base is *minimally adjusted*. Here we see, for the first time, a real need to postulate an additional procedure, next to combination, namely editing (i.e., erasing and rebuilding structure or, better, minimally modifying structure). We need a repair rule that turns the *a* structure into the *b* structure.

We also can demonstrate the need for repair rules at the level the phonemes themselves. Consider the following words:

> in elegant
> in nocent
> iŋ credible
> im possible
> il logical
> ir rational

We see that the negative prefix has 5 different phonological forms, which depend on the combination that they occur in. This phenomenon is called **allomorphy.** An obvious account of this variation is to choose one form as basic and derive the others in terms of adjustment rules. For the moment we will assume that this is the correct way to go about it. This means we need repair rules that change /n/ into a variety of other phonemes. Why does this happen? Let us assume that there is a set of phonotactic constraints that rule out certain combinations of phonemes, such as /nk/, /np/, /nl/ and /nr/. In fact such clusters are nearly absent in simplex words, which shows that they are phonotactically deviant. There is a way of stating these constraints in a unified manner (i.e., as one constraint), but we will not bother about that now. These constraints are essentially of the same type of constraints that rule out certain combinations within syllables (like /kn-/ or /rk-/), except that here we deal with sequences of phonemes that belong to different syllables. Given these constraints the result of adding the negative prefix leads to a result that is phonotactically illformed whenever the base starts with a consonant other than /n/:

*in credible
*in possible
*in logical
*in rational

However, instead of throwing these forms in the garbage the phonological system has a repair strategy in the form of a small set of rules that change /n/ into the appropriate phonemes. Repair rules, then, are mechanisms to remove violations of constraints.

There is another negative prefix, *un-*, which has a different vowel, and you might wonder whether there also is a rule changing /i/ into /u/, but there isn't. There is no reason for why, for example, *inwise* would be phonotactically illformed and there is thus no repair rule that would make the change. It seems that *in-* and *un-* are different prefixes in Modern English (although they are historically related). Some words take the *in-* prefix and others take the *un-* prefix. There is some regularity in how the choice is made, but we won't go into that here.

Summarizing, we can say that the phonological module at the word level specifies (a) a finite set of phonemes as primitive building blocks, (b) a finite set of constraints that characterize all the permissible, i.e., wellformed combinations of phonemes into word forms (here called phonotactic words), and (c) a set of repair rules.

Both aspects of word phonology need to be fleshed out further. In Chapter 10 we will go into more detail and learn that the phonotactic structure is more elaborate (but strictly binary) and also that there are many more (types of) repair rules.

A Note on Compositionality

We now have to ask in which sense complex phonological units are compositional. Related to this we have to ask what the status is of the labels *syllable* (σ) and *phonotactic words* (ϖ). Instead of providing higher nodes in the structure just with these labels, we bring out the notion of compositionality more adequately if we provide those nodes with the sum total of the phonemes of the lower parts, in the right order:

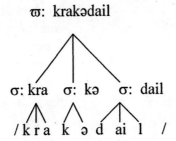

We can then say that the labels *syllable* and *phonotactic word* are nothing more than names for the first and second layer of organization in the phonological structure. These labels are not compositional properties. Compositionally, each syllable is the combination of the phonemes that compose it. It is important, though, to keep track of the layers because phonotactic constraints make reference to them. A combination /rk/ is illformed when it is the beginning of a syllable, but fine if the /r/ and /k/ belong to different syllables, as in *orca* /orka/.

I will make one other remark about phonological compositionality here that will be developed in a later chapter. I mentioned the property of *stress*. One syllable in a word is said to be stressed. Is stress a compositional property? It does not seem to be. The extra prominence of the stress syllable is not due to an intrinsic property of the syllable in question. Somehow, then, combinations of units can have emergent properties, properties that cannot be derived from the parts but that are properties of the structure as such. In Icelandic, for example, the first syllable in the phonotactic word structure is always the one that carries stress. In a later chapter I will examine the nature of this kind of **structural property**.

A Note on Binarity

Note that the structures in the phonological organization are not always binary branching. It might be that the binarity claim only holds for merge structure and is carried over in the phonotactic structure only to the extent that the phonological material comes from different norphemes (as in the example *walker*). In Chapter x we will revisit this issue and suggest there are good reasons for adhering to strict binarity of structure. This will necessarily entail postulating more layers in between the phoneme layer and the syllable layer, and in between the syllable layer and the word layer.

The Categorial Structure of Words

Here are some additional examples of complex words:

Complex word	Category	Morphemes
friendship	noun	friend - ship
crocodile	noun	crocodile
armchair	noun	arm - chair
warmly	adverb	warm - ly
soccer	noun	soccer
sleeper	noun	sleep - er
occasional	adjective	occasion - al
readable	adjective	read - able
reread	verb	re - read

We have just discussed how such combinations are checked for their phonological properties. Let us now investigate the categorical structure of morpheme combinations. Take a look at the word *unfriendly*. This complex word consists of three morphemes, and the question can now be raised whether, at the level of category labels, these three morphemes just form a simple linear string or whether there is a more detailed grouping. We have three possibilities:

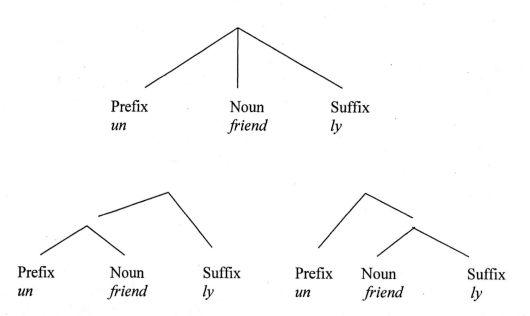

(The italics represent the *name* for each morpheme, which has no official status but is put in so that we can keep track of which morphemes we are talking about. When we talk about the phonological or semantic structure we do no need such remains because the notations we use for form and meaning are sufficient reminders.)

Which one do you think is correct? And why? If we assume that the merge structure is binary and we assume that this also holds for the categorial structure (by default), the first structure is out. However, there are independent reasons for ruling this option out. If we believe that the second structure is correct, we seem to be saying that the sub-structure *un + friend* is a possible word. The problem is that there is no such word as *unfriend* and, more crucially, we cannot add the prefix *un-* to nouns so *unfriend* could not exist; it is not a **possible word**. Rather we add *un-* to adjectives (*unfair, unprepared*). The third structure lacks both problems. *Friendly* is a possible, and, in fact, an **actual word**, and because it is an adjective we can add *un-* to it. Thus the best categorial structure is one in which only binary combinations are used. This implies that the categorial structure of words with more than two morphemes is hierarchical.

We will make this hierarchical structure more complete by adding category labels to all the nodes in the structure. After all, *friendly* is a noun and the whole thing is an adjective:

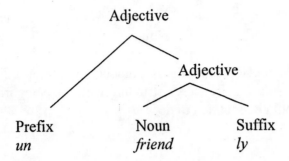

A space-saving way to represent hierarchical and linear structure is to use brackets (which do not make it easier to see what the structure is, though).

$$[[\ un \ ]_{Pfx} \ [[\ friend \ ]_{Noun} \ [\ ly \ ]_{Sfx}]_{Adj}]_{Adj}$$

First we put square brackets around each morpheme and again around each combination of morphemes. Then we attach the category labels to the right-hand brackets (]). You have to make sure that each opening bracket ([) corresponds to a closing bracket (]). The reason for putting the category labels in the flat structure as subscripts is to bring to the surface that we are talking about a categorial structure. In fact, the higher level labels have no other place to go, so to speak, because they are not part of the properties of any morpheme.

We can also use the flat notation for the phonological tree diagrams:

$$(\ (kra)_{\sigma} \ (k\partial)_{\sigma} \ (dail)_{\sigma} \ )_{\omega}$$

The use of parentheses rather than square brackets is irrelevant, but in practice it is useful to differentiate the brackets for the different dimensions, as I will do. (We'll later see that tree and bracket notations can also be used for semantic structures.)

The grammar allows the speaker to make new words though derivation and compounding. There are, of course, other ways to get new words. Especially important is borrowing. Every language that is in contact with other languages borrows words from those languages.

The categorial structure and the phonological structure are independent from each other and can be thought of as existing in separate dimensions or planes.

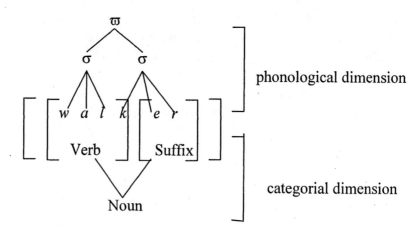

The merge structure is indicated using the flat bracketing notation. Recall that we will, at some point, consider conflating the merge structure with the categorial structure, which is what must linguists would be inclined to do.

Another Note on Compositionality

In which sense, precisely, is the categorial label of a complex unit compositional? Consider again the structure of *walker*:

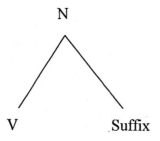

Why is the top label *N*, and in which sense can this label be said to be predictable from the labels of the units that have been combined? We can answer this question by considering some examples of compounds.

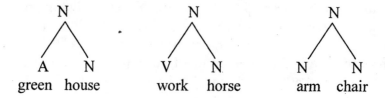

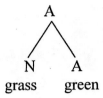

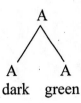

In each case the compound is a noun when the right-hand morpheme is a noun, and an adjective when the right-hand member is an adjective. This seems to suggest that, in compounds at least, the category label of the whole unit is identical to the category label of the right-hand unit. The category label of the left-hand unit is immaterial. This is a kind of compositionality in the sense that the category label is predictable from one of the subunits, more specifically the one that occurs in the second position. It is a different kind of compositionality from what we saw in the case of phonology and will see in the case of semantics because the top label is not, somehow, a combination of the labels that have been brought together.

Suppose now that this right-hand effect is true for all complex words (let us be cautious and say that it holds in English). Returning to *walker* this would suggest that the suffix *–er* is some sort of noun.

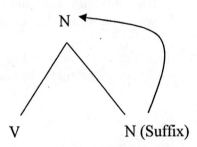

In other words, the suffix *–er* is a *noun maker*, and in fact this is always so. Every derived word with *–er* (meaning AGENT) is a noun.

In conclusion, we can say that the categorial label of complex words *is* predictable from one of the category labels that enters into the complex unit. The other label is not compositionally incorporated into the categorial label of the whole construct, which seems to tell us that the nature of this label is irrelevant to determining how the complex structure can be incorporated into larger categorial structures. (When we get a chance to be more precise on these issues, we will learn that the categorial kind of compositionality, in fact, also occurs in the cases of phonological and semantic structure, which in addition have the normal kind of compositionality. And we will learn why such differences exist.)

Categorial Repair Rules?

Are there any reasons for postulating repair rules in the categorial word system? And what would such rules look like? For the sake of the argument, let us construct a potential case of repair. Suppose we have attached the suffix *-able* to a noun, whereas this prefix requires a verb as its base.

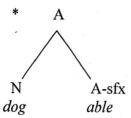

Instead of rejecting this structure, one might imagine a repair rule that changes the class label of the base from N to V.

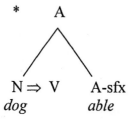

It is conceivable that such cases exist, although it is difficult to check whether the change from N to V has taken place. If words like *dogable* exist, they might also simply be exceptions.

At this point I will leave these questions open, but I will say here that it has not been customary to recognize the necessity for rules that edit the categorial structure of complex words.

Different Types of Structures

The phonological structure and the categorial structure of words are both hierarchical. The phonological structure did not appear to be binary, but, as mentioned, that is perhaps only because we have not gone into sufficient detail. However, there is another difference between the two structures that is perhaps real.

Note that phonological structures have the property of **strict layering,** meaning that each grouping creates a new layer with its own label. Phonemes group into syllables, and syllables group into phonotactic words.

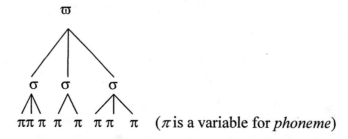

However, categorial structures are not strictly layered, or, rather, they are *self-containing.*

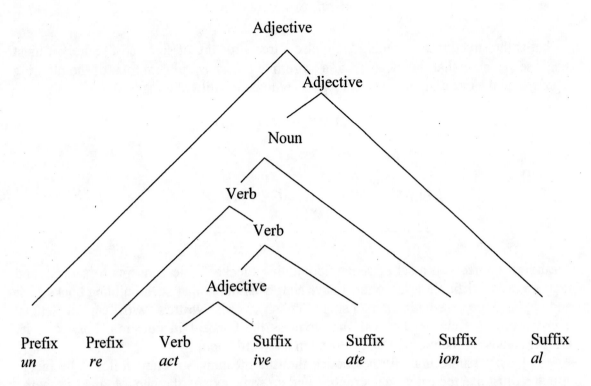

Each case of affixation creates a word, and we thus see that words are contained in words, apparently without limit. This is what I meant by self-containing. In the phonological structure we do not see syllables inside syllables, or phonotactic words inside phonotactic words. Schematically we can represent the difference as follows:

    a.   Phonology   b.   Categorics

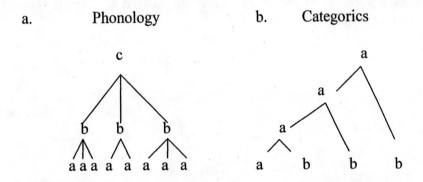

A self-containing structure is also often called **recursive**, a concept that we will define more precisely later on.

    We now turn to the third dimension of complex words, namely the semantic dimension.

The Semantic Structure of Words

What is the structure of meaning? Is it also a tree structure of some sort? Surely it must be. It seems clear that the meaning of a word like *player* is the sum total of the meaning of *play* and the meaning of *-er* (i.e., there is compositionality of meaning).

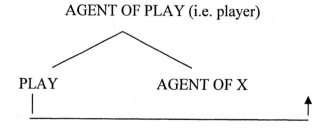

AGENT OF PLAY (i.e. player)

PLAY   AGENT OF X

We haven't agreed on a set of semantic building blocks (basic concepts or semes), and that is a rather difficult task. So far, I have simply assumed that such building bocks exist and I have represented them using English words written with capital letters. Those words are chosen because they express the concept in question. For example, GOOD stands for the concept that we find in the word *good*.

I will assume until further notice that the meaning structure follows the merge structure, just like the categorial structure and, to some extent, the phonological structure. The tree structure indicates that {PLAY} and {PERSON, ACTOR OF X} are two semantic units that together form a larger semantic unit. (I'll use braces from now on for semantic structure.) During the semantic composition, the meaning of *play* is plugged into the **variable** in the meaning of *-er*. Rather than seeing PLAY as the unit that is substituted for a variable in the suffix, other linguists might argue that the variable is located in the meaning of the base.

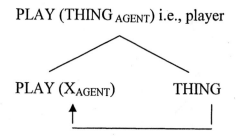

PLAY (THING $_{AGENT}$) i.e., player

PLAY (X $_{AGENT}$)   THING

PLAY, after all, is a *predicate*, which takes one argument, the semantic role of which is AGENT. (The predicate PLAY may be said to take two arguments, the second argument being the THEME (i.e., what is *played*).

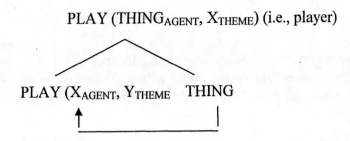

The theme argument can be **satisfied** by adding another level of complexity at the word level by creating a compound.

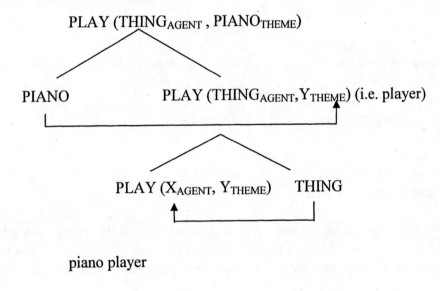

piano player

Semantic Repair Rules

We need to raise the question whether we anticipate the need for semantic adjustment rules. Here, as in the case of categorial structure, there is no obvious example of what such repairs would be. I postpone answering this question in more definite terms until later.

Syntax

We now turn to the three dimensions of syntax, the formation of sentences out of words. A single word *can* form a sentence, for example: *Go!* or (Who did that?) *Me!* More typically, however, sentences consist of several words, each with its own form, category, and meaning. In our discussion of the three dimensions of sentences, I will start with the categorial dimension. Before we start with the categorial aspect of *sentences*, we need to say more about word categories.

Word Categories

Which word categories do we have or need? It turns out that all human languages that we know of have **nouns** and **verbs**. Some will argue that these two word classes function in what is perhaps the most basic communicative act, namely **naming** entities in the world (perhaps often accompanied by pointing to them as well) and then **predicating** a piece of information about these objects.

A typical feature of nouns and verbs in all modern languages is that these classes are **open**. This means that through morphology speakers can add new members to these classes:

derived verbs	*derived nouns*
beaut(y) + ify (beauty)	play + er (play)
black + en (black)	excite + ment (excite)
be + witch (witch)	pian(o) + ist (piano)

In English, the **adjective** class is also an open class:

parent + al
clown + ish
read + able

But in some modern-day languages the class of adjective is closed. Hausa (an African language) is claimed to have around 12 adjectives with no morphological means to add new ones (Whaley 1997: 59), and other languages are claimed to have no adjectives at all.

Just as adjectives can specify a property of an entity (expressed by the noun), we also have words that specify properties of the actions to which verbs refer. In some cases it would seem that these words are adjectives:

A fast car   He runs fast

But there are other cases in which we have to add the suffix *-ly* to the adjective in order to use it as a modifier of a verb:

A steady pace   He walks steadily

And then there are words that can only be used to modify verbs:

*An often visitor   He visits often

In short, we seem to have a special word class that consists of words that can modify verbs; this class is called **adverbs**. In English, the class of adverbs is somewhat open, since we can make adverbs from adjectives by adding the suffix *-ly*.

Adjectives and adverbs themselves can also be modified:

> a tall man
> a very tall man
>
> he walks very fast
>
> *a very man
> *he walks very

Thus, *very* is a modifier of adjectives and adverbs; it cannot be used as an adjective or an adverb by itself. Still, linguists call *very* an adverb. That is confusing because it really seems to belong to a separate class. The class of adverbs is, as any linguist will admit, a rather broad category that seems to contain many subclasses, including words that express a time indication, or negation:

> The man ate *yesterday*
> The did *not* eat

I do not intend to give a complete list of all word classes. Firstly, that would take too long, and secondly, there are lots of discussions about what a complete list should look like. Let me say right away that whatever the complete list is, we do not want to say that all languages have all of them. We already saw that there are languages that perhaps don't even have adjectives, where what looks like the equivalent of an adjective in English is something that behaves more like a verb (e.g., by taking tense affixes).

Here are some other important word classes that, I believe, all or most languages have:

> prepositions: in, before, after, between
> conjunctions: and, or
> complementizers: that, whether, if
> determiners: the, a, those, some
> pronouns: she, they, who

A characteristic of these classes is that they are all closed, i.e., there are no morphological means for making new prepositions, pronouns, and so on. Each language has a fixed set of these kinds of words, although languages can differ in the number of words that they have in each class.

An important issue is that some classes seem to contain subclasses, and once the distinction is made between two subclasses the question arises why we do not simply speak of two different classes. For example, I assumed that it is a typical property of nouns that they can occur with a number-affix to indicate more than one (or technically, **plurality**). There are words that share a number of properties with nouns (like being able to occur with a determiner) that do not allow the plural suffix:

> the gold melts (noun verb)
> *I bought several golds

Nouns like gold are called **mass nouns**, but one could propose to regard such words as a different class altogether.

Another example is the class of so-called **auxiliary verbs**:

> The man *is* going home
> The dog *has* eaten the meat
> We *must/may/should* go

These verbs always occur with another verbs. However, they can also usually occur by themselves as independent verbs, which means that they belong to two classes.

Ultimately it turns out to be the case that all word classes can be divided into subclasses which can be further divided into subclasses and so on. As mentioned, the population of the lexicon is constantly subjected to processes that lead to speciation. Specific words or groups of words may develop special and unique properties in the sentence, and such developments may then effectively lead to a new (sub)classes.

What are the properties that make us decide that a number of words form a word category? It might seem that it is their meaning, but meaning is actually a problematic criterion. More reliable is the criterion of the company that words keep, i.e., what they can combine with. This is technically called the **valency** of a word. Another criterion is the kinds of inflectional affixes that words take. In English, for example, all words that can take the plural suffix *–s* are a class, which we call the noun class. All words that take the past suffix *–ed* are a class that we call verbs.

Lexical and Functional Categories

The distinction between open and closed classes is often referred to in different terms. Open classes are called *lexical categories*, while closed classed are called *grammatical categories*, of late also called *functional categories*.

The Categorial Structure of Sentences

The combination of a noun and a verb can perhaps be seen as the prototypical sentence. By expanding the noun and verb parts, one can make increasingly complex sentences:

noun	**verb**
man	*sleeps*

article noun	**verb**
the *man*	*sleeps*

article adjective noun	**verb**
the *tall* *man*	*sleeps*

article	adjective	noun	verb	adverb
the	*tall*	*man*	*sleeps*	*deeply*

It seems obvious in the above examples that each sentence is not just a linear string of words. Rather, to take the last example, it would seem that the string *the tall man* forms a unit of some kind, just like the string *sleeps deeply* forms a unit.

We call such units **phrases**. In each phrase we have a central unit with which the other units are combined. In the first phrase the central unit is a noun, and therefore we will call this a Noun Phrase (NP). It is justified to call *the tall man* a noun phrase because it behaves just like a noun in that it can be combined with a verb to form a sentence. Other conceivable groupings of words cannot be combined with a verb to form a sentence:

*in the yard	sleeps
*very nice	sleeps
*walk a mile	sleeps

Arguably *in the yard*, *very nice* and *walk a mile* are also phrases, but they cannot be combined with verbs to form a sentence; hence they are not noun phrases.

In the second phrase, the central element is a verb, and therefore we will call this a Verb Phrase (VP):

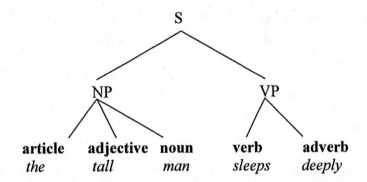

The nodes at the bottom (the leaves of the tree) are word category labels, while the labels higher up are phrase category labels. The top node is labeled *S* for sentence. Notice that, as in the case of the categorial structure of words, labels of non-terminal nodes are derived from one of the labels that enter into the combination. Thus, the label *NP* is determined by the label *N*; in fact, despite tradition, we *could* take *N* rather than *NP* to be the label of the phrase.

Once the notion of *phrase* was introduced, linguists proposed to use it in all cases, i.e., also when a noun or verb occurs without modifiers. In English, plural nouns or mass nouns occur without an article, for example, and verbs, such as *sleep*, can obviously occur by themselves.

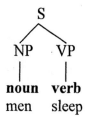

Having defined a phrase as a central word with (or without) modifiers, let us take a close look at the following sentence:

article	**adverb**	**adjective**	**noun**	**verb**	**adverb**	**adverb**
the	*rather*	*tall*	*man*	*sleeps*	*very*	*deeply*

At first sight one might be inclined to assign the following tree structure to this string of words:

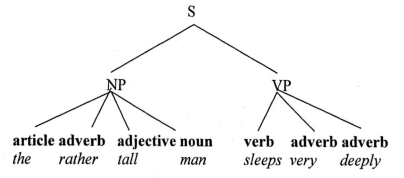

But look again. Is *rather* a modifier of *man*, and is *very* a modifier of *sleeps*? This is not how we have introduced these items. It would seem that *rather* modifies *tall*, while *very* modifies *deeply*. It would seem that we have to have to admit that modifiers, like adjectives, can be central units themselves:

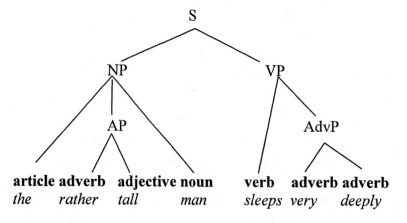

The adjective *tall* is the central unit of an adjective phrase, while the adverb *deeply* is the central unit of an adverb phrase.

What we see here is that phrases can be contained in other phrases! This is a very interesting and important feature of the categorial structure that we also encountered at the word level; I called that kind of self-containing structure **recursive**.

Earlier we listed four additional word classes (prepositions, conjunctions, determiners, and pronouns). One might ask whether all words can form phrases by taking modifiers. This is a rather difficult issue, since it depends a lot on how one wishes to analyze things. I will return to this issue later.

Pronouns are often regarded as NPs, not because they themselves can take modifiers, but because pronouns can take the place of a whole NP.

The men	are	outside
They	are	outside

Another view is to regard pronouns as determiners because, in fact, they can be combined with nouns, as in:

We men don't like to cry

As for determiners (which contain several subclasses, like articles) and conjunctions, we will simply say that these word classes do not form phrases. Determiners are just modifiers and conjunctions are just connectors. (That, we will have more to say about below.)

Prepositions are words that form phrases, though. Consider the following example:

The man works [in the yard]

Clearly, the unit *in the yard* functions as a whole as a modifier of *works*; it indicates the location where the work takes place. Within this unit *the yard* modifies *in*, which by itself just means IN X (where X is a variable). Or perhaps we should see *the yard* as an argument of *in*, which in that sense is like a predicate. In any event, the preposition is combined with an article-noun combination, which is an NP, which presents us with another example of a phrase inside a phrase. In fact, since the PP is contained within a VP, we have a double nesting of phrases:

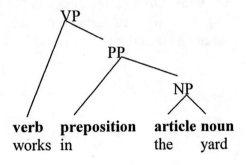

If you have digested all this, you're already getting to be quite a syntactician, but as always, there's more.

Different Types of Verbs: Subcategorization

In our listing and discussion of word categories we have seen categories like noun, verb, etc. I mentioned that several of those categories can be divided into smaller categories. Here we discuss such further divisions for the category verb. Consider the following examples, focusing on the VPs:

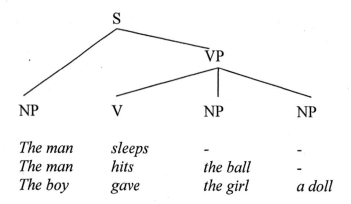

NP	V	NP	NP
The man	*sleeps*	-	-
The man	*hits*	*the ball*	-
The boy	*gave*	*the girl*	*a doll*

In the second and the third sentences, the VPs are more complex than what we've seen so far. Whereas every verb occurs with an NP with which it forms a S (recall that we call this NP the **subject** since it function as the AGENT of the verb, as well as for other, perhaps better, reasons that we discuss later), it now appears that verbs can differ in terms of occurring or not occurring with an NP *inside* the VP.

One might ask how we know that the NP to the right of the verb belongs to the VP rather than being directly linked to the S node. I'll answer this by referring to the meaning of the verbs in question. It would seem that the verb *sleep* has a complete meaning, as is evident from the fact that the sentence above is fine. Of course, one can add things like *the whole night*, which is also an NP, but that addition is **optional**. But one could not say:

>   *the man hits
>   *the boy gave the girl

The second sentence is complete if *girl* is understood as the **theme** of giving (i.e., what is given), but not if *girl* is meant as the **recipient**. We then *must* add an NP that expresses the theme. One could say that the meaning of *hit* has one variable (or one argument slot) in that it needs to be filled by the meaning of an NP. Likewise, *give* has two variables:

>   hit :   HIT X_{THEME}
>   give: GIVE $X_{\text{RECIPIENT}}$ Y_{THEME}

Thus, verbs differ in that some want specific phrases to be part of the VP. Here's the relevant terminology:

sleep	=	**intransitive**
hit	=	**transitive**
give	=	**di-transitive**

We even have verbs that require other kinds of units, such as a sentence:

I [said [that I fell] s] vp

The verb *say* is, in a sense, transitive, but what is being said is expressed in terms of a phrase of the category sentence, rather than of the category NP. Here we see another striking case of recursion, namely a whole sentence that occurs within the VP. Perhaps it is clearer when we draw the tree:

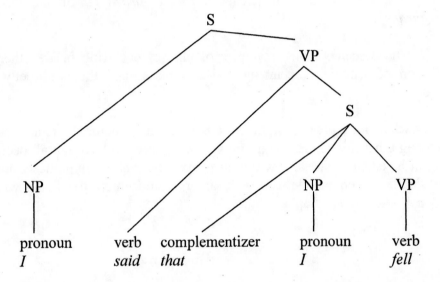

It is quite striking that a sentence can (indirectly) occur *inside* another sentence. Note that the inner sentence starts with the word *that*, which belongs to a word class that you haven't seen before, that of the **complementizers**. Some transitive verbs can take an NP or an S:

I promised [that I would come] s
I promised [a story] np

The technical term for the requirements that verbs have is **subcategorization**. This means that there are different subcategories of verb based on their valency requirements.

I mention finally that not all sentences have an NP as their subject, the subject can also be a sentence:

[That the will lose] is evident

Summarizing:

- We have seen that sentences can be quite complex in the categorial dimension. Except for sentences like (*Who did that?*) *Me!*, or *Walk!*, each sentence contains a verb which takes a phrase that is its subject (an NP or an S).

- The verb can form a VP by itself or require phrases that go with it. The verb is the central unit of the VP.

- Each NP has a noun as its central unit, which may occur with various modifiers. Some modifiers may themselves be phrases, i.e., APs (Adjective Phrases), which have an adjective as their central element.

- A fourth type of phrase is the PP (prepositional phrase), which can function as an optional modifier of verbs (*... works [in the garden]*) or of nouns (*the man [in the garden]*).

- We have seen various examples of phrases occurring inside other phrases and even of sentences occurring inside phrases (and thus indirectly inside other sentences).

There is a whole lot more to learn about the categorial structure of sentences and phrases. Note among other things that the groupings in this section have not all been binary. This should not be taken as an early withdrawal from the binarity hypothesis. Later on, when we will deal with sentence level categorial structure in more detail, we will see that the binarity hypothesis can be upheld.

Categorial Repair Rules

In a Chomskyan approach to sentence structure, two types of repair rules have been proposed that seem to be triggered primarily by the categorial structure. These two types of adjustments are inflection and transformations. The first type enriches words with categorial features that often come with a phonological form and a meaning aspect. These enrichments are assigned given the position of words within the categorial structure, and we traditionally think of them as inflectional affixes. The second type of enrichment is transformations, rules that have more dramatic effects on the categorial structure and, in fact, on the merge structure as a whole.

I will introduce these two types of adjustment rules as belonging to the categorial dimension of sentences, but the above wording has already made it clear that these operations do not affect the categorial structure alone. The consequences of that will be discussed later on.

Inflection

Consider the following sentence:

>A man bites a dog

In English it is clear that [a man] is the subject NP, but there are many languages in which the order of NP with respect to the verb does not tell you anything about which one is the subject and which one is the object. For whatever reason, the order of phrases can be rather free. With such freedom, how does one differentiate between a message in which the man is the biter and one in which the dog is the biter? Languages with free word order have developed a system to keep track of the relationships between words and phrases. This system is called **inflection**. The basic idea is that phrases that have a certain function (such as being the subject) or phrases that belong together are marked with affixes that reveal their function or coherence.

Just imagine an affix that means *subject* or *object*, let us say *-su* and *-ob*:

>A man-su bites a dog-ob
>A dog-ob bites a man-su
>Bites a dog-ob a man-su
>Bites a man-su a dog-su
>A dog-ob a man-su bites
>A man-su a dog-su bites

We can now place the words and phrases in any order we want. It will always be clear who is doing the biting and who is the victim.

Inflectional systems can get quite sophisticated. We also find the trick of marking words that belong together with the same suffix:

>the-su tall-su man-su kisses the-ob old-ob lady-ob

We can now even mix up the words of different phrases:

>the-su tall-su kisses the-ob old-ob lady-ob man-su

In principle, all orders are possible. As long as there are inflectional affixes we can figure out what goes with what.

If we regard inflection as a part of the categorial system, we can say that inflectional rules are categorial adjustment rules. The also take categorial phrase/sentence structures as input and perform operations on the category labels that add information to these labels, in effect creating subcategories.

The type of inflection that we have discussed signals the grammatical functions of noun phrases (subject, object) as well as the going together of words that belong to the same phrase. We also find inflectional affixes on verbs, sometimes to indicate whether their subject is plural or singular, this information also usually being encoded on the subject itself:

boy-sing   play-sing
boy-plur   play-plur

This is called subject-verb **agreement**. The agreement does not involve identity in the phonological form of the inflectional affix. In fact, in the case at hand, English has:

boy-sing   play-sing
-                 /s/

boy-plur   play-plur
/s/   -

Singular on nouns is phonologically empty, while on a verb it is -/s/. Plural has the opposite marking. The point is, however, that there is a systematic correlation between singular and plural marking on nouns and verbs.

In other cases verb endings must appear because of the occurrence of other words in the sentences that are not necessarily subjects of the verb. To give some examples, consider what happens when we combine words (as parts of speech) into sentences in English. Take the verb *(to) play*:

I like to *play*
I don't want to be disturbed when I *play*
When a child *play*-**s**, the parents are happy
Yesterday we *play*ed the whole afternoon
Be quiet, he is *play*ing

In all these sentences we encounter the same verb *(to) play*. We note that this verb takes on various endings in these sentences, and the crucial point to take home is that these endings are forced upon the verb by the properties of the sentence's context. For example, as already mentioned, in English a suffix *–s* must be added to a verb if the **subject** is a third person (like *he* or *the child*), at least in the present tense. Likewise, when the sentences refer to a situation in the past, we must add *–ed*.

Once an affix is designated to be inflection (because there are cases where its presence is dependent on other words in the sentence), it is always considered to be inflectional, even if its occurrence in some cases seems to be a free choice:

John walks fast   John walk*ed* fast

John has the dog*s*   John has the dog

In the first pair the choice between *walk* and *walk-ed* does not seem to be dependent on any other word in the sentences. In the second pair, the same holds for the choice between *dog* and *dogs*.

Hence we have a set of inflectional rules that add endings to nouns, determiners, adjectives, verbs, etc. These rules look a lot like word formation rules (in particular derivational rules), but they are not word formation rules. Inflectional rules that add endings to words that are enforced by the syntax are called **inflectional rules**. These rules specify affixation of words that is necessary for these words to occur in specific categorial environments. They do not, like derivational rules, make new words; they make variants of the same word.

Inflectional rules are repair rules because these add features to words that would otherwise not be wellformed in a given configuration. There are thus categorial constraints of the following sort:

A subject Noun must bear the feature [+subject]

In the very first versions of generative grammar, inflectional rules were actually called *adjustment rules*. If it is correct to regard inflection as an example of categorial adjustment, the focus of attention should here *not* be on the phonological or semantic properties of inflectional endings, but rather on their categorial properties. Thus, from a categorial point of view, plural inflection is a change that affects the category label N, turning it into a complex category label [N, +plural], *plural* being a **non-lexical category label**. Likewise, an inflectional rule that marks a noun phrase as being the subject rather than the object adds a label *subject* (often called *nominative* rather than *subject*) to the label NP. Understood in this way, inflectional rules can be assumed to operate in *all* languages. If that is so, languages would differ in whether inflectional features correspond to a phoneme combination that is glued to a noun (in which we properly can speak if an affix), or to a fixed *position* that the noun must occupy in the sentence, as in English, where the subject NP must occur before the verb. In other words, *word order* can be seen as an aspect of the phonological dimension.

Since the categorial side of inflection (features) is hard to separate from a phonological aspect (affix, or position) and, indeed, from a semantic aspect (certain categorial features are associated to a clear meaning such a [+plural]), we might want to reconsider location inflection in the categorial system. Below, I will consider instead seeing inflection as more intimately linked to the merge system.

Phrases that Move?

One specific aspect of sentences that we will now focus on is the phenomenon that phrases sometimes seem to occur out of place.:

[Who] ₙₚ did the man hit - ?

The pronoun *who* seems to have the grammatical function of the object of *hit*. Yet it does not occur directly after *hit*, as is the case in:

The man hit [who] ₙₚ ?

The latter sentence is called an *echo question*. In some languages echo questions and normal questions have the same word order, but in English normal questions must have the question word at the beginning of the sentence.

How do we account for the fact that the [who] in the front goes with *hit*? Chomsky proposed that in addition to phrase structure rules and inflectional rules a third type of categorial rule is needed which moves phrases:

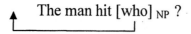

The man hit [who] NP ?

Such movement rules have been called **transformations** because, indeed, they transform some basic form of a sentence that violates a constraint against locating *who* directly after the verb into a correct form.

Another example of a transformation can be seen in this example:

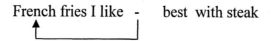

French fries I like -   best with steak

Here the sentence with the moved unit is merely a variant of the sentence, *I like French fries best with steak.*

The effects of transformation can be quite spectacular:

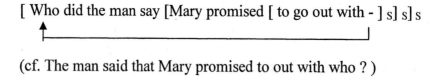

[Who did the man say [Mary promised [to go out with -] S] S] S

(cf. The man said that Mary promised to out with who ?)

In this case, the [who] has been moved from "two sentences down." There seems to be no limit on the distance that phrases can be moved.

Transformations are a different type of adjustment rules than inflection rules: they take a phrase/sentence structure and move units around, whereas inflection modifies the the basic units (words).

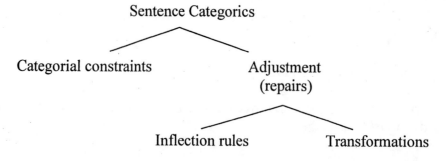

In what sense can transformation be taken to be operations on categorial trees? We can simply assume that the *Qnoun* (the category of words like *who* and *which*) is moved to the beginning and combined with the S (sentence) creating, let us say, a QS (Q-sentence):

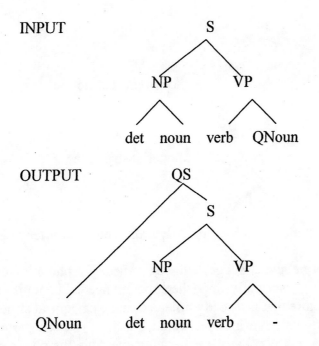

This movement is necessary because there is a categorial constraint that disallows Qnouns to occur in the VP even though that is where they seem to belong.

Clearly, Qmovement must be matched by a similar operation in the phonological dimension, and perhaps also in the semantic dimension, i.e., the movement seems to involve the word *who* with all its properties, not just its word class label. This suggests (as in the case of inflectional rules) that transformations should perhaps not be placed in the categorial sentence module, but rather in the merge module where we deal with the packages of form, meaning, and category. I suggest that inflection, too, perhaps belongs to the merge module. I will return to this issue below.

The Phonotactic Structure of Sentences

When words are merged into sentences they drag their phonological properties with them. Is the phonological structure of a sentence more than the linear sequences of the phonological structure of its words? Specifically, (a) are these phonological word structures arranged into a well-defined hierarchical structure (that is distinct from the basic merge structure)? and (b) are there any changes (repairs) in the phonemic or syllabic make-up of the words that are being combined? These are reasonable questions since we have seen that at the word level the answer to both of them is yes (recall (a) the discussion about the syllable structure of the word *walker* and (b) the allomorphy of the negative prefix).

Let us first discuss the matter of structure. On the phonological side it would seem that *he* and *is* form a unit given that a normal pronunciation is: *he's sick.*

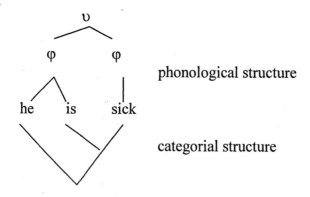

(φ stands for phonological phrase and υ for utterance.)

The apparent grouping of *he* and *is* suggests the existence of a phonological structure in the phonological dimension, especially since the structure needed is not isomorphic to the most obvious merge structure that is directly reflected in the categorial structure.

At the same time we have also answered question (b). The argument for the phonological structure is precisely that there are adjustments in the phoneme structure of the words *he is* → *he's*. Adjustment rules at the sentence level are often called **sandhi** rules.

Here is another example showing that the phonological organization of phrases is not just a linear concatenation of the phonological organization of words. The syllables that make up French words do not like to end in particular kinds of consonants such as /p/, /t/, or /k/. Now consider the two different ways in which an adjective *petit* (small) can be pronounced:

> petit ami   little friend
> peti garçon   little boy

The adjective has a final /t/ when the following word starts with a vowel, but it lacks such a consonant when the following word starts with a consonant. We can understand this as follows. The /t/ is part of the phonological make-up of the word and it can stay if it can form the beginning of a syllable with the vowel of a following word, while it gets deleted (or remains unpronounced) otherwise.

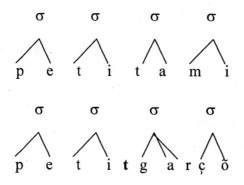

In other words, the /t/ is removed (or silent) when it cannot find a home in a syllable. But when the next word starts with a syllable that begins with a vowel, the /t/ gets incorporated into this syllable. This kind of sandhi is called **liaison** in descriptions of French.

The Semantic Structure of Sentences

When words are combined into sentences they contribute their meanings to the total meaning of the sentence. It stands to reason that the words' meanings add up to the meaning of the sentence, although, following the compositional principle, we also expect the linear order and grouping of words to matter. But how exactly does this adding up work? Simple adding up occurs perhaps only when two words (or phrases) are combined in terms of a conjunction *and*. In this case there is an explicit "adding up word," but that is not always the case. In *the man runs* we combined the meanings of *the* (A SPECIFIC X) and *man* (MAN) into {A SPECIFIC {MAN}} and this unit we combine with the meaning of *runs* (X_{AGENT} RUN) into {{A SPECIFIC {MAN}} RUN}. We can say that the meanings of *the* and *run* contain an *open slot*, a **variable**, symbolized by the X in which we link the meaning of the unit that we combine these words with.

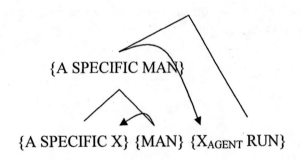

{A SPECIFIC MAN}

{A SPECIFIC X} {MAN} {X_{AGENT} RUN}

We can regard the semantic representations that have variables as *functions* that take another unit as their *argument*. The function {X_{AGENT} RUN} applies to the argument {{A SPECIFIC {MAN}} (itself the result of an earlier functional application) to deliver {{{A SPECIFIC {MAN}} {RUN}. (Here I've ignored the semantics of the inflectional suffix – *s*.)

Verbs like *hit* or *kiss* have two arguments:

hit:　　{X_{AGENT} HIT Y_{THEM}}

In the case of verbs, as I have argued, the variable(s) will actually supply information regarding the *semantic role* of its argument. Consider the following sentences:

The dog bit the cat	X = AGENT
The cat bites the dog	X = AGENT, Y = THEME
The key opened the door	X = INSTRUMENT
The park disallows dogs	X = LOCATION

Note that these roles are not referred to by terms such as *subject* or *object*, which are not semantic notions but rather categorial notions. Linguists have made the point that the phrases that function as subject (or object) can have different semantic roles:

The boy kicks the ball	AGENT
The boy us in love	EXPERIENCER
The boy receives a present	BENEFACTOR
The boy is beaten	THEME
etc.	

In all the sentences *the boy* is the subject, but from a semantic point of view *the boy* has different roles.

Are the Primitives Universal?

We have seen that in each dimension merge causes the structural integration of the phonological, semantic, and categorial material of the parts that have been put together, and the constraints check whether the resulting structure is wellformed in each dimension. In this section I will focus on the status of the *primitives* or building blocks that we find *at the bottom* of each structure:

Dimensions	Primitives
Phonological	phonemes
Categorial	labels
Semantics	semes (i.e., concepts)

Let us first establish that we need primitives to begin with. The first step is to acknowledge that morphemes as a whole cannot be innate because the particular combinations of forms and meanings are grossly unpredictable (or arbitrary), whereas the relations between meanings and categories are strong tendencies at best. Does this mean that their forms, meanings, and categories *taken on their own* cannot be innate either? Logically that does not follow. What we established is only that the particular *combinations* are not universal and thus are not innate.

Could it be then that there are separate innate lists of meanings, categories, and forms? And is morpheme learning a matter of figuring out links between members of these three sets? Things are probably not that simple. It is hard to imagine that every member of our species is born with, for example, the ingredients /dog/ (form). However, it might be argued that the semantic concept DOG (meaning) and the label noun (category) are perhaps innate.

We have been assuming that at least the form (/dog/) and perhaps the meaning (DOG) of morphemes need not be unanalyzable wholes. Rather in each of these two dimensions, at the bottom of each structure, we find the ultimate building blocks, the smallest units in that dimension. In phonology these units are called *phonemes*, in semantics *concepts* (or *semes*). In the case at hand DOG need not be a basic seme; rather it may be a complex concept composed out of truly basic semes like ANIMAL, DOMESTIC, etc. (As mentioned before, it is not so clear what the basic semes are.) In the categorial dimensions the labels that are associated with morphemes *are* the primitives because morphemes, by definition, belong to one category (and not to a combination of categories, whatever that would be). Could it be then that there are innate lists of such primitive phonological, semantic, and categorial building blocks, and that languages merely differ in the combinations of building blocks that the constraints allow and, in addition, in the combinations of forms, meanings, and categories?

To start with categories, a universal list would presumably be not too large and, even though the nature of such a list has not been decided on by linguists, the list of categories is the best candidate for having full innate status. The matter is, however, not uncontroversial, and there are linguists who claim that there may be no universal definition of category labels and that these labels group together language-specific sets of words. Another matter is whether the labels Noun, Verb, Adjective are truly atomic. It is possible perhaps to decompose these labels into a smaller set of "ultimate primitives." Such ultimate primitives are often seen as features that are either present or absent. One proposal to this effect is that the four major categories (N, V, A, and P) can be represented in terms of two such binary features:

	+V	-V
+N	Preposition	Noun
-N	Verb	Adjective

The features N and V can be read as "nouniness" and "verbiness," if you wish. In addition, there are other categorial features such as the ones that are introduced by the inflectional system. Perhaps, thought of things in this way, the list of categorial features is no going to be that short!

As for meanings, it seems unlikely that our prehistoric ancestors were born with meanings or concepts like BICYCLE or COMPUTER or WHEEL and that there was no incentive to use these concepts until bicycles, computers, and wheels were invented. But, as I already indicated earlier, we should not look for innate meanings at this gross level, we should look for true semantic *primitives*, basic buildings blocks of meaning (basic concepts or semes), perhaps a small set, out of which complex meanings can be constructed. This is indeed a viable position, and certainly one that has its defenders. The semantic buildings blocks, in fact, need not be thought of a linguistic in nature. Rather, these units, or combinations of them, could have a more general cognitive status and be understood as the elements of our mental lives in terms of which we think, fear, hope, and desire, or, as the philosopher Jerry Fodor puts it, of **the language of thought**. What we call word meanings are those thought concepts that happen to be linked to a phonological form and category so they can play a role in the linguistic system.

Is it feasible, however, to decompose the meaning of the word *computer* into basic building blocks that were present in the minds of our ancestors that were wandering around in the African savanna some 150,000 years ago? Or should we say that this "meaning" should be split up into a meaning proper (composed of universal concepts) and a layer of **encyclopedic knowledge** that comprises all the culture-specific and time-sensitive ingredients? But where do we draw the line between concepts and encyclopedic knowledge?

Despite having its defenders, there is no generally accepted system of universal concepts, although there certainly is a small industry that tries to develop such a system. If a set of basic concepts could be established, the members of which could be shown to be universally present in the minds of all people, it seems plausible to hypothesize that this set is innate. That members of that set, of combinations thereof, can characterize morpheme meanings entirely, is doubtful, which suggests that a layer of learned encyclopedic features would seem to be necessary.

This brings us, finally, to the form. Again, it is unimaginable that the forms of morphemes are innate as such. It seems much more reasonable, as in fact we have assumed, that the forms consist of building blocks that can be combined into a large variety, perhaps an unlimited set of constellations from which every language uses a fairly coincidental subset. A reasonable candidate, as we have seen, for such building blocks is the speech sound, or phoneme. It does seem to be the case that the set of phonemes used in all languages together is a small set (perhaps consisting of 200 or 300 members), one that perhaps could be taken to be entirely innate.

Postulating innate sets in all three dimensions does not have to imply that the members of all three sets *must* be present in all languages. A milder hypothesis, which admittedly weakens the notion of *universal*, would be that the lists, while initially present in the minds of all people, reduce on the basis of experience to smaller sets, whichever one is necessary for the language that the learner is exposed to. Another way of saying this is that languages (or rather their speakers) make different choices from each set. In this view, while categories like Noun and Adjective and so on would be held to be universal, languages would be allowed to not have, say, adjectives. This view certainly makes sense in the phonological dimension because it is rather obvious that languages differ in the set of phonemes that are used (although the picture changes when indeed we find that phonemes are not the basic units, but instead are composed of even smaller units. We will later learn that there *are* proposals to decompose the phonemes into smaller units called **phonological features** or **phonological elements**.)

In summary, while the word *dog* is itself not universal and thus not innate, it is possible to argue that the basic units out of which each of its three dimensions is composed are chosen from a universal set:

(the word) *dog*

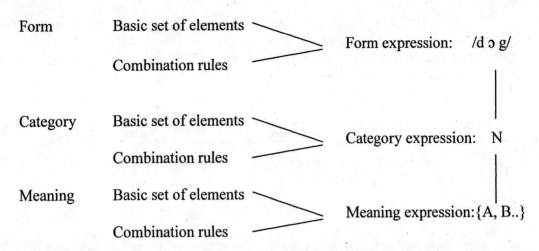

Summarizing, we can attribute the fact that the set of derived expressions can differ from language to language to (a) different choices from the set of primitives, and also to (b) different combination of the primitives. This raises the question of whether the combination rules that any language uses differ randomly from language to language or are chosen from a universal set of rules that is innate. If we assume that the way of combining primitives is not unlimited, we allow languages to differ, yet we also claim that they can differ in unlimited ways. The interaction between nature and nurture would be relevant in both the domain of primitives and combinations, in that experience guides the choice of both primitives' and combinations' rules that any given language requires.

The Variability of Linguistic Units

In the preceding sections, we have seen that each grammatical module has the same general organization. We have a set of "basic units" (primitives) and a set of "combination rules" (stated in the form of constraints). For example, in the case of (word) phonology, our basic units are the phonemes (as we assume for the moment), and our combination rules are the phonotactic constraints. We have also seen that when combinations are checked, sometimes *adjustments* are necessary in the end product which, taken at face value, would be in violation of some constraint. By applying an adjustment. the structure can be repaired (after which it is necessary to check the structure again to see that it is not the case that now some other constraint is violated). Thus we have seen that the form of morphemes (as in the morpheme /in/-) sometimes changes depending on the form of neighboring morphemes. I refer to this phenomenon as **the variability of linguistic units**.

We have seen examples of variability in word and sentence phonology resulting from rules that change the hierarchical and/or phoneme structure of morphemes and words. I also have identified variability in sentence categorics resulting from inflectional rules, which change the categorial structure of words (adding inflectional features). In addition, we have seen that the categorial structure at the sentence level is subject to transformations, which cause variability in the basic structure of sentences (statement versus question, for example).

The basic idea is that linguistic units are like chameleons. They adapt to the environment in which they appear.

But the need for adjustment rules is not obvious in all grammatical modules. In principle, we might expect to find them in all three dimensions both at the word and sentence level, but we don't, at least not at first sight:

	word level	sentence level
semantics	?	?
categorics	?	Inflection Transformations
phonology	allomorphy rules	sandhi rules

Given the gaps in this table, we might question the need for adjustment rules. In the next section we will see that the effect of inflection and transformations can perhaps be built into the merge operation. The question of whether we can also get rid of allomorphy rules and sandhi rules is a project that I will pursue in Chapter 10.

Is Categorial Structure Central?

Let us summarize the conception of grammar that we have developed so far:

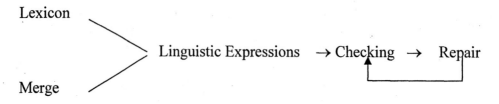

Checking applies to all three dimensions both at the level of words and sentences. Although constraints may perhaps refer to information in more than one dimension (although we haven't seen examples of that), it seems that repairs pertain to specific dimensions. Phonological repairs, for sure, make changes in the phonotactic shape of linguistic units. However, it would seem that the categorial adjustments that we have talked about (inflection and transformations) are *not* internal to the sentence categorial level because both affect the phonology and semantics as well.

As long as inflection merely introduces categorial features (like [plural] or [nominative]) all seems to be confined to the categorial dimension. However, such features sometimes have semantic consequences (such as the feature [plural]) and this, therefore, requires action in the semantic dimension as well. Finally, we see that inflectional features have **overt consequences**, either in the form of affixes (phoneme strings, like -/s/ in the case of plural nouns in English, -/ed/, corresponding to the categorial feature [past]), or in the form of specific word orders (e.g., a [nominate] Noun (phrase) occurs before the verb in English). Ignoring the effect of inflection on word order for the moment, it would seem that inflection introduces *morphemes* that, as such, contain all three dimensions.

Transformations also do much more than affect category labels. They move (or copy) not just category labels, but rather complete words/phrases including their semantic and phonological properties.

While it is still true that inflectional rules and transformation are triggered by categorial constraints, their affect is not limited to the categorial dimension. The **cross-dimensional effect** of inflectional rules and transformations suggests that these adjustments must be integrated with the merge procedure which, in turn, makes it necessary to project the categorial information of affixes and words *into* the merge tree and have categorial checking apply so that categorial adjustment can affect the insertion of morphemes and movement/copying of words/phrases.

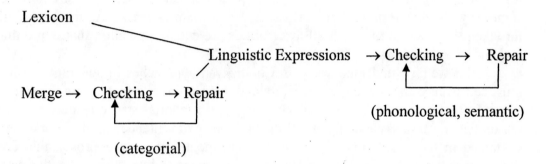

In this conception of grammar categorial structure is, in some sense, central, in that its checking takes priority over the checking of phonological and semantics properties of linguistic expressions, while the repairs that it triggers take scope over all three dimensions.

The claim that the categorial property is central can be formally expressed by seeing the representation of a morpheme (e.g., *walk*) not as (a) but as (b):

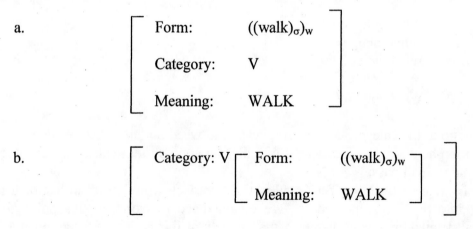

The difference is that in (b) we make the category property an extrinsic property of the sign proper. The sign *proper* comprises its form and meaning, while the extrinsic label indicates its combinatory properties. Being an extrinsic property the category is the first thing that gets checked when a combination is made, and if the combination is wellformed the resulting structure is a wellformed categorial structure. Then, in the second instance, the grammar checks whether the combination in question has led to wellformed structures in the form and meaning dimension.

Note that the use of phonological adjustment rules does not seem to entail an asymmetry in the three checking systems, i.e., it does not entail that the phonological checking has to take priority over categorial or semantic checking. The reason for this is that phonological structure and semantic structure have an existence in their own right, whereas categorial structure is nothing by itself; it is merely an *external* labeling of signs which are packages of form (phonology) and meaning (semantics). Therefore any rules that would affect the categorial information necessarily have repercussions for the intrinsic properties of the signs.

The claim that categorial structure (often called *syntax*) is central is clear in the approaches that follow the ideas of Noam Chomsky. **Ray Jackendoff** (1945) calls this idea that categorial structure is central, with phonological and semantic structure being in some way *dependent* on that central structure, *syntacto-centrism*. As mentioned, I've so far taken the position in which all three pillars are equal, a position that is prominent in Jackendoff's own work.

But we now understand *why* in Chomskyan approaches in generative grammar it must be assumed that the merge structure and the categorial structure are the same thing, which is tantamount to saying that checking the categorial structure gets priority. The reason lies in Chomsky's treatment of the variability of sentence structures and the words contained in them in terms of categorial adjustment rules. An approach that crucially relies on categorial adjustment rules *must*, as we have just seen, take the categorial structure as central. Grammatical models that reject adjustment procedures (such as Jackendoff's, but before him several other so-called non-transformational generative approaches) *can* view all three dimensions as equal. Such models must build the effect of the alleged adjustment directly into the merge procedure. For example, strings in which question words occur at the beginning must be generated, just like strings with question words in other positions:

> What did you buy what
> did you buy what
> What did you buy
> you buy what
> What you buy

It is now up to the categorial constraint system to weed out all structures except the third one. If the phonology is fine with it and the semantic system can deal with it, too, the third sentence will pass.

To avoid inflectional repair rules, this approach would build inflectional features directly into the merge procedure. We do not need to worry at this point about the technical details, but I can guarantee that models of this sort have been developed with great care and success. The categorial check would only allow categorial configurations in which words have the right kinds of features. In this view, then, there would be no categorial adjustment at all, only checking and then acceptance or rejection of linguistic expressions. (Other linguists might argue that it makes sense to view the semantic structure as central because, as they say, the fundamental property of linguistic expressions is WHAT is said, not how you say it. This is a view, however, that seems to view the grammar as the system for transforming preverbal thought into linguistic expressions, rather than as the system that checks the wellformedness of these expressions.)

Isomorphism Again

By attributing equal status to the three dimensions we do not deny that there is a strong tendency for structures in all three dimensions to be very similar. Nor do we fail to explain this high degree of **isomorphy** (meaning "similarity in structure"). In order to explain that the structure in the three dimensions tends of be isomorphic, it is necessary to distinguish the merge structure as being distinct from the semantic, categorial, and phonological structure. Merge structures impose isomorphic structure in all three dimensions simply because each merge operation delivers packages of information in the phonology and semantics.

Summarizing the Model

On the basis of a preverbal message (a thought of some sort), a set of morphemes and words are rounded up from the lexicon, which the merge system organizes into a binary structure that needs to be checked in the categorial, phonological, and semantic dimension.

In a model that uses categorial adjustment rules there are reasons for viewing the categorial structure as central (i.e., integrated with the merge structure). After checking and repair of the categorial properties, two additional systems home in on the semantic and phonological dimension of the morphemes and words that have been organized into a wellformed categorial structure, each checking the word and then the sentence level:

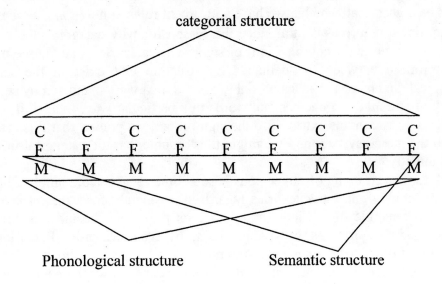

We can visualize the centrality of the categorial organization by modifying Take 6 in Chapter 2 simply by directing the merge operation directly to the categorial dimension:

The Organization of the Grammar (take 6 - revised)

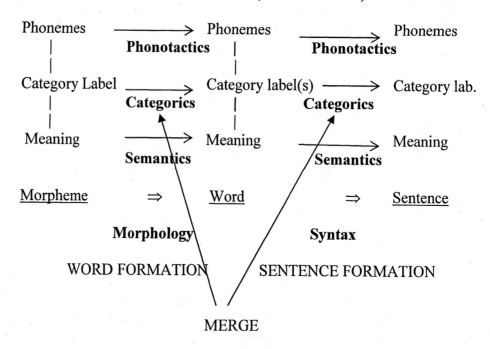

However, we have seen that the centrality of the categorial structure is not mandated in a model that does away with categorial repair rules.

A Compromise

It might be argued that, whether we have adjustment rules or not, it *makes sense* to regard the categorial structure as central since the reason for why category labels exist in the first place is to guide the combinations of signs. The categorial system, one might say, is the compromise between the demands on structure that exist in the semantic and phonological dimensions. The categorial system is, in a way, mandated by semantics and phonology to arrange morphemes and words in a particular way. Indeed, if we represent the categorial structure as extrinsic to the sign proper, we predict that this information *is visible* to the merge system, and we might thus assume that the categorial information is checked directly.

A further grouping of dimensions is sometimes suggested, namely when it is said that the phonology and the categorics regard, in a general sense, the *form* of language, whereas the semantic dimension stands alone as providing the meaning. Indeed, both phonology and categorics, as we have just seen, involve linear order. Phonology needs to stipulate linear order (of phonemes) at the morpheme level (sometimes called the *second articulation*), whereas categorics stipulates linear order (of morphemes) at the word and sentence level (sometimes called the *first articulation*). This suggests the following hierarchical (tree) organization of the three dimensions of linguistic expressions, or of the grammar modules that account for these expressions:

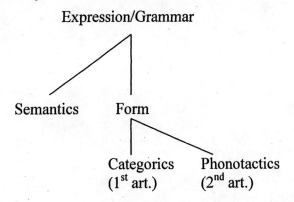

Both the 1st and the 2nd articulation regard structure that *is not* meaning as such. Simplex expressions of form (category labels) are associated with (complex) expressions of form elements (phonemes). In turn, these expressions (simplex and complex) of form are associated with meaning. We can insert this hierarchical organization in our diagram:

The Organization of the Grammar (take 7 [final])

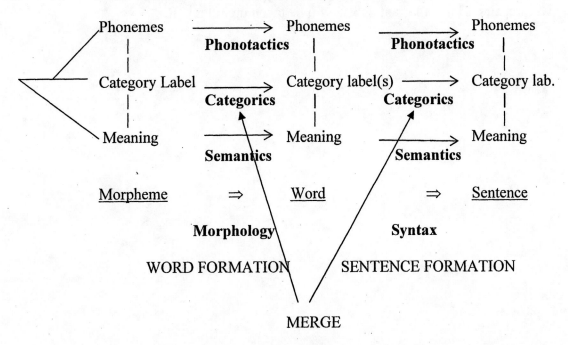

It might seem that the central place of categorial information is at odds with calling this information extrinsic. However, we will see that centrality and being extrinsic are two sides of the same coin when we see that information is called central precisely because it **projects to the whole unit** that is expressed in the tree diagram.

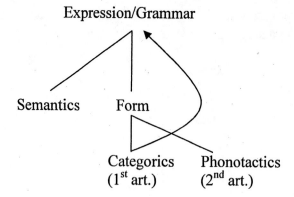

These are matters that we will discuss in more detail in Part III.

Conclusions

We have seen in this chapter how the grammar as a checking system operates at two levels and in three dimensions. There is controversy about whether a distinction must be made between constraints and repairs. Perhaps a richer set of constraints can do away with repairs. This important debate will be taken up in Part III.

Chapter 9

Hierarchical Structure Everywhere

Introduction

The human mind imposes **structure** on everything that it experiences. Sensory experiences are organized into categories (tables, lions, things, good things, bad things, nouns, phonemes like /p/, etc.) and these categories are organized into mental networks of various kinds that express all sorts of relationships between the categories, either general relationships or specific relationships that can vary depending on need and context. There is nothing we can do about this; it is simply part of our nature. It happens in art, in daily life, and in science.

This chapter introduces a common way to represent certain types of networks, namely by using the **tree diagram**, which is particularly suited to represent networks that limit the kinds of relations between categories to **hierarchical organization**. We have used various kinds of tree diagrams in the preceding chapters, and we are thus somewhat familiar with them. In this chapter we will discuss their properties in somewhat more detail.

Tree Diagrams

In the most general sense, we can think of the notion of *structure* as some kind of organization consisting of **units** (things, events, people, dates, whatever) of some sort (*building blocks, ultimate constituents, primitives*) that are grouped into a larger unit. The structure indicates **relations** between the units. When one thinks of a structure that indicates the relations between the cities in some country (where the relations indicate, for example, the roads and highways that connect them), we call the diagram that expresses this structure a **network**.

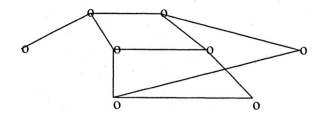

Networks are interesting objects to study. In this day and age we find researchers who study the network that is constituted by the World Wide Web, for example. They discover interesting properties that tell us how the Web actually works and how both its speed and resistance against breakdown (including sabotage) can be improved.

Now imagine a very simple network, one in which all units have no relation to the others at all, except that all are connected to one specific unit.

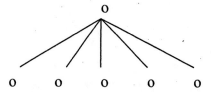

This network displays the kind of structure that can be represented with a tree diagram, as, in fact, I have show above. The node that all other nodes connect to (the *root* of the tree) has a special status, which is why we have represented it on a higher **tier**, but this is actually irrelevant. We could also have chosen to put the root on a lower tier.

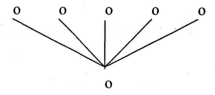

This tree diagram, then, has a modest amount of hierarchy; it has two tiers. We can also have tree diagrams with more than two tiers:

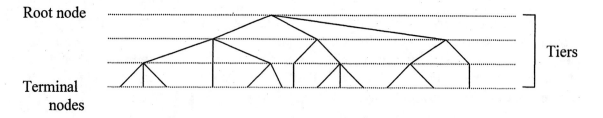

In the preceding diagram, each unit (also called **node**) is linked to a higher unit that itself belongs to a higher unit, until we reach the unit that forms the root of the tree. The units that form the leaves or the outermost branches of the tree are called the **terminal nodes**.

To increase the informational value of a tree diagram we can **label** the tiers or, alternatively, each node:

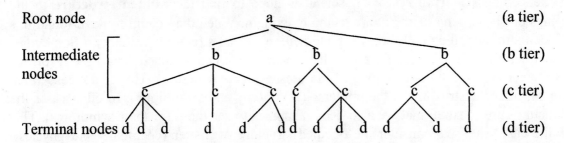

For a specific purpose, we could identify each individual node with labels that stand for entities of some sort. For example, for the terminal nodes we might choose names of people or names of animal species and so on. Still, the definition of a tier is that each node at that tier is of the same type (d type, c type, b type, etc.).

When it comes to man-made matters (organizations, things), we can think of such concrete examples as the following:

> d = people (Tom, Dick, Harry ....)
> c = teams (of people, working on a specific subject: team 1, team 2, etc.)
> b = departments (formed by teams working in a related subject)
> a = the whole organization (a business of some kind)

Or:

> d = art objects
> c = specific artists (i.e., makers of these objects)
> b = artists belonging to the same artistic movement or period
> a = the whole collection (for example, of a museum)

Or:

> d = paragraphs
> c = sections
> b = chapters
> a = the whole book

Social constructs or systems (e.g., organizations such as universities or states), or, more generally, products of human culture are also man-made products, and it would seem that the human mind has a strong urge impose hierarchical structures with several tiers.

As mentioned at the beginning of this section, grouping, hierarchical or not, is not the only kind of organization. In some organization where Tom, Dick, and Harry work more might be going on than relations between bosses and employees. For example, it might be that Tom and Harry are cousins, a network type of relation. The point is, however, that when we analyze the organization we need not express that relation because it is not relevant (at least in shouldn't be).

Science: The Search for Hidden Structures

When doing **scientific research**, scientists hope to find the **hidden structure** in the things or phenomena that they are trying to explain. When they claim to have found this hidden structure, they call their characterization of that structure "a theory." Sometimes the structure is so big or so far away that it takes complicated machines to see it (or just to see certain symptoms that suggest the presence of a structure). This is the case when we consider the structure of the universe (astronomy and cosmology). In other cases the structures are so small that we also need machines to see them (or their symptoms). This is the case when we consider the detailed structure of matter (chemistry and physics). These natural (as opposed to cultural) structures appear to also often be hierarchical in nature. (We can never be sure how much of that structure is really there and how much is due to the scientist's perception and understanding of it, but I'll stay away from that philosophical question here.)

Consider physics, for example. Since ancient times (starting with the Greeks in the 6th century BCE) philosophers and, later, scientists have been searching for the basic (i.e., ultimate) constituents of matter. We now "know" (i.e., hypothesize) that matter has some sort of hierarchical organization. The smallest elements were first thought to be **atoms** (a term which actually means something like "indivisible") that cluster together into **molecules**. Then it was discovered that atoms consist of smaller things (**electrons, protons, neutrons**), and subsequently it turned out that these things also consist of even smaller units (**quarks**, etc.). Thus, we have at least four levels (ignoring **string theory**). At each level—except the lowest—units can consist of several units at the previous level.

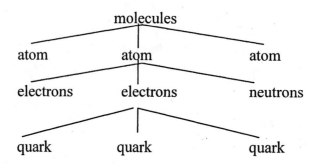

This structure is multi-tiered with, at each tier, units of the same or a comparable type.

In **biology**, where we turn to organic, living things, we can often clearly see the gross aspects of structures (of our body, for example), but when we literally wish to go deeper (below the skin), we again need fancy equipment. The most fascinating unit of our structure is the **cell**, and within the cell the notorious **DNA** (deoxyribose nucleic acid) molecules (studied in genetics). DNA molecules consist of (among others) four chemical units (**bases**) that form substrings called **codons** (sequences of three bases), which in turn make up **genes**; genes are grouped together on **chromosomes**. Again, we clearly see a hierarchical organization.

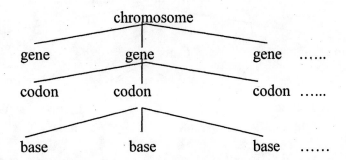

In short, wherever we look we "see" structure (or symptoms of structure) involving **tiers** and **repetition**, and much of science is about revealing these hidden structures. Linguistics is no exception. For linguistics the hidden structures are in the mind.

Structures in the Mind

The mind itself can be seen as a hierarchical organization of different modules.

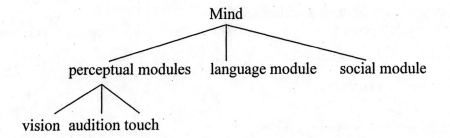

In previous chapters we also learned that each of these modules can be divided into submodules. The **language module** (earlier called the mental grammar), for example, must have components that deal with the different aspects of language, such as the sound side of language, the structure of sentences, the meaning of words and sentences, and so on.

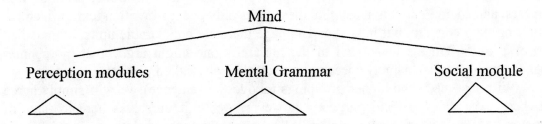

Other modules of the mind undoubtedly also have an internal organization, here indicated by closed triangles, and in fact modules themselves may be grouped in related sets of modules (as shown in the case of perceptual models).

Recall that the mental grammar contains six subcomponents. Those subcompenents themselves form a hierarchical structure.

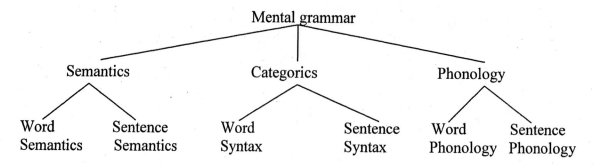

Each module at the bottom of this structure contains **basic units**, **combination rules** (**constraints**), and **adjustment** or **repair rules** (depending on the approach).

More Hierarchical Structure

We have learned that the function of all these modules is to characterize or check entities (called **representations** in the jargon of linguistics) that express an aspect of the hidden structure of **words** and **sentences**. We have also learned that representations themselves are also understood as hierarchical structures. In this section I want to discuss certain more detailed properties of these structures.

Recall that sentences are composed of words, which can be composed of morphemes:

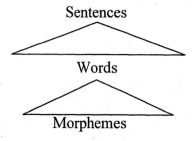

At first sight one might argue that there are even more levels than three tiers. After all, sentences can be organized into **paragraphs,** paragraphs into **sections,** sections into **chapters,** and so on. You might say that these units only occur in written texts, which are not our primary concern, but in spoken language there are comparable units, often called **discourse units**. On the lower end of the hierarchy one might argue that morphemes consist of smaller units, namely speech sounds, technically called **phonemes**.

With respect to the higher groupings (above the sentence) we will simply agree that these exist. For practical purposes, however, we limit ourselves here to units of language like the sentence and smaller. All sciences impose limitations on what they study; often it is necessary to first understand smaller things before you turn to bigger things. There are, however, branches of linguistics that deal with larger units (i.e., discourse structure) than the sentence, using whatever knowledge is now available with respect to sentence structure.

What about the idea that there are smaller units than morphemes, namely phonemes? We will not deny that phonemes are viable units of linguistic analysis.

However, as the reader will recall, I have rejected the idea that morphemes **consist** of phonemes. After all, there is more to a morpheme than its *sound side*. Morphemes also have a meaning and a category label. The meaning side of a morpheme need not be thought of as atomic, that is, unstructured. The meaning of a word like *cat* (let us use CAT as a label for that meaning), can be thought of as consisting of smaller semantic building blocks (or basic concepts) like ANIMAL, FURRY, DOMESTIC, and so on. There is not much agreement about the question of how to analyze meanings into basic building blocks, but if we accept for the moment that something like this is required, we arrive at the conclusion that morphemes can be thought of as consisting of both phonemes AND semantic primitives. But phonemes and semantic concepts are units of a very different nature. How can morphemes consist of both?

The solution was to say that the building blocks of morphemes exist in **three dimensions**: phonology, categorics, and semantics. Take the free morpheme *cat*:

-   Noun   **category** (word class label)
-   /kæt/   **form** (phoneme(s))
-   ANIMATE, MAMMAL, FURRY, ...   **meaning** (semantic concept(s))

A morpheme has, by definition, a simplex category label (noun, verb, adjective, conjunction, etc.). A morpheme, though simple in terms of its category label, can be simplex or complex at the phonological or semantic side. The morpheme {/-s/} (as in *dog-s*) consists of just one phoneme, while, as just demonstrated, the morpheme {/kæt/} consists of three phonemes. Examples of morphemes that are simplex in semantic terms are more difficult to give, because a good system of basic semantic concepts has not been developed.

In any event, the three dimensions of morphemes are not tiers that enter into a hierarchical relationship. Rather, they exist side-by-side on equal footing, together *constituting* the morpheme. We then made the further point that morphemes, words, and sentences have an important characteristic in common: They ALL have three dimensions. After all, when morphemes are combined to form words they carry their three dimensions with them. Hence, we have to modify the tree diagram to show how morphemes, words, and sentences are hierarchically related:

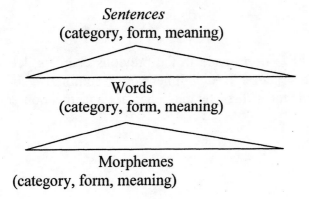

But we have seen that phonological structure is more than just a linear arrangement of phonemes, that is, there is also hierarchical structure there. The semantic structure is represented in terms of groupings of semantic concepts, and groupings of such groupings, and this also, then, involves hierarchical structure. Thirdly, when category labels are combined at the word and sentence level we also see hierarchical structure emerging. However, this simple diagram does not bring to the surface that each dimension has its *own* hierarchical structure, nor, for that matter, that the categorial organization can (or must) be thought of as central. The following, fancier diagram perhaps brings out more clearly that each unit has three dimensions, one of which is central. Morphemes are represented by a triple line. Think of the thick line as the central categorial information, which directs the merge structure. The other two lines represent the Form and the Meaning dimensions, which are organized in hierarchical structures of their own.

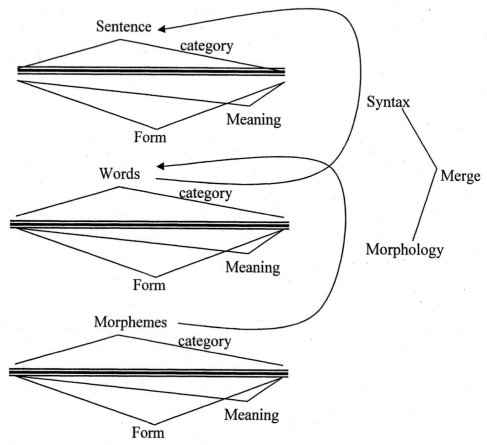

Recapitulating some points that have been made in the previous chapters, let us again take a closer look at nature of the structure in each dimension to summarize some of the properties that we have learned about in the previous chapters and mention some new ones.

The Categorial Structure of Words

Let us start with the words themselves. We have seen that the relationship between morphemes and words is hierarchical, i.e., a complex word is more than a linear string of morphemes; there is grouping, most likely binary grouping of morphemes into larger units, which themselves can group with additional morphemes into increasingly larger complex words.

Here's a word that I just made up: *refinalization*. In an example like this, it is easy to see that there are four morphemes:

re   final   ize   ation

(Some linguists suggest that *ation* is two morphemes: *ate* and *ion*.)

A moment of reflection will show that these morphemes have been combined in a series of three steps:

final + ize   to make final
re + finalize   to again make final
refinalize + ation   the act of again making final

Each step adds an affix that adds a semantic ingredient to the new word. We can represent the hierarchical structure using the following **tree diagram**:

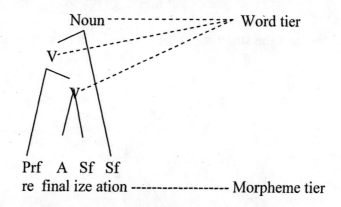

We note immediately that the units on the morpheme tier are not all directly related to the one word tier. Rather what we note is that the word tier is repeated several times, namely each time a new morpheme is added. Clearly, the following flat structures that lack internal organization would not be an adequate categorial representation of the word in question:

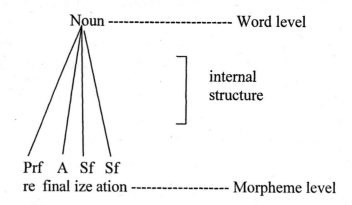

The repetition of a tier type is called recursion. Due to recursion, the distance between the terminal nodes and the root node increases with each new application of merge. We might say that merge itself is recursive and that the categorial structure follows suit.

The Categorial Structure of Sentence Structures

Let us now look in more detail at sentences and reaffirm that sentences also have a hierarchical *and* recursive structure. The following sentence is not just a string of words in some linear order:

John and Mary built that large house.

We can represent the structure as follows, using a **tree diagram**:

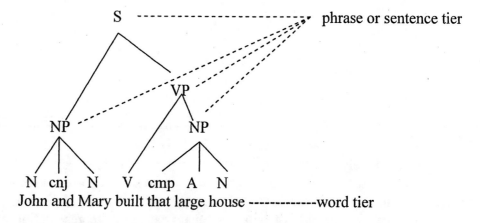

In this tree diagram, the highest level is the **sentence** (the **top node**), whereas the lowest level in this tree is formed by the **words** (the **terminal nodes**). Thus, we can provide the highest level with the label *sentence* and lowest units with the label *word*, or more specifically with a **word label** that indicates the category (or word class) that each word belongs to: *noun, conjunction, verb, demonstrative, preposition, determiner*, and so on. [John and Mary] forms a phrase that functions as the **subject** of the sentence. They perform an activity, namely, [built that large house]. What they [built] is [that large house]. This seems a plausible structure. Of course, we need to say more than that in order to motivate it properly. Assigning such structure to sentences is often called **parsing**.

In the above diagram we see that the relationship between the unit *Word* and the next higher unit *Sentence* is **not direct** because there are groupings of words into **phrases.** Note in particular that phrases can occur inside other phrases; the phrase [that large house] occurs inside the phrase [built [that large house]]. This phrase-within-phrase pattern gives categorial sentence structure its recursivity. If the relationship between the word and the sentence level *would have* been direct, the structure of our sentence would have been as follows:

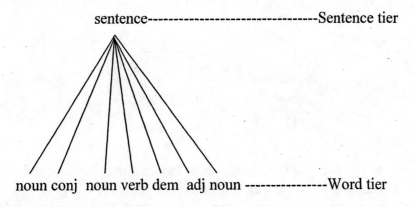

sentence--------------------------------Sentence tier

noun conj noun verb dem adj noun ----------------Word tier

John and Mary built that large house

This tree, however, does not give us an adequate representation of the structure of the sentence. It merely displays that a certain string of words forms a sentence, while it says nothing about the internal structure of the sentence.

We note that for the top node I use the label *sentence* or *phrase*. What this indicates is that a sentence is just a particular kind of phrase. Recursivity, in fact, might involve sentences within sentences.

[John heard [Mary say [that Bill was sick]$_S$] $_S$] $_S$

The important point to keep in mind is that all categorial structure, both at the word level and the sentence level, shows recursion.

The Semantic Structure of Words and Sentences

Semantic structures, like categorial structures, are hierarchical, and I will assume without demonstrating this in detail that semantic structures look very much like the categorial (merge) structures, including the property of recursion. Semantic structures will be discussed in more detail in Part III.

The Phonological Structure of Words and Sentences

We have seen in Chapter 6 that phonological structures are also hierarchical and that the phonological structure of words and sentences has several intermediate tiers. At the word level phonemes get organized into syllables, which then get organized into words.

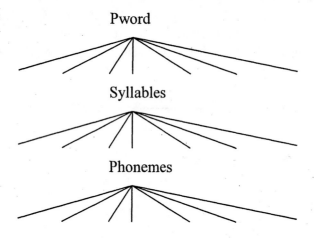

The grouping of phonotactic words into larger phonological units has been less motivated, but as we have seen it can be argued that such a grouping is necessary to explain the occurrence of the sandhi process. Pwords are organized into Phonological phrases, which then make up the Phonological unit corresponding to the sentence.

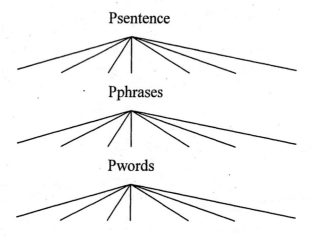

The Pwords that emerge from the morphology and the Pwords that are grouped into Pphrases may differ slightly in that small words like *the* and *a*, or pronouns, in short closed class words, may get to be incorporated into bigger Pwords. So for example the sequence of Pwords *he is* is turned into one Pword, *he's*. These little words, that in the sentence appear to be incapable of standing on their own, are called **clitics**.

Tiered and Recursive Structure

We have discussed earlier, and will do so here again in more detail, that categorial structures (and semantic structure) differ in one important respect from phonological structures, and this difference relates directly to the notion of recursion. When it comes to the phonological organization it does not seem that there is recursion in the sense of tiers of a certain type containing tiers of the same type. However, the phonological structure of words is not entirely flat either, i.e., it is not:

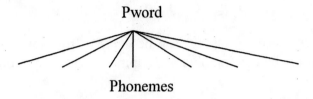

Nor is the phonological structure of the sentence:

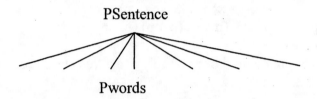

Instead we see a variety of intermediate tiers. This difference between categorial and phonological structure was noted in chapter 7 where I represented it as follows:

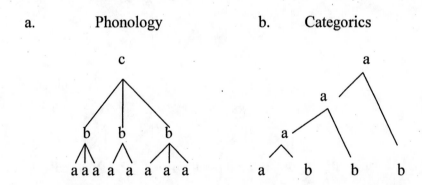

To go from the morpheme to the word level or from the word to the phrase level categorics has a self-containing recursion with one tier (word or phrase) repeating itself, while phonology involves the introduction of new intermediate tiers. Thus, in the categorial dimensions we saw that words occur inside words, whereas at the sentence level we saw that phrases occur inside phrases. In the phonological dimensions, however, we have not seen that phonotactic words contain phonotactic words, not have we provided arguments for syllables occurring inside other syllables, or Pphrases inside other Pphrases.

This difference in organization calls for an explanation, which, at this point, I am unable to spell out in detail. Here is a hint. Phonological structure is foremost a categorization of phonetic properties of linguistic expressions which, among others, involve rhythmic alternation of units of increasing length. In other words, rhythmic organization involves alternation of units at different levels which we can represent by a graph that depicts each rhythmic beat by an x; p stands for the sequence of basic units, i.e., phonemes:

```
x
x                             x
x           x       x         x         x
x     x     x   x   x   x     x
p  p  p  p  p  p  p  p  p  p  p  p  p  p
```

It seems that phonotactic structure (i.e., grouping) can be derived from this hierarchical nature of rhythmic structure simply by making binary groupings at each rhythmic level.

```
(x)
(x                                   x)
(x                 x)      .  (x                 x)
(x        x)    (x      x)    (x        x)    (x)
(p    p)(p    p) (p    p) (p    p)(p    p)(p    p) (p    p)
```

Another way to represent the grouping would be to simply use a tree structure:

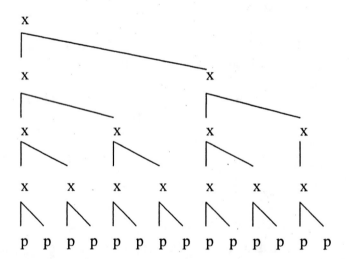

This looks, pretty much, like a strictly tiered phonotactic structure. Perhaps, then, rhythmic organization, which I take to be a property of phonetic structure, is the point of departure for hierarchical phonotactic organization.

Categorial structure, on the other hand, is mostly catering to semantic structure, i.e. conceptual structure (the language of thought), which is inherently recursive in that our thinking patterns typically show the embedding of one thought into another.

We can summarize the causes for the differences between categorial and phonotactic structure as follows. I put the categorial and phonotactic structure between thicker lines because, as some linguists claim, these two systems form the core of the mental grammar. After all, the conceptual system is a more general system that must exist independent from language as the home of all aspects of our conscious mental life. Likewise, it might be argued that the phonetic system is external to language proper in that it involves the control of articulatory and perceptual mechanisms, which, just like the conceptual system, in part have been put to use for the purpose of language.

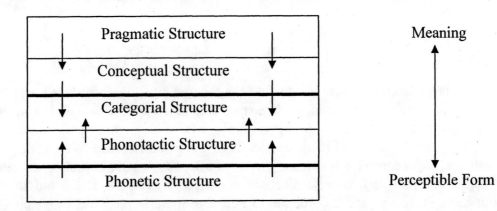

Even though it would seem that the categorial structure is largely catering to the conceptual structure, some aspects of it may also be dependent on the phonotactic structure. The categorial structure, then, tries to compromise between the needs of conceptual structure and phonotactic structure. I have also included a level called *pragmatic structure*, which captures all aspect of meaning that are dependent on the actual realization of a linguistic expression. Phonetic structure, like pragmatic structure specifies the properties of linguistic expressions that are dependent on the context of use and in this sense, pragmatic structure and phonetic structure both come into play when a linguistic expression is used as an actual utterance.

Binarity

An apparent difference between the categorial and the phonological grouping is that the latter does not seem to be binary. However, as I will show in chapter 10, that is a consequence of the fact that we have not gone into much detail. There are more tiers in the phonological structure than I have mentioned so far. Clearly a more-than-binary (a) structure can be made binary by adding an extra level X, as in (b).

Whether this is a sensible move depends on the argument that we can provide for postulating the X layer.

It must be added that the binarity hypothesis, in the end, may be better motivated for phonological structure than for categorial or semantic structure. As for merge structure, I have assumed that this is a binary procedure (which makes the categorial structure binary, too, if merge and categorial structure are identified). This is not a necessity, however, and I will come back to the binarity hypothesis in Part III.

Grouping and Linear Order

There is an essential resemblance between the tree structure introduced here to represent linguistic representations and the tree structures that we discussed earlier in this chapter, which captures the structure of, for example, a large company. In both cases we indicate grouping and hierarchical relations, but there is also a difference. We can think of the tree structure that represents a company as a **mobile**. We have a grouping at each level, but there is no necessary **linear order** within each level. If Tom, Dick, and Harry all work for Boss Pete, they are subordinate to Pete, but there is no sense in which Tom comes first, followed by Dick and finally by Harry. However, when we use a two-dimensional medium to represent a tree we are forced to impose a left-to-right order. Thus, on paper, we have to write the nodes in a linear order (one after the other on a line), but it is important to understand that this is just because paper poses a two-dimensional limitation.

Now in some cases we perhaps do want to state a specific linear order between a set of nodes that is dominated by another node such as in the phonological and categorial properties of words and sentences. Certainly in the case of sentences the linear order seems to matter: The words actually occur in some specific **linear order**, and that ordering is an important part of the linguistic utterance, at least in English. But within words we have seen that morphemes also, crucially, appear in a certain order. In the phonological dimension phonemes also occur in a specific order, and so do syllables, and so on.

We could express the relation of linear order *explicitly* in the diagram, thus expressing that each group is a network in that there is a relation of precedence holding between its members. Consider the sentence:

John and Mary built that large house

The categorial sentence structure:

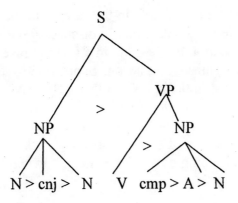

The phonotactic sentence structure:

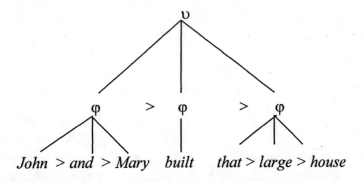

I have left out the ">" symbol in between all the phonemes, but assume they are there.)

However, we usually suppress the symbol ">" when we talk about the linguistic structures that express properties of words and sentences.

But let us now ask to what extent linear information is a *necessary* ingredient of linguistic structures. It has been argued that the only structures that *must* express linear relations are phonetic structures. After all, the reasoning goes, the cause for placing words in some linear order (and within them phonemes) is phonetic because human beings cannot pronounce more than one word or phoneme at the same time. At the same time it is likely that the perceptual system imposes a linear organization of speech (perhaps less of signs; see Chapter 15).

But this can't be the whole story because, as we will see, many linear precedence relations can be predicted from either the categorial structure or the phonotactic structure, either in terms of universal principles or in terms of language-specific principles.

The linear ordering of morphemes in words and of words in sentences does not follow from phonological principles. There is no conceivable phonological reason preferring [*that large house*] over [*that house large*] or [*house large that*]. Yet some languages have one, while others have another. Having one or another is a property of the categorial-merge system, and in fact it is an arbitrary property in that it does not follow from the phonological or the semantic system. Thus, morpheme and word order is categorial in nature.

In what way are linear relations predictable in the categorial dimension, and how do we express this predictability? Here's an example. In discussing the nature of phrases we have noted that phrases have a central unit, a noun in a noun phrase, a verb in a verb phrase, an adjective in an adjective phrase, and so on. Suppose now that in any given language the central unit is always last in the phrase so that we always get *the big house* (and never *house big*), *apples eat* (and not *eat apples*), *very small* (and not *small very*), and so on. Clearly, one might say, it is now **redundant** to specify this fact in each constraint that governs the wellformedness of a particular type of phrase. We could state all these constrains as referring to grouping only, and make one general constraint about the location of the central unit.

Grouping constraints:

[N, A] $_{NP}$
[NP, V]$_{VP}$
[A, Adv]$_{AP}$

Linearization constraint:

The central unit comes last

Similarly, linearization constraints have been proposed at the level of word categorial structure.

What this discussion shows is that phonetic structure does have a certain impact on categorial structure in that the ordering of morphemes and words is enforced by the inherent linear organization of speech. At the same time we see that within the categorial constraint system the linear demands can be stated in a separate set of constraints. I do not wish to suggest that all specification of linearity can be extracted from the categorial constraints, and it might be that, in the end, the so called predictability of morpheme and word order follows tendencies rather than hard and fast rules.

Let us now turn to linearity within the phonotactic structures. Which aspects of linear order follow from phonological principles? It might be argued that the linear precedence relations among phonemes do not *fully* follow from phonological principles at all. Firstly, in as far as morphemes and thus words bring in phonological material it seems natural to expect that the linear order of these larger units carries over in the order of their associated phonological material. In other words, we do not expect that the phonemes of two morphemes that are combined into a word will end up completely intermixed due to phonological principles. Interestingly, this is not always so. In certain languages (such as many Semitic languages), the vowels and consonants of words are introduced by separate morphemes such that one morpheme brings in all the vowels, while the other morpheme brings in all the consonants. In the final result, consonants and vowels are then intermixed so that the word ends up being sequence of consonant+vowel syllables. In such cases, however, each type of morpheme contains its phoneme in a specific linear order:

$$\begin{bmatrix} X \\ kbt \end{bmatrix} \begin{bmatrix} Y \\ iau \end{bmatrix} \Rightarrow \begin{bmatrix} X\,Y \\ kitabu \end{bmatrix}$$

This intermixing would be due to a repair that responds to the fact that the sequence *kbtaiu* is not wellformed phonotactically.

This seems to suggest that the linear order of phonemes within morphemes is given and cannot be considered redundant, i.e., derivable from phonological principles. However, in many cases there are predictable aspects to the linear order of phonemes.

Consider the three phonemes /k/, /æ/ and /t/. It is not the case that these can occur in any conceivable order. The following three orderings are all phonologically wellformed in English: /kæt/, /ækt/, /tæk/. Both consonants can be on either side of the vowel, but when they are on the same side only /kt/ is possible, and only after the vowel. This shows that the linear order among phonemes is, at least in part, predictable, which would make it possible to split the constraint set into constraints that characterize grouping and constraints that characterize the linear order of phonemes within groups.

Concluding, we have seen that the linear structure among morphemes and words is characterized by the categorial-merge system and that the linear order of phonemes is characterized by the phonotactic system. In both cases it is possible that some aspects of linear order follow from special linearization constraints. The fact that the categorial systems must deal with linear order (which finds its cause in phonetic structure) indicates that this dimension of grammar is partly dependent on phonetic structure.

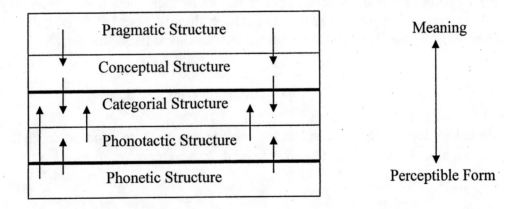

This, then, raises a further question. Are there grounds for saying that conceptual structure can influence phonotactic structure? Perhaps there are. In Part I we learned about iconicity, which is the phenomenon that aspects of the phonotactic form of words can be motivated by aspects of the corresponding conceptual structure. For example, if a word corresponds to a conceptual structure that includes a reference to some sort of sound, the phonotactic form can try to mimic this sound and create a so-called onomatopoeic word. Since this kind of relationship does exist in languages, we can say that conceptual structure can influence phonotactic form.

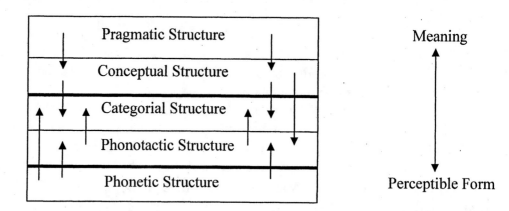

We will pursue these issues that concern the relationships between the various dimensions in greater detail later on. For example, it is in fact possible to argue that conceptual structure, even though we assume that this kind of structure does not involve linear order as such, influences the linear organization of the categorial structure. For example, it would presumably be a task of conceptual structure to express whether certain concepts are more prominent or relevant within the broader message than others. This kind of informational prominence can then be encoded into the categorial structure, for example, by systematically placing old information before new information, or, seemingly in conflict with that, more important information before less important information. It is often assumed that this kind of information forms part of a particular kind of conceptual structure which is called **information structure** but that is irrelevant to the point I am making here, although it does perhaps show that the various dimensions might contain not just the kinds of structures that we have been discussing, but perhaps additional (related) structures or various annotations to these structures.

Arborial Terms

In talking about trees we have used terms like *root node*, *terminal node*, and so on. There are additional useful terms that refer to relationships between nodes.

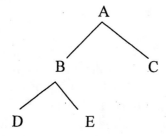

In down to earth terminology, A is called the **mother** of B and C, which are called **daughters** of A and with respect to each other **sisters**. Likewise B is the mother of D and E, which are daughters of B and sisters to each other.

Mother nodes are also called **dominating nodes**. A directly dominates D and E, and **indirectly** D and E. B in turn directly dominates D and E and nothing else. Dominating nodes are also said to be **superordinate** to lower nodes, and lower nodes are said to be **subordinate** to higher nodes.

Conclusions

Tree diagrams are a common way to represent hierarchical structure. We find tree structures in all sectors of life and science. In order to understand the workings of language (or, rather, of the mental grammar), we use lots of tree diagrams, not only in characterizing the organization of the mental grammar itself, but also with respect to the linguistics units (words and sentences) that the mental grammar delivers.

In Part III we will discuss, again in greater detail, the modules of the mental grammar. We start with the phonological word and sentence modules (focusing mainly on the word module). Then we turn to the categorial word and sentence modules, each treated in separate chapters. Finally we discuss the semantic word and sentence modules in one chapter.

Chapter 10

Phonological Structures
(Word and Sentence Level)

Introduction

We now embark on a detailed examination of the six grammatical components. In all cases I will explain the component in terms of the ingredients introduced in the previous chapter (primitives/building blocks, combination rules/constraints, and where seemingly necessary adjustment/repair rules). There will be repetition in these chapters in that basic concepts introduced in Part I will be briefly mentioned and defined again.

Does Phonological Wellformedness Exist?

Given that each language has a fixed number of **phonemes** (**consonants** and **vowels**), one can, as a first approximation, characterize wellformed words as permissible **linear arrangements** of these phonemes. Clearly, not all arrangements of consonants and vowels are permissible or **grammatical**. It is important to understand that being grammatical does not depend on being an actual existing word. For example: *pront* and *skal* (we may wish to spell the latter word as <skall>, but we are not talking about spelling here) are not actual words, but *as phoneme strings* they are grammatical according to the phonological system of English; these strings *could* be words of English, just like the actually occurring *print* and *skull*.

Hence there must be **rules** that allow speakers to make this assessment, and these same rules allow them to say that *rpont* and *ksal* are *not* grammatical. Note that there is an important difference between words that don't exist but *could* exist (*pront, skal*) and words that don't exist and could not exist (*rpont, ksal*). We can refer to these two cases as **possible** and **impossible words**, respectively. And when we say *words* we mean, in this context, the phonological dimension of words. In each language only a subset of the possible words are actually occurring words.

We will see that the relevant rules are not all universal (although some of them may be). In certain languages words can start with the consonant group /rd/ (e.g., Polish *rdest* "knot grass"), but this is not possible in English and many other languages which have the phonemes /r/ and /d/. Both English and Polish allow combinations of consonants of considerable length, especially in between two vowels, but there are languages where no combinations occur at all so that each word has the structure CVCVCV... (where C stands for consonant and V for vowel). Combinations of vowels are uncommon in most languages, but they nonetheless occur in some.

Normally, we do not just make new word **forms** (to be used as free morphemes). Why would we? The forms of morphemes are *given* in the lexicon. But we can do it for fun, for example, in poetry (if we can't find a word that rhymes, we can make one up) or if we want to cheat when playing Scrabble®. However, people in the advertising business do make up new word forms as proper names for new products. In that case, the "meaning" of the new word form will be that specific product. Over time, such a product name may become an actual word that we use generally for the *kind of thing* that product is. For example, *kleenex* has become a word for "tissue," even though it started out (and still is) a specific brand name (see Chapter 14).

We have seen in the previous chapters that there are *two* phonological modules—one for the word level and one for the sentence level. In this chapter I will mostly discuss the **word** level system.

The general structure of the phonological word module is as follows:

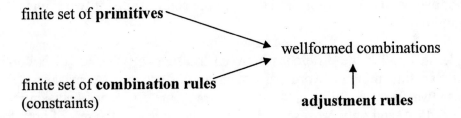

I will now discuss each of the three boldface ingredients.

The Primitives of Phonological Structure

The first step in describing a language is to make **phonetic transcriptions** of individual words using **IPA (International Phonetic Alphabet)** symbols, a set of symbols (letters, many taken from the Roman alphabet) and diacritics that allows a unique representation of each speech sound that has so far been shown to exist in the languages of the world. The linguist elicits these words from an **informant**, and he writes them down in IPA. It is not always easy to decide how many sounds a word consists of, because there are no clear divisions between the sounds that make up words.

The exact total number of different speech sounds that the linguist registers (for the language as a whole) will depend on how detailed (the technical term is how **narrow**) the transcription is. For example, the first sound of the English word *pot* may differ slightly each time it is pronounced (even by the same person). Also, the first sound of *pit* will be different from the first one in *pot* because of the fact that it is followed by a different vowel. (We'll soon see that sounds influence each other, as one might expect.) In making a transcription linguists abstract away from such individual and contextual

phonetic differences among speech sounds *if they are very small*. In other words, in the transcription we collapse into one symbol those speech sounds that differ only minimally. (What is regarded minimal and what is not is not ease to say in a few words.)

Transcriptions in IPA symbols are placed between square brackets: [kæt] (for *cat*). This is done to make it clear that we are not talking about a representation of the word in terms of phonemes, in which case we use slant lines around the IPA letters, for example as in /kæt/.

From Transcription to Phonological Analysis: Phonemes and Allophones

The next step is to distinguish between speech sounds that are **contrastive** and those that are not. This leads up to what is called the **phonological analysis**, the reduction of speech sounds (or phones) to phonemes. We cannot determine whether a sound is contrastive by just listening to it very carefully. To determine contrastivity we always need *two* sounds, and we need to compare them *as they are used in actual words*.

- Two sounds are called *contrastive* in some language L if the difference between them causes two different "sound events" in L.
- A pair of two words in L that is used to prove the contrastivity of two sounds is called **a minimal pair**.

For example, in English the difference between the sounds [p^h] and [b] is contrastive because we can find minimal word pairs such as *pin* and *bin*. A speaker of English regards these two forms as different words *because of* the difference between the initial sounds [p^h] and [b], and only because of that difference because the rest of both forms is the same.

Why do we say that the word pin starts with a [p^h] rather than [p]? What is that little *superscript h* doing there? The little *h* indicates (according to IPA convention) that the initial sound of *pin* is **aspirated**. (Pronounce the word *pin* while holding a piece of paper before your mouth; you'll see that the paper is blown away when you pronounce *pin*, but not when you pronounce *bin*. The extra puff of air is called aspiration.). In addition to the difference in aspiration, [p^h] and [b] also differ in terms of vocal fold vibration, which is why [p^h] is often called voiceless and [b] voiced. We will assume that the voicelessness and aspiration form a phonetic package which, as a whole, makes up the contrastive aspect of [p^h] as opposed to [b]?

English, in fact, does have a sound [p] (without the aspiration). In the word *spin* there is a plain [p]. A trained linguist describing English in terms of IPA symbols will notice a difference between the initial sound of *pin* and the second sound of *spin*, and will transcribe them as [p^h] and [p], respectively. Now, it so happens that in the English spelling system we use the same letter in both cases, <p>, and this might be the reason why speakers of English (unless they are linguists) think of *pin* and *spin* as containing the same "p" sound. However, a linguist describing language utterances is trained to ignore spelling and listen carefully to the actual sounds. (In fact, many languages don't even have a spelling system when they are first described.) Having found instances of the sounds [p] and [pʰ], the question is now going to be whether the difference between these sounds is contrastive in English.

It isn't! There are, in English, no minimal pairs like [pIn] and [pʰIn]. In fact, if you would pronounce the word *pin* as [pIn] it might sound somewhat funny perhaps; you would probably regard that form as an odd pronunciation of the word *pin,* something a foreigner might say. It is also possible that one hears the form [pIn] as the pronunciation for *bin*. The sound [p] is somewhere in between [pʰ] and [b]. So an English speaker is likely to hear [pIn] as either [pʰIn] or [bIn]. In any event the difference between [pʰ] and [p] is not contrastive. We compare [pʰ] to [p] because they are so similar. It is important to realize that the difference between [p] and [pʰ] is not too small to make a contrastive distinction between two words. In other languages than English, such as *Thai*, minimal pairs can be formed that contrast only in this difference:

[pɔ:n]	to wish	[pʰɔ:n]	also
[tɔp]	to support	[tʰɔp]	be suffocated
[kat]	to cut	[kʰat]	to polish

Hindi is another language that has minimal pairs for these two sounds. Thus, whether a phonetic difference is contrastive or not depends on the language. The linguist can only establish whether a phonetic difference is contrastive by finding minimal pairs. If he can't find such pairs, the difference is non-contrastive.

(It also depends on the language whether a given speech sound occurs at all. *Dutch*, for example, does not have the sound [pʰ], although it has [p]. I will come back to this point, but I was taking for granted here that you already know that languages differ in their inventory of speech sounds.)

To understand why contrastivity is such an important matter, realize that the essential function of speech sounds is to supply each morpheme with a perceptible form that is different from the form of other morphemes. Morphemes *must* have a perceptible form because otherwise one would have to be a mind reader to know what a person wants to communicate. To make communication successful each word must have a perceptible form, and in the ideal language each morpheme has a unique form. But to know what counts as different there must be a tacit agreement among speakers of a given language about which phonetic properties of words matter to make such differences. These are the contrastive differences.

Compare this to chess; the different pieces must have differences in their form, but the kinds of differences can differ from one set of pieces to the next. Sometimes a tower looks like a real medieval tower, sometimes just like a straight column; really, the form that represents a tower could be anything as long it has a property that makes it different from the other pieces that have behave differently and as long as the players agree that it *represents* a chess piece that can make certain moves but not others.

English is not as ideal as chess because, like all other languages, it does have cases where two or more different words have the same form. We call such words homophones (they sound the same). An example is: <to>, <two>, and <too>.

So English has both [pʰ] (in words like *pin*), [p] (in words like *spin*), and [b] (in words like *bin*). The difference between [pʰ] and [b] is **contrastive** (because we can find minimal pairs), but the difference between [pʰ] and [p] is not. Once we have established that there are no minimal pairs for two sounds, we know one thing for sure: The two sounds cannot occur in the *same* environment (i.e., position in the word, adjacent to the same other sounds). Why? Well, if they could occur in the same environment they would be (potentially) contrastive, that is, they would constitute the only difference between two (possible) words and we ought to be able to find a minimal pair. (Make sure you completely understand this point; it is crucial. I call the idea of contrastivity the Central Dogma of phonology.) In other words, the sets of environments that non-contrastive sounds occur in must be **complementary** (or at least non-overlapping). In the case at hand we can say that [pʰ] occurs at the beginning of a (stressed) syllable (not preceded by an *s*), and [p] elsewhere. A linguist will refer to the environments that a sound occurs in as the **distribution** of the sound. Two sounds that are not contrastive must therefore have a **complementary distribution**.

According to this account [p] can occur in a word's final position such as in *cup*. Indeed, we often say that the final sound of this word is [p]. In actual fact this final [p] differs somewhat from the [p] in *spin*. It is *non-released* (it doesn't have the same explosive force as the [p] that is followed by a vowel). We could note this in IPA by using the symbol [p˺]. Again we can show that the difference between [p˺] and [p] or [pʰ] is not contrastive and that their distributions are non-overlapping. For now I will limit the discussion to just [p] and [pʰ].

Given, then, that [p] and [pʰ] are in complementary distribution (more precisely: non-overlapping), we will regard them as two possible versions of the same "sound intention." It is as if the speaker **intends** to use the same sound in both cases, but due to the differences in environments the sound comes out slightly differently. A technical term for the *sound intention* is **phoneme**. We used this term informally already, but now we have a better understanding of the way in which a linguist uses the term. A phoneme, then, is not the same thing as a speech sound. As a sound intention it is not a physical sound at all. Rather, it is a mental unit that represents speech sounds.

In this example we will say that the phoneme underlying both speech sounds is /p/, which would make [p] the "direct" realization of this phoneme. We will then also say that the sound [pʰ] is a non-direct realization of /p/. Realizations of a phoneme (whether direct or indirect) are called **allophones**. Allophones, like phonemes, are not to be equated with speech sounds. Allophones are still cognitive entities, just like phonemes. Allophones are derived from phonemes in terms of a **cognitive computation**, an adjustment rule converting /p/ into [p] or [pʰ]. The former computation is *vacuous* because it is direct; the latter involves *adding aspiration*.

We indicate that we talk about phonemes by using slant lines: /p/; allophones, as shown, are put between square brackets, as if we were dealing with IPA transcriptions of speech sounds. However, we have to keep in mind that allophones are cognitive units and in terms of their composition (see below) not really different from phonemes. As cognitive units they ought to be distinguished from phonetic transcriptions, which are symbols on a piece of paper or a screen meant as an approximation of the actual speech sounds. Even more clearly should we distinguish between allophones (as mental entities) and the actual speech sounds (which are acoustic entities that one can display in the form of spectrogram). Where this distinction becomes crucial to keep track of I will put references to actual speech sounds between double square brackets [[pʰ]] and use the single square brackets to indicate allophones. Below we will see that the allophones of a given phoneme can be seen as being derived from the phoneme in terms of an adjustment rule that, in the example at hand, adds aspiration in certain contexts. Such adjustment rules are also called **allophony rules**. (The term *allophone* is sometimes used in a slightly different way in that it is said that the phoneme /p/ has *one* allophone, namely [pʰ]. However, I have chosen to say that /p/ has two allophones [p] and [pʰ]. As discussed, /p/ actually has more allophones, such as [p']; I will return to this point below.)

Why do we use the symbol "p" for the phoneme, rather that "pʰ"? In other words, why do we not regard /pʰ/ as the phoneme from which we derive [pʰ] vacuously and [p] by an adjustment rule that deletes aspiration in certain contexts?

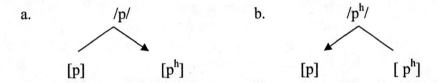

a.   /p/   b.   /pʰ/

[p]   [pʰ]   [p]   [pʰ]

The non-vacuous derivation is here represented in terms of an arrow, the other derivation involves an "identity rule" that we do not even bother to mention any further.

The basic reason for choosing one of the allophones as the basic allophone that is identical to the phoneme refers to distribution. As a rule of thumb, we will say that the allophone with the widest distribution is the basic allophone. In this case we can say, for example, that [pʰ] occurs initially before a stressed vowel, while [p] occurs in all other environments, or, as we say, elsewhere (i.e., everywhere else).

A second reason for choosing a particular allophone as basic is when it is in some sense to be defined as "simpler" than the other one(s). In our example we could say that [pʰ] is more complex than [p] because it is basically [p] <u>plus</u> [ʰ].

There is another question that should be asked. I tried to make it clear that we cannot find a minimal pair involving [p] and [pʰ]. So this difference is non-contrastive, and we then decided that both phones are allophones of the same phoneme. Someone could now say that the difference between [p] and [b] is not contrastive either because again we cannot find a minimal pair [pɪn] or [bɪn]? But this is incorrect. It is true that these two sounds cannot be contrastive initially (at the beginning of a word), but they can be finally: *cap* and *cab*. Hence [p] and [b] cannot be allophones of one phoneme.

How Many Allophones?

Earlier I mentioned that a linguist, *when doing a transcription*, abstracts away from minute differences. Many of these differences have to do with the gender, size, mental, or physical state of the speaker (we call these difference *paralinguistic*), but others are due to the context or environment (in terms of neighboring sounds or position in the word) in which they occur. For example, the difference between the *p* in *pot* and *pit* is ignored. The difference between [p] and [p'] is also often ignored. So why would we not ignore the difference between [p] and [pʰ] in our transcription, and transcribe both as, say, [p], which then leads to recognizing only one allophone [p] for the phoneme /p/? First of all, when making a narrow transcription we *could* note such small differences as that between *pit* and *pot* or the p's in *spot* and *top*. However, when making a broad(er) transcription a linguist tries to register only those differences that he thinks **could** be contrastive. Here he has to rely on his experience and knowledge of languages in general. If the linguist knows a language in which some property X is contrastive, he will note it in his transcription of the language he now works on even though he doesn't know yet whether X is contrastive in this language too. In addition, he will register differences that are **clearly noticeable**, even when he is unaware of any other language in which that difference is contrastive. After all, it could be that the language under analysis is the first to show evidence for the contrastivity of a certain phonetic difference. A third factor that contributes to noting or non-noting a small distinction in the transcription has to do with how automatic the difference is. For example, the difference between the p's in *pot* and *pit* in English can be regarded as an automatic consequence of the way that human articulation works. It is humanly impossible to not make such small differences, and we will find them therefore in all languages; they are universal. The phenomenon that sounds always influence each other is called **co-articulation**. The same cannot be said for the difference between [p] and [pʰ] in English. Many languages do not have such a difference. Dutch has a plain [p] wherever English has [p] or [pʰ]. This makes the aspiration of p's in the initial position a specific fact about English. In transcriptions, linguist will tend to register such language-specific facts.

Thus, the linguist would know that the difference between the first sound in *pot* and *pit* has never been noted as constituting a contrastive difference in any language, and moreover would surmise that the difference is so subtle that probably no language will ever use it contrastively. Furthermore, he would try to show that this difference is outside the control of people and due to the universal way in which our articulatory system works. The idea is that a /p/ *cannot* be articulated in exactly the same way in *pot* and *pit* because a following vowel will *always* exercise some influence on its articulation. Hence, such differences fall outside the domain of phonology and would be the object of study by **phoneticians**, people who study the universal workings of the articulatory and auditory systems of humans. In terms of the separation between a model of competence and a model of performance (which we made in Chapter 7), we would locate an account of minute differences like this in the performance module.

The status of the difference between [p] and [p'] is not so clear. We do not know any language where such a difference is contrastive. However, to release or not release a final p depends on the language that you study. Therefore, we are not dealing with a phonetic universal here, and we might want to note it in our transcription even though we believe the difference is not potentially contrastive.

Thus, ignoring the influence of paralinguistic factors, we can say that each phoneme has many, many different allophones, one for each different context in which it can appear, but we ignore many of those when they are due to universal processes (co-articulation) and in a so-called broad transcription in which a linguist is anticipating, as it were, the phonological analysis, he will ignore everything that is not potentially contrastive.

(Sometimes a linguist might wish to register every possible detail in the transcription when it is made for a special purpose such as pinning down the minute differences between two related dialects, or when noting down the way young infants pronounce words, or patients with speech defects. For these latter reasons we even have special symbols at our disposal which are not part of the official IPA.)

Summarizing: Although the difference between [p] and [pʰ] in English has been noted, and thus not ignored, in the phonetic transcription, and also having established that the difference is not contrastive, we can now conclude that this difference *can* be ignored when it comes to listing the phonemes of English. This means that, in stating the inventory of phonemes for English, we will abstract away from the presence of aspiration. We choose one of allophones as basic and consider the other allophone(s) to be derived from it by adjustment rules (allophony rules). In this case the adjustment rule will assign aspiration to the /p/ in certain positions.

The Many Allophones of /t/

In English, the phoneme /t/ is perhaps the champion in terms of having a high number of pretty noticeable allophones. We already discussed [t], [tʰ] and [t']. I also briefly mentioned the flap [ɾ]. But there are more:

- [t]   stop
- [tʰ]   top
- [t']   pot
- [ɾ]   little, writer
- [ʔ]   button ([ʔ] is the sound that you make twice when you say oh-oh)

We will not dwell here on the question as to why /t/ has so many allophones.

Allophones and Phonemes

Because the distinction between phoneme and allophone is so central, I repeat the difference. When we look at the distribution of [p] and [pʰ], we get the feeling that, somehow, [p] and [pʰ] are the same sound, or, rather, two variants of the same sound. **A central claim in phonological analysis is that in the mind of the speaker [p] and [pʰ] are indeed the same entity.** This mental entity is a (mental) image of a sound that has certain properties that are shared by [p] and [pʰ], but as a mental entity is it neither one nor the other. The things that we put between square brackets are also mental entities, but they are one step closer to the actual pronunciation. We refer to the deeper mental images as **phonemes** and the shallower entities as **allophones**. To make it clear that we talk about a phoneme and not an allophone we put the phoneme between slant lines: /p/. (We choose "p" and not "pʰ" as the phoneme symbol because the sound [p] has a more general distribution than the sound [pʰ].)

When considering two allophones of the same phoneme, the differences between them can be predicted from the environment that one of them occurs in. The allophone with the predictable properties is the one that is limited in distribution to a certain context. The elsewhere allophone (the basic allophone) does not have properties that can be predicted from the environments it can occur in; these environments do not form a homogeneous (or natural) class.

Another way to look at phonemes is to call them *sound intentions*. Thus, there is a sound intention /p/ which comes out as a bunch of different actual sounds.

If we now assume that only allophones that belong to different phonemes can be in contrast with each other, we can say that our hypothesis that [p] and [pʰ] are manifestations of a single phoneme /p/ EXPLAINS that the two sounds are in complementary distribution.

Phonemes as Sets of Allophones

It may sometimes be convenient to define phonemes as *sets of allophones* and to use so-called Ven-diagrams to represents these sets, e.g.:

/t/

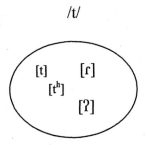

With such diagrams we can depict phonemic overlap as overlap of the sets that are associated with two phonemes.

A variant of this interpretation of phonemes is to regard phonemes as mental **concepts** that refer to a set of articulations, just like our mental concept of *dog* refers to the set of all dogs.

Free Variation

Recall our discussion of [pˀ], the unreleased p that we find word finally (i.e. at the end of words). It is possible to release a final p, however, and it is sometimes said that there is free variation between [p] and [pˀ] in final position. This means we have two allophones that can occur in the same position, and doesn't that mean that they should belong to different phonemes? The answer is no, because the difference between these two sounds is not contrastive. There are no minimal pairs just involving this difference.

It is an open question whether the variation is really free. It could be the release or non-release is dependent on whether a following word starts with a vowel or consonant. It could also be that the difference is dependent on the rate of speech or what is called the style of speech (or register). We know that we can speak our language in many different ways depending on all sorts of factors that are involved in terms of the situation, who we are talking to, and so on. What we call free variation may simply be variation that is dependent not on neighboring sounds inside the word, but on sounds in other words or the extra-linguistic, situational context, which brings us eventually back to the paralinguistic factors that have a bearing on the details of pronunciation.

Phonemes are Meaningless Yet Functional

It is very crucial to see that phonemes *as such* have no meaning. /p/ does not mean anything, nor does any other consonant or vowel. Phonemes just *distinguish* different meaning units (e.g., words) from each other. Thus the /p/ in *pin* distinguishes this word (i.e., a meaningful unit) from *bin, tin, sin*, and so on.

Phonemes and Morphemes

It will be clear at this point that the form side of morphemes can be said to *consist of* phonemes, i.e., the form of a morpheme is a particular sequence of phonemes of the language in question. Typically morphemes consist of several phonemes, but in the limiting case a morpheme can consist of just one phoneme, in which case you might wrongly think that we are dealing with a case where a phoneme has meaning. Consider the English morpheme {/z/} (I place morphemes between braces).

> {/dɔg/}[dɔg] dog   {/dog/} + {/z/} [dɔgz]   dogs

We have other morphemes that consist of just one phoneme. Usually they are bound morphemes, e.g., the suffix for past tense which seems to be {/d/}.

> {/ple/}   [ple]   play   {/ple/} + {/d/}   [pled]   played

So keep a clear distinction between a phoneme (the mental category that corresponds to a family of allophones) and a morpheme (a mental representation of a meaningful unit consisting of an array of phonemes, a meaning, and categorial information such as word class membership).

Two Levels of Representation

By establishing a distinction between phonemes and allophones we have constructed a phonological theory that has two levels of representation:

> phonemic level
> |
> phonetic or allophonic level

The phonemic level represents the sound structure of words as they are recorded in long-term memory, in our mental lexicon. The allophonic level represents a level that speakers process on-line when they speak. In this process, each phoneme is pronounced *as is* (in terms of the basic allophone) unless there is an allophonic rule that intervenes by selecting an allophone that differs from the basic allophone.

The Reality of the Phoneme

It is sometimes argued that only the phonetic level should be recognized. This viewpoint then denies the reality of phonemes. There is, however, independent evidence for the reality of phonemes as a type of entity that is distinct from their allophones.

Firstly, and most importantly, it seems abundantly clear that many allomorphy can only be accounted for in terms of operations that recognize the unit phoneme.

Secondly, one could point to alphabetic writing systems, which tend to have separate symbols for different phonemes and not for different allophones of phonemes. If phonemes did not exist it would be unexplained why alphabetic writing systems represent units that are not there, but fail to represent units (allophones) that are there.

Other evidence comes from speech errors. If someone says *brint pook* for *print book*, we notice that the p sound, which in print is unaspirated, ends up as [pʰ] in *pook*. This can only be understood if we make it possible for the substitution to occur at the phonemic level because at the phonetic level we only have [p] in print, which would lead to *pook* with an unaspirated p.

Finally, we can refer to so-called **word games**, i.e., games which involve the formation of secret languages by changing the order of phonemes or inserting phoneme chunks at specific location in the string.

The Phonological Combination Rules

We have now discussed the way in which we arrive at the finite set of phonemes that a language has. A representation of a word in terms of its phonemes is often called a phonological representation, while a representation in terms of allophones is called a phonetic representation. I might use these terms sometimes. However, I prefer to speak of phonemic and allophonic representation, respectively, and I consider both phonological in nature. (Phonetics, as opposed to phonology, deals with the actual production of allophones, their acoustic properties and they way in which our hearing apparatus registers speech sounds.)

We also established that we need adjustment rules that add non-contrastive properties (such as aspiration) to phonemes in the relevant environments, thus creating allophones that differ from the basic allophone, which is identical to the phoneme. I will come back to the adjustment rules in more detail. First, we now need to discuss the combination rules.

The combination rules (also called **phonotactic rules**) specify which combinations of phonemes are wellformed. In the beginning of this chapter we saw that such rules exist because speakers of languages have judgments concerning these matters. Here is another example. Speakers of English know that no word can begin with the cluster /bn/, whereas /bl/ and /br/ are fine:

bnik
blik
brik

Only the third sequence is an **actual word** (that would be written as *<brick>*). The first and the second words both do not exist. However, whereas the second sequence is a **possible English word**, the first sequence is not. This means (again) that speakers of English have a system of rules that tells them which combinations of phonemes are wellformed words.

I will now give a specific fragment of the system of combination rules for English, starting with some general remarks about the format of these rules.

Whenever a rule specifies a certain combination, it assigns a "label" to the product of that combination. These labels are the linguist's name for the grouping (or **constituent**) that is formed when two things are combined. Thus, combination rules have the following general form:

$$X \Rightarrow Y + Z$$

We read this as: *When Y and Z are combined they form a constituent of type X*, or: *constituent X consists of Y and Z.* You might be inclined to ask why we don't write the rule as follows:

$$Y + Z \Rightarrow X$$

Meaning: Y and Z together form X. We might just as well have done this. However, linguists have chosen the former rule format. The best way of reading this format is thus: *A constituent of type X consists of a Y and a Z.* More on this later.

Here's a bunch of combination rules that we need for English:

Phonotactic rules
a. Word ⇒ Syllable (& Syllable) (& Syllable)
b. Syllable ⇒ (Onset) & Rhyme
c. Onset ⇒ *Consonant (& Consonant)*
d. Rhyme ⇒ Nucleus (& Coda)
e. Nucleus ⇒ *Vowel*
f. Coda ⇒ *Consonant*

All non-italic terms used in these rules are labels for constituents. I will explain the status of the italic terms later on; they essentially refer to subclasses of the phonemes.

Rule (a) specifies a **choice** (indicated by using parentheses): A word can be one, two, or three **syllables**. In real life English words may be longer, of course, although it is not clear whether there is an upper bound. (We could try to invent a special notation that means "a word can consist of any number of syllables except zero," but I'll leave that for another occasion.)

Rule (b) says that syllables consist of two parts: an **onset**—the consonant(s)—and a **rhyme**—the vowel and following consonant(s). The parentheses indicate that the onset is **optional**; that is, syllables in English can start with a vowel (e.g., the first syllable of *a.pril*).

In rule (c) we also specify a choice: An **onset** can consist of one or two **consonants**.

Coming back to the rule format issue, we note that phonotactic rules are also sometimes called **rewrite rules** because they can be understood as instructions to rewrite what's on the left of the arrow by what's on the right. This rewriting can be represented in different ways. We start with the symbol *word*, which we appropriately call the **start symbol**.

Step 0: Word	
Step 1: Syllable	rule a
Step 2: Onset Rhyme	rule b
Step 3: Consonant Sonorant Rhyme	rule c
Step 4: Consonant Sonorant Nucleus Coda	rule d
Step 5: Consonant Sonorant Vowel Coda	rule e
Step 6: Consonant Sonorant Vowel Consonant	rule f

In those cases in which the rules allow a choice, we have made one in the preceding **derivation**. We can also represent the derivation in the form of a **tree diagram**:

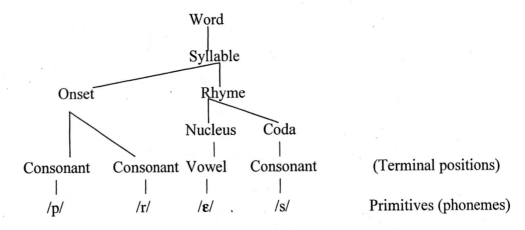

The phonemes occupy, or are associated to, the **terminal positions** of the structure. You might ask how we guarantee that they end up in the appropriate terminal positions; after all, we do not want to place the phoneme /p/ in the vowel position, or the vowel /ɛ/ in a non-vowel position. Following we will learn that phonemes are composed of **elements** (i.e., units that are even more basic than the phonemes themselves), some of which correspond to the terminal labels of the hierarchical structure. Thus, these elements will guide the placement of phonemes in syllabic positions. Thus the phoneme /p/ consists of several elements, some of which are called *consonant* (C) and *vowel* (V).

Structure Above the Syllable

We have seen that phonemic representations are more than just a linear string of phonemes. The phonemes are organized in terms of a hierarchical structure. Here's a representation of the word *albatross*:

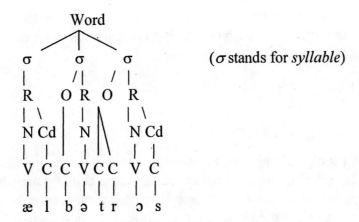

(σ stands for *syllable*)

Linguists have argued that there is perhaps intermediate structure in between the syllable and the word, structure that captures the rhythmic grouping of syllables that is especially present in longer words:

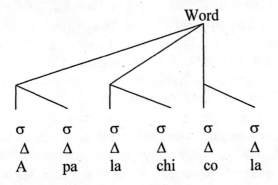

These constituents formed out of syllables are called **feet**. In this diagram the little triangles stand for the syllable structure. We sometimes use such triangles if we don't bother to spell out the internal structure of a constituent. Also, note that I give the phonemes, not as IPA symbols, but in terms of letters that spell them. Again, this is a sloppiness that we sometimes allow if we do not wish to go to the trouble of using the technical IPA symbols.

The combination of phonemes in syllables and of syllables in feet delivers what we call the **phonological representation**. This is a cognitive level of representation, which means that it is assumed that this representation exists in the mind of the speaker/hearer.

We can now say that a word is wellformed (phonologically speaking) if and only if it can be organized into a tree diagram that can be generated by the phonotactic rules. We can say that the phonotactic rules assign a tree structure to the string of phonemes to check whether the string forms a wellformed word. I hope that you realize that this is much the same as assigning a tree diagram to a string of words in order to check whether the string is a wellformed sentence, syntactically speaking (more on this in Chapter 15).

Where Do the Phonological Labels Come From?

The astute observer will have noticed that the tree diagrams used so far in this chapter have a peculiar property. In each constituent one daughter is dominated by a vertical line, while the other is dominated by a slant line:

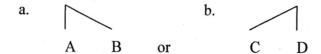

Why? What I indicate with this notation is the idea that units that form a constituent, whatever it is, enter in an asymmetrical relationship called **dependency**. What the slant line indicates is that the unit dominated by it is dependent on the other unit. The non-dependent unit is called the **head**. Thus, in (a) A is the head, while B is the dependent. In (b) C is the dependent, while D is the head.

Headedness correlates with a variety of properties and so does dependency. What these properties are precisely depends on the what the constituent consists of. For example, if we combine a vowel and a consonant to its left, the vowel is the head because it is the obligatory unit in such a constituent (which we call a syllable). By obligatory we mean that a syllable, at least in English, can consist of a vowel alone, but not of a consonant alone. A consonant needs a vowel to be part of a syllable; it is thus dependent on the presence of a vowel. A vowel can also form a constituent with a consonant to its right, in which case we call the constituent a rhyme. Again, the vowel is the head because a rhyme can consist of a vowel alone, but not of a consonant alone.

Feet also consist of a head and a dependent. In this case the head is the syllable that is stressed, while the dependent is the unstressed syllable. In *Apalachicola*, the first, third, and fifth syllables have stress, all others are unstressed. In English unstressed syllables can only contain the reduced vowel [ə]. Proof that syllables with this vowel (called the schwa) are dependents is that a word cannot consist of a single syllable that has a schwa.

We can now define labels like *rhyme, onset, coda, syllable* and *foot* in terms of the head-dependency organization of the structure that is formed over the string of phonemes. For example, a rhyme is a combination of a vowel and a consonant to its right. In such a combination the vowel, which is the head, is called the nucleus, while the consonant is the coda. All these labels, then, are merely convenient shorthand for heads and dependents at the various levels in the hierarchical structure.

Phonological Constraints

The phonotactic rules that we have discussed in the previous section stipulate the global restrictions or constraints on what constitutes a wellformed word form. These rules essentially regulate the combinatorial possibilities of consonants and vowels. In fact, instead of using the term *rule*, linguists often refer to these statements as *constraints*, currently a popular word in linguistics.

However, these rules, or constraints, are insufficiently specific to completely determine what is wellformed. For example, it is one thing to say that onsets can consist of two consonants, but that still allows any combination of consonants. No language on earth is that liberal. In all languages there are additional phonotactic constraints, which stipulate which specific combinations are allowed. Whereas the rules introduced in the previous section seem to take the form of positive constraints (they say what is allowed), the more specific statements that we need to rule out all sorts of bad combinations typically take the form of negative constraints. For example, for onsets we can make a list of combinations that are no good:

*lp, *lt, *lk, *ls, etc.

Below we will learn that we often can collapse these specific statements into more general constraints, but to do that we need to acknowledge that sets of phonemes can be referred to in terms of certain phonetic properties that they share. The point that the constraints that regulate specific combinations need to be formulated in the negative is not hard and fast, and in many cases we simply have the option of either focusing on the combinations that are allowed, adopting the practice that what is not mentioned as allowed is not allowed. For example, in many languages codas allow only a subset of all the consonants that the language in question has. In Japanese, for example, word final codas can only contain the phoneme /n/. In this case it is easier to state this fact positively than to have a constraint that mentions all other consonants than /n/. However, we can simply refer to this latter set as "¬/n/":

Positive Coda constraint: Cd   Negative Coda Constraint: *Cd
                               | |
                              /n/   ¬/n/

So, in fact, when we use a positive constraint we must always add in our mind that any other structure of that kind is excluded. It would seem that using negative constraints sometimes will drive home that point more clearly.

Next to positive and negative, we also seem to need implicational (or *if-then*) constraints. In this case we state that if a unit has a property A, it must also have the property B. Take English again. In word initial position onsets can actually consist of three consonants (as in *spring* or *strong*). But such clusters are very restricted in the sense that the first consonants is always /s/. This means that we can write an if-then statement which says:

IF a cluster consists of three consonants THEN the first one is /s/

CCC   → /s/ CC

Again, whether we use the implication format or negative or positive formats is often dependent on what looks most conspicuous. After all, an implicational statement can always be shown to be equivalent to a negative statement:

$$\neg\,(\neg\ /s/\ \&\ CC)$$

In conclusion, wellformedness of word forms is captured in terms of a set of constraints (earlier also called combinatorial rules) which state the permitted structure of syllables in terms of consonants and vowels, of feet in terms of syllables, and of words in terms of feet. In addition, there are constraints that further limit the combinatorial possibilities of specific phonemes.

The Phonological Adjustment Rules

We now turn to a more detailed discussion of the adjustment rules. We will discover that there are two types of adjustment rules. So far I have only mentioned **allophonic adjustment rules**, but there is a second class of phonological adjustment rules that I will call **phonemic adjustment rules**.

Example 1: Aspiration

Earlier, we motivated, for English, an adjustment rule that assigns aspiration to a /p/ in syllable-initial position before a stressed vowel. (The same rule also derives the allophone [tʰ] from the phoneme /t/, and [kʰ] from /k/.) The initial consonants of words like *top, tea, teach, tree, pit, pot, press, cat, cool, cross,* and so on are all aspirated. (In the words *tree, press,* and *cross,* the aspiration is simultaneous with the /r/.). The medial consonants in words like *raccoon, platoon, repel,* and so on, are also aspirated, by the same rule.

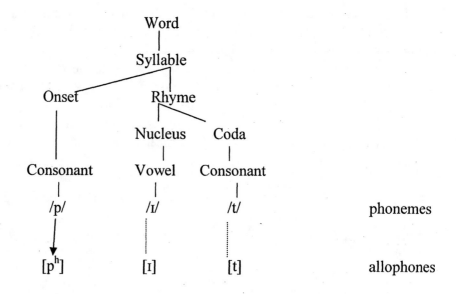

Note that the phoneme /t/, which has an aspirated allophone when occurring initially, does not trigger the aspiration adjustment rule because it is not in the correct environment for this rule to apply. The plain line here represents the identity rule (i.e., the allophone is identical to the phoneme).

In all words given so far the initial and medial phonemes will *always* be aspirated, because they will *always* be in the required syllable-initial prestress environment. However, we will now learn something new. Given that phonemes can have allophones, it may happen that a given *morpheme* ends up having two realizations due to the aspiration rule. Consider the following pair:

invite [ɪnvait]   invitee [ɪnvait^h + í]

The two phonetic shapes of the morpheme *invite* are: [ɪnvait] and [ɪnvait^h], with a plain and an aspirated allophone of the final phoneme /t/, respectively. The reason for this variation in shape is that the suffix –*ee* [í] is stressed. When we add it to the base /ɪnvait/ the final /t/ will be in a syllable-initial position before a stressed vowel and thus it must be aspirated.

We can construct a similar example for the medial consonant of the word *metal*. If we add a suffix –*ic* [ɪk], we get *metallic*, in which the stress is on the second vowel. As a result, the /t/ must be realized with aspiration:

metal   [mɛtəl]   metallic [mət^hælɪk]

We see how this kind of variation in the realization of morphemes is simply the result of an allophony rule. (The two variants of the morpheme *metal* also differ in their vowels, because there is another adjustment rule that turns unstressed vowels into the vowel allophone [ə]. Actually, the /t/ in metal does not sound as [t], but rather as a weak kind of [d]; this *weak d* is called a *flap*, for which the IPA symbols is [ɾ].)

The phenomenon that a morpheme ends up having two realizations (because it contains a phoneme that can have more than one allophone) is called **allomorphy**. As far as we have seen things now, allomorphy results from allophony that is caused by combining morphemes. I will call this kind of allomorphy **allophonic allomorphy**.

Example 2: Korean Liquids

We have seen that the same pair of sounds may count as allophones of one phoneme in one language, while it may count as two phonemes in another. Consider the sound [r] and [l]. In English these sounds represent different phonemes, /r/ and /l/, and it is easy to find the minimal pair to prove this:

read   –   lead
rip   -   lip
hour   owl

In Korean (and several other languages) these two sounds are allophones of the same phoneme, with [r] occurring between vowels and [l] elsewhere.

Example 3: Dutch Obstruents

Suppose you are describing Dutch. You would quickly learn that the sounds [t] and [d] belong to different phonemes because there are minimal pairs:

> dam =/= tam
> matras =/= madras

We must conclude that there are two phonemes /d/ and /t/:

```
/d/          /t/
 |            |
[d]          [t]
```

Then you notice a **gap**: [d] never occurs at the end of the word. You have noticed that other consonant sounds normally occur in this position in Dutch; there are many words ending in a consonant, but [d] is not one of them. In other words, the difference between [d] and [t] is not contrastive word finally.

At first sight, there are two possible explanations for this fact:

> Analysis A: the phoneme /d/ cannot occur word finally (phonemic analysis)
> Analysis B: the allophone [d] cannot occur word finally (allophonic analysis)

In both cases we are dealing with a phenomenon that phonologists call **neutralization**. In analysis A, /d/ has been eliminated as a contrastive option at the phonemic level *in certain positions*. In analysis B, however, the contrast is maintained at the phonemic level but not at the allophonic level. This, as we will see, leads to a situation that is called **phonemic overlap**, a term that will be explained shortly.

Analysis A should be exploited first. This analysis, as stated, assumes a phonotactic constraint which bars /d/ from final position and that is the end of it. We can show that this analysis does not work. Consider the following facts from Dutch. The word for *dog* is [hɔnt], but the plural (dogs) is [hɔndən]. The plural is formed by adding a suffix /-ən/ to the singular word. In many cases this is the only change we see:

[kɑt]	cat	[kɑtən]	cats
[bom]	tree	[bomən]	trees
[ze]	sea	[zeən]	seas
[wɑnt]	mitten	[wɑntən]	mittens

So why would the plural of [hɔnt] all of a sudden have a [d] at the end of the noun before the plural suffix? In other words, what accounts for the allomorphy [hɔnt] – [hɔnd]? Following the usual strategy we assume that the two allomorphs can be derived from underlying form. The question is, what is this form? We can narrow this question down to asking what is the final phoneme of the morpheme for dog?

a.

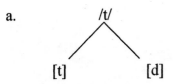

/X/ is realized as [d] before a vowel and as [t] elsewhere

b.

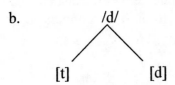

/X/ is realized as [t] word finally and as [d] elsewhere

How can we decide which analysis is the correct one?

One rule of thumb (as we have seen) is that we take the phoneme symbol to be the one of the sound that has the widest distribution, and this correlates with the *elsewhere* case. In this case, however, we can come up with a plausible elsewhere statement for both options. However, we can show that the first solution doesn't work. Look at the word for *mitten*. It has a [t] in both the singular and the plural and thus an underlying /t/. The plural form, in particular, shows you that there is no rule that assigns a [d] to the phoneme /t/ in the plural.

Since the second analysis is correct, and the final [t] in [hɔnt] derives from the phoneme /d/, we arrive at the conclusion that the sound [t] is one of the allophones of the phoneme /d/, as well as being an allophone of /t/. We can represent this as follows:

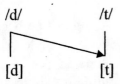

This is a new situation that we have not encountered thus far. I might have lead you believe that each phoneme has its own set of allophones. However, we now see that, in Dutch, /d/ and /t/ share an allophone, [t] (which happens to be the only allophone of /t/). In other words, the allophones of /t/ and /d/ overlap, a phenomenon that is referred to as **phonemic overlap.** (This is the traditional view of these Dutch facts. Recently, it has been argued that the [t] that comes from /d/ may not be exactly the same as the [t] that comes from /t/. If this is correct, there is no phonemic overlap in this case. Still, in other cases, we appear to have phonemic overlap, so we have to reckon with this possibility.)

Example 3: English Plurals

Consider the addition of the plural affix in English. The English plural suffix appears to have three phonetic variants:

- [s] in plurals like *cats*
- [z] in plural like *dogs*
- [ɪz] in plurals like *kisses*

When we look at the spelling of this suffix, one might think that the plural form of both *dog* (*dogs*) and *cat* (*cats*) is formed by adding a morpheme that consists of the phoneme /s/. However, when you listen closely to how both forms are pronounced, you might observe a difference:

    [dɔgz]   [kæts]

So, what is the plural suffix, really? Is it /s/ or /z/? Rather than saying that there are two suffixes that have the same meaning and a very similar form, linguists believe that the best way of looking at this situation is to assume that there is one **basic form**, from which two **allomorphs** are derived. Just like we immediately accepted that [ɪnvait] and [ɪnvaitʰ] are two allomorphs of one basic form which had to be /ɪnvait/ because we had already decided that [tʰ] is derived in terms of an adjustment rule. And we also accepted that [hɔnt] and [hɔnd] can be derived from one basic form which we argued is /hɔnd/.

For the plural suffix we now need to decide which form is basic. As a first approximation, let us say that the basic form of this suffix is /z/. We say this because when we add it to a word like <eye> (phonologically: /ai/; phonetically: [ai]) it comes out as [z]. There is nothing about the phonological shape of <eye> that forces us to choose the [z] sound because a word like *ice* (/ais/; [ais]) tells us that the sound [ai] *can* be followed by the sound [s]. Hence, if the underlying form of the suffix was /s/, why would it have to change to [z] when the noun ends in a vowel?

If we add this basic form (i.e., /z/) to *dog*, everything is fine because there is no phonotactic rule that disallows the sequence /gz/); however, if we add it to *cat*, we get an illformed sequence /tz/. Indeed, no word of English ends in (or even contains) this sequence, which means that there is a phonotactic rule ruling out this sequence. Thus we need an adjustment rule that changes /tz/ into /ts/, in other words this rule assigns a voiceless allophone to a phoneme like /z/ (that is normally voiced) if it occurs next to a voiceless consonant (like /t/). (The phonemes /p/, /t/, /k/, /f/, /s/ are **voiceless**, whereas /b/, /d/, /g/, /v/, /z/ are **voiced**).

As a consequence, the realization of the plural suffix in this case is going to be [s], due to this allophonic rule:

/z/

↓

[s]

(In this case, again, we deal with an allophonic rule that causes **phonemic overlap**. Here, [s] is an allophone the phoneme /z/, but it is also an allophone (via an identity rule) of the phoneme /s/.)

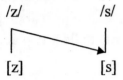

/z/   /s/

[z]   [s]

Let us now look at the variant [ɪz]. If we simply add the plural affix /z/ to, for example, the noun *kiss*, and apply the allophony rule for voicing we will get:

$$/kɪs/ + /z/ \quad \rightarrow \quad *[kɪss]$$

(The singular form *kiss* ends in one /s/, despite the double spelling. Recall that the "*" means *not wellformed*.)

We would have to pronounce the plural with a long [s] at the end. But English does not have long consonants. (Don't get confused by spelling: *happy* does not have a long consonant, nor does the word *press* or *kiss*. Why we spell two identical letters in these cases is a story that I don't want to go into here.) In any event, because English has no long consonants, [kɪss] cannot be the plural form. This means that we need an additional adjustment rule that will insert the vowel [ɪ]. It is difficult to see, however, how [ɪz] as a whole could be an allophone of /z/. Allophones are never combinations of two sounds. What we need here is an **insertion** or **epenthesis** rule:

insert [ɪ] in between a stem ending in /s/ and the plural suffix.

Since this is not a rule that regards producing allophones, we have to see it as a phonemic adjustment rule. This explains why this rule has to be applied before the allophony rule that turns /z/ into /s/ when the stem ends in a voiceless consonant, because otherwise we might derive the wrong surface form:

a.		kɪs + z	b.		kɪs + z
voice assimilation		s	insertion		ɪ
insertion		ɪ	voice assimilation		---
output		*kɪs ɪ s			kɪs ɪ z

By regarding insertion as a phonemic adjustment rule we explain why it precedes voice assimilation, which is an allophonic adjustment rule. The ordering between the rules is called intrinsic because it automatically follows from the analysis. It has been argued that sometimes a phonological analysis needs to establish the specific order two adjustment rules of the same kind. In that case, the ordering that needs to be stipulated is called **extrinsic ordering**. I do not discuss cases of extrinsic ordering here.

Before we wrap up this example we need to take care of one final detail. The plural of *wish* also gets the extra vowel. But the final phoneme of *wish* is [ʃ]. If we only apply the original rule we would get [wɪʃs], and in that case we do not have two *identical* consonants at the end. Clearly, I was simplifying the matter. The real problem with [kɪss] (two s's) and [wɪʃs] is that the English languages does not allow two consonants next to each other that are too similar.

Example 5: Velar Softening

Now consider the following pair, which also displays allomorphy:

electri[k]　electri[s] - ity

Here it would seem that the two forms, *electri[k]* and *electri[s]*, are allomorphs of the same morpheme. Let us assume, for simplicity's sake, that the form ending in [k] is the basic form. In that case we need a rule that changes *k* into *s*. Here, however, it is difficult to regard [s] as an allophone of the phoneme /k/. These two entities are just too different. Indeed, English does not appear to have an allophony rule to that effect. This is evidenced by forms such as *bookish*, *working*, where the /k/ does not change into [s] before a similar kind of vowel as the one of the suffix *–ity*. In other words, there is nothing wrong with having a /k/ before a vowel /ɪ/.

Although it seems that we need an adjustment rule here, it certainly is not going to be an allophonic rule. Thus, it must be a phonemic adjustment rule:

/k/ → /s/ when it occurs before the morpheme *–ity*

In other words, the *k-to-s* rule **substitutes** one phoneme with another phoneme in the environment of specific morphemes (like *–ity*). Actually, the *k-to-s* rule applies in more cases than just before *-ity*, as is clear from words like *criticism*. The suffix *-ism* apparently also triggers this rule.

Below, we will see that this rule perhaps should have a different status from the rule of [ɪ] insertion. The latter seems to truly avoid a violation of a phonotactic constraint (i.e., a constraint against two adjacent near-identical consonants). The *k-to-s* rule lacks this kind of phonotactic motivation. The sequence …/kɪ/… is not ill-formed as such, shown by the fact that many words have this sequence (such as the word *king*). The mandated change from k to s seems to be motivated by nothing more than the presence of certain affixes. In other words, the motivation for the rule is not phonotactic or phonological, but rather morphological.

Let me, once more, try to avoid one misunderstanding: The application of adjustment rules does *not* create a new level of representation; that is, adjustment rules are operations on and internal to the phonological representations, either at the phonemic or at the allophonic level.

Allophones and Allomorphs

First we have seen that phonemes can have different manifestations that are called **allophones**. Then we talked about the fact that morphemes can also be looked at from the viewpoint of how they are realized. The different realizations of a morpheme are called **allomorphs**.

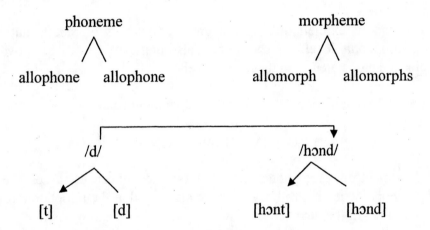

The allophony rule that derives [t] from /d/ causes allomorphy for morphemes that contain /d/ in the relevant environment. But not all cases of allophony cause allomorphy, and not all case of allomorphy are due to allophony.

- For an allophony rule to cause allomorphy it must be the case that the environment for one of the allophones can be created by putting morphemes together. We saw that the rule deriving [tʰ] from /t/ presents such a case because a suffix like –*ee* creates a context for the rule. If English didn't have suffixes that changed the stress in the base, our allophony rules would never have a chance to cause allomorphy. It might be pretty hard to find a case of allophony that does not create allomorphy (more precisely allophonic allomorphy). A good case would be a rule that only affects word initial consonants in a language that has no prefixes so that the rule affects initial consonants in all their occurrences. Still, if such a language would change and adopt prefixes, allomorphy would be the result because then initial consonants would cease to be initial when a prefix was added. I conclude that all allophonic adjustments potentially create (allophonic) allomorphy.

- On the other hand, allomorphy does not imply allophony either. Sometimes when morphemes are combined rules apply that delete or insert phonemes. That causes variation in the shape of morphemes that is not due to allophony rules. For example:

electri[k] => electri[s] - ity

Rules that cause such allomorphy have been called phoneme substitution rules.

Another category of rules that cause allomorply but not allophony (at least not in the usual sense) is rules that insert phonemes. We have seen such a rule in the case of the English plural suffix. Likewise, rules that delete phonemes do not cause allophony while causing allomorphy. Consider the Dutch pair:

piano   pian – ist

The vowel /o/ is deleted before the suffix *–ist*, creating the allomorphy [piano] – [pian]. There is no allophony here.

All this means that allomorphy can be due to allophonic adjustment rules or to phonemic adjustment rules.

Earlier we made it explicit that we recognize two levels of representation, the phonemic and the allophonic level. We should now also make explicit that the two kinds of adjustment rules are associated with these two levels:

Phonemic level   (Phonemic adjustment rules)
|
Phonetic level   (Allophonic adjustment rules)

The phonemic adjustment rules are phonotactically motivated, except for cases like the k-to-s rule, which is phonotactically arbitrary. Can we also say that the allophonic rules are motivated by something? In the next section I will answer that question positively.

The Interaction Between Constraints and Adjustment Rules

Let us first try to get more mileage out of the idea of phonotactic motivation. We have discussed the fact that the phonemic level is characterized in terms of a set of phonotactic constraints. How can we flesh out the idea that there seems to be a close relationship between these phonotactic constraints and phonemic adjustment rules?

Let us first make explicit that phonemic adjustment rules come into action only when morphemes are combined. Take the rule of [ɪ] insertion. This rule needs to operate when we combine a noun with a plural suffix:

a. Insert /ɪ/ in between two consonants that are too similar
b.   kɪs ɪ z

Now apart from forms that contain the plural suffix, it is simply a fact of English that no word contain an immediate sequence of two (near-)identical consonants. In other words, this is a phonotactic fact of English that needs to be captured in a phonotactic constraint:

*two consonants that are too similar

Note the similarity between this constraint and the insertion rule. Essentially, the insertion rule repeats the information that we already have in the constraint. This suggests the following account. Given that we have a set of phonotactic constraints, we can say that the addition of the plural suffix /z/ to a noun kiss incurs a constraint violation. The form *kɪsz is illformed and should be rejected. Adjustment rules can now be seen as mechanisms that save the day; they adjust the illformed form so that it becomes wellformed. Let us say then that adjustment rules are somehow linked to constraints:

> Constraint: *two consonants that are too similar
> Available adjustment: insert [ɪ]

It is important to see that the repair doesn't come for free. For starters, there could be no repair and the grammar might simply mark certain plural forms as illformed, in which case the speaker needs to find another way to say that there is more than one kiss. But other repairs could be used. For example, there could be a repair that chances the stem-final consonant into a /t/ so that eventually the plural of kiss would be [kɪts], or there could be a rule that deletes the stem-final consonant, and so on. In fact, if we develop this approach we will see that languages sometimes differ in precisely this way: they share some phonotactic constraints, but differ in the associated adjustment.

Let us now turn to allophonic rules and ask whether we can treat these rules as responses to a violation.

Let us return to the rules of final devoicing in Dutch. According to this, rules voiced consonants like /d/ have a voiceless allophone in word final position. We argued that this was the correct analysis because, as we noticed, Dutch has no words whatsoever with these voiced consonants in final position. But now note that this fact goes beyond the cases in which we find an alternation, such as:

> [hɔnt] dog   [hɔndən]   dog (plural)

We can derive the singular form in terms of a rule:

> /d/   →   [t]   word finally

But can we regard this rule as an account of the general fact that there is no Dutch word that ends in [d]? Let us split up this rule into a constraint that blocks word final [d] and an adjustment rule that repairs a violation:

> Constraint: *[d] word finally
> Available repair: [d] → [t]

The constraint (which is an allophonic constraint and not a phonotactic constraint) that bars the allophone [d] in final position will prevent [hɔnd] as the singular form, but it does not tell us how we can pronounce the singular form. In other words, we need to know what kind of adjustments can be made. There are several logical possibilities:

[hɔndə]	add a schwa at the end
[hɔn]	delete the /d/
[hɔnn]	assign an allophone [n] to the /d/
[hɔnt]	assign an allophone [t] to the /d/ (or choose [t] instead [d])

We need to specify in the analysis that the fourth option is the one that is chosen, so we need to state the rule of devoicing.

The constraint states a true fact about the phonetic representation while the repair is an instruction on what to do if a form will otherwise end up with a violation of this constraint. Let us conclude that this is how we will treat allophony.

We end up with the following picture:

phonemic level (phonotactic constraints, phonemic adjustment rules)

allophonic level (allophonic constraints, allophonic adjustment rules)

The mapping between the phonemic level and the allophonic level is performed by an identity rule, which is overruled or corrected just in case it will create a violation of an allophonic constraint. Whether the identity rule is overruled or corrected leads to a subtle difference in how we write the allophonic readjustment rule, namely rule (a) or (b) respectively.

a.   /d/ → [t]
b.   [d] → [t]

If we wish to formulate adjustment rules as computations internal to a level, we should prefer the second option.

Back to Rules?

Since we need to link the right repair to the right constraint and we might regard this relationship as an IF – THEN relationship:

(IF)	Constraint:	¬ [d] at the end of the word
(THEN)	Repair:	Eliminate the property "voice"

Direct linking of constraint and repair seems to imply a return to the original rule format in which we conflate constraint and repair in one statement. Still, it seems useful to separate the constraint and repair part formally because it is possible that a given constraint is linked to more than one repair if different repairs apply depending on additional environmental factors. For example, imagine a constraint against any combination of two consonants:

(IF)	Constraint:	¬ CC
(THEN)	(IF)	initial
	(THEN)	delete the first C
	(IF)	final
	(THEN)	delete the final C
	(IF)	medial
	(THEN)	insert [ɪ]

Another reason for maintaining the separation between constraint and repair is that in this way we can more clearly state that two of more languages share the same constraint while differing in the associated repair.

Now, I mentioned that constraints can be positive, negative, or implicational (if-then). This raises the question as to whether a constraint and repair pair can be regarded, as a whole, as an implicational constraint? This would, in a way, make all constraints implicational. An implicational constraint is, after all, a constraint with a built-in repair. Does this mean that we are back to *rules*? In a way we are, with the proviso that all rules must state generalizations that are true of the level that they apply to.

Two Kinds of Computation

We have two levels (phonemic, phonetic) each characterized by its own constraints and each provided with its own set of adjustment rules. Earlier I mentioned that representations are stored in memory, while phonetic representations are produced on-line. This implies that the allophonic adjustment rules are also on-line computations.

It is interesting to note that these allophonic computations are both difficult to learn and to unlearn. That sounds paradoxical. What I mean is this. It seems that the allophonic computations are easy to learn as part of the task of learning your first language. Chomsky would argue that this kind of early learning is made easy because it relies on innate capabilities. However, these innate capabilities seem to diminish as we get older, and we notice this when we try to learn a foreign language later in life. Firstly, it is difficult to learn the fine details (read: allophonic variation) of a new language and, secondly, we tend to transfer the fine details of our first language into the new language, which means that we apply the allophonic computations of our first language in trying to articulate the newly acquired language. We speak the new language with a foreign accent, although *foreign* here really means that we, unwillingly, try to "nativize" the foreign language, introducing pronunciations that, indeed, are foreign to that language.

What about phonemic adjustment rules? Are these also computations that happen on-line? We don't know exactly. Phonologists usually assume that they do, at least in cases where they are triggered by a morpheme combination that is newly formed by the speaker. After all, the forming of a new morpheme combination is itself an on-line computation, and this means that the phonotactically motivated adjustment rule that needs to apply to such a complex word must too be computed on-line.

A Selection Alternative to Phonemic Computation

Instead of having phonemic adjustment rules as actual computations, an alternative exists which simply stores allomorphs in memory. For example, for the English plural suffix we could say that two variants are stored:

/z/ ~ /ɪz/

We would still have a constraint that blocks /kɪs+z/ of course, because this constraint expresses a true fact about the phonemic level. We could now adopt a convention that the allomorphs are *ordered* and that we only use the second form if the first one fails to produce a wellformed output. This is the so-called *item-and-arrangement* (I would prefer *item-and-selection*) approach to allomorphy as opposed to the *item-and-process* view that we have been advocating thus far.

It may even be possible to conflate the two allomorphs into one representation if we use the parenthesized notation to indicate material that can be omitted:

/(ɪ)z/

Not ordering is now necessary, and the convention would be to choose the shortest form first, i.e., /z/.

This approach runs into a problem when we consider cases that involve a deletion rule under the item-and-process approach. Consider the case *piano – pianist*. How do we represent the noun? If we adopt:

/pian(o)/

We cannot see that we try the short form first because the form /pian/ would not violate any phonotactic constraint. So in this case we would never choose the form with the /o/.

Hence, if one wants to stay away from computations at the phonemic level, it seems that allomorphs have to be stored as an ordered list. If more than two allomorphs exist, even the ordered list approach might not work and each allomorph (except for one, the elsewhere case) would have to be provided with an *insertion frame* that indicates in which context it must appear.

Free Rides?

I mentioned that phonemic adjustment rules only work in contexts that are created by combining morphemes. We call such contexts **morphologically derived contexts**. It could be argued that we can get more mileage out of these rules if we also apply them in certain non-derived environments. For example, we could argue that the phonemic representation of a word like analysis is /analɪss/, willingly allowing a phonotactic violation in this form. This, one could argue, buys us that the form as it is stored in the lexicon is simpler. However, the violation would be noted if we assume that all forms that are taken from the lexicon for use are checked against all phonotactic constraints. Subsequently, the insertion rule would insert [ɪ]. Now the rule applies in a non-derived environment. In this case, it would seem that no harm is done. We have gained some simplicity in the lexicon, although we pay the price that one more computation is necessary. But since the rule is already there anyway, we could say that the computation is free (although it really isn't).

We can extend the idea of free rides to all phonemic adjustment rules that are truly phonotactically motivated. However, in cases where we are dealing with deletion rules or rules that substitute one phoneme for another there is really no gain. For example, suppose a language has a constraint against V+V (two vowels immediately next to each other). This constraint is truly phonotactically motivated if there are no non-derived words that have such a sequence. Then, if a vowel initial suffix would be added to a vowel final stem, we would expect an adjustment rule. Let us say that this rule deletes the first vowel:

kata + om => katom

We could now say that morpheme-internally every vowel in every morpheme is preceded by some other vowel. Thus, the word form *moon* (which is pronounced as [kam]) would be stored un in the lexicon as /koam/. Since this form violates a constraint it would trigger the adjustment and become /kam/. But what is the point of doing this? Clearly there is no gain whatsoever and there is only the loss that the vowel deletion rule has to apply in this form.

By all means, it seems extremely plausible that forms are stored in the lexicon in a way that minimizes the amount of computation that is necessary. This means that in case there is no allomorphy, the lexical form is identical to the form that will be sent to the phonetic level. This also makes sense from an acquisition point of view. Why would a child learning our imaginary language ever come up with the idea that the lexical form for moon is /koam/ when it only ever hears [kam].

Lexical Exceptions and Morphological Contexts

There is another reason for being skeptical of the free-ride mechanism based on phonemic adjustment rules that are not phonotactically motivated. Consider the k-to-s rule. If we allow this rule to apply to all words in the lexicon, it will turn *king* into *sing*. We can't have that. Likewise, the Dutch rule that deletes /o/ before the suffix *–ist* (presumably because it start with a vowel), cannot be allowed to apply to words like *coalitie,* which in the first two syllables has a vowel /o/ immediately followed by another vowel. These rules cannot be phonotactically motivated precisely because there are words that violate them in non-derived contexts, or sometimes even in other types of derived contexts. The latter applies in English where the k-to-s rule is violated in cases like *book-ish*.

All languages have rules like this. How do we deal with them? We could simply stipulate (as a general property of phonemic adjustment rules) that these rules apply only in derived environments. This would allow non-derived words to actually be in violation with these rules, and this would be OK since these rules are not linked to a phonotactic constraint. But that raises the question of how those rules are written such that they will apply in the correct derived environments:

$$/k/ \quad \rightarrow \quad /s/ \quad \text{before} \;/ɪ/$$

The idea would now be that rules that have a context built in can only apply if this context is morphologically derived.

This does not solve to non-application before *–ish*, so perhaps the rule needs to be more specific:

$$/k/ \quad \rightarrow \quad /s/ \quad \text{before -ity, -icsm}$$

Now the rule will not apply in *book-ish*. But if that is the correct formulation it immediately follows that the rule will not apply in any non-derived environment (like *king*).

In fact, if we allow direct reference to specific lists of suffixes we could even split these rules up into constraints and repairs:

    a. Constraint: * …/k/ + ity
    b. Adjustment: $/k/ \rightarrow /s/$

It is an open question whether there are rules that only apply in derived environments while not being triggered by specific morphological contexts. I suspect the answer is no.

The Phonological Periodic Table (Elements)

Before concluding this chapter, I return to the primitives, that is, the phonemes. I have presented phonemes as the basic building blocks of phonological structure. It turns out, however, that phonemes themselves are composed of even smaller entities that we will call **(phonological) elements**. Another frequently used name for these smaller entities is **features**. The argumentation in favor of subphonemic elements comes from what I will call **group behavior**:

- A first kind of group behavior can be demonstrated when we examine the sets of **phonemes** (consonants and vowels) that languages have. These sets appear to have very regular structures. As can be seen below in the (partial) consonant table of *English*, consonants indeed occur in regular patterns, and this suggests that they result from the systematic combinations of a small set of properties. Phonemes that share properties form subgroups within the group of phonemes.

- A second form of group behavior is apparent in the **combination rules**. For example, a certain class of phonemes, sonorants, can occur in the second position of two-consonantal onsets. Thus, these consonants, as opposed to all the other consonants, form a group.

- The third case of group behavior comes from the **adjustment rules**. For example, I mentioned the fact that the phonemes /p/, /t/, and /k/ all have aspirated variants in exactly the same environment (syllable-initially, before a stressed vowel). In other words, these three phonemes behave as a group vis-à-vis the aspiration rule.

We have seen that the phonological module has three ingredients: a set of primitives, a set of combination rules, and a set of adjustment rules. Apparently, all three ingredients provide hints for the idea that phonemes consist of smaller units!

The study of the languages of the world indicates that the same groupings show up in language after language; this phenomenon suggests that these groupings are not random.

The only reasonable explanation for **group behavior** is that phonemes that form a group share **one or more properties**. I will call these properties **elements** and name them in terms of the articulatory phonetic property that they correspond with. For /p/, /t/, and /k/, one shared property is |closure|, because /p/, /t/, and /k/ all have a complete closure in the mouth when these phonemes are realized. (Note: Element names will be put between |vertical lines|.) Phonemes like /b/, /d/, and /g/ also have the property |closure|, but they differ from /p/, /t/, and /k/ in also having the property |voice|, which refers to the fact that the vocal folds are vibrating when these phonemes are realized. The difference between /p/, /t/, and /k/ (all having the property |closure|) lies in the fact that they have their closure in different places in the mouth. This means that we need a couple of place properties, like |labial|, |dental|, and |velar|. These same place properties differentiate /b/, /d/, and /g/. Elements, like phonemes, are cognitive units within the mental grammar.

We can now arrange phonemes in a table (much like we arrange the elements in physics and chemistry in the periodic table):

	|closure|		|friction|		|gliding|	|nasal|
		|voice|		|voice|		
|labial|	/p/	/b/	/f/	/v/	/w/	/m/
|dental|	/t/	/d/	/s/	/z/	/y/	/n/
|velar|	/k/	/g/	/x/	/ɣ/	—	/ŋ/

This is a simplified table. It has most, but not all, of the English consonants in it. In a complete table we also have places for all the vowels.

The discovery of the phonological periodic table (which is still subject to changes, based on new research) has been very important in the study of phonology because it helps us to understand *why* phoneme systems have systematic patterns and why phonemes show group behavior with respect to combination rules and adjustment rules.

It perhaps does not come as a surprise that the elements seem to correspond exactly to the phonetic properties that have the potential of being contrastive in the languages of the world.

Natural Classes

Now that we have recognized that phonemes and allophones (jointly referred to as **phonological segments**) can be decomposed in terms of elements, we can introduce the concept of **natural class**. Any maximal group of segments that share one or more elements is called a natural class. For example, the class of segments that have the element |voice| is a natural class. I say that the group has to be maximal because we have to include all segments that possess this element.

With elements we can describe constraints and repairs in simpler, more generalizing terms. Consider final devoicing:

> A-Constraint: ¬(| voice | & |obstruent|) word finally
> A-repair: delete |voice|

Or aspiration in English:

> A-Constraint: ¬ (|obstruent| & ¬| aspiration | & ¬|voice|) word initially before
> |vowel|
>
> A-repair: add |aspiration|

Another advantage of elements, as you can see, is that the repair rules can refer to the elements rather than having to state replacement operations of whole segments by other segments.

Recall that the aspiration allophony in English holds not only for p's but also for k's and t's. In all three cases the element of aspiration must be present when these sounds occur word initially followed by a vowel. If we did not have elements we would have to state three separate constraints and three repairs:

> A-constraint: *[t] word initially before vowel
> A-repair: replace [t] by [tʰ]
>
> A-constraint: *[k] word initially before vowel
> A-repair: replace [t] by [kʰ]
>
> A-constraint: *[p] word initially before vowel
> A-repair: replace [t] by [pʰ]

Instead, as we did above, one constraint and one repair can be stated if we can use elements to refer to segments.

Another advantage of elements is that the repair rules can now be said to make sense. Consider the change of [z] to [s] that we need for the plural form of cats and compare the following two statements of the relevant constraint and repair:

(a) with elements

A-constraint: * ¬ |voice| & |voice|
A-repair: delete |voice|

(b) without elements

A-constraint: * [t] & [z]
A-repair: replace [z] by [s]

The statements that make no use of elements are, in a way, random. They do not provide any insight into what is wrong with the illformed combination or why the replacement would make things better. The statements with elements fare much better. The constraint says that a sequence of two segments with opposite voicing properties are illformed and the repair makes things right by ensuring that the two segments no longer differ in their voice property. Making this explicit (in this case and all other cases) allows us to see constraints typically militate against disharmony, i.e., unlikeness with respect to the properties that adjacent segments have.

Segmental Constraints

Note that by seeing phonemes as being composed of elements we have added a further instance of the general structure of grammatical components. In other words, we have seen that the general architecture (primitives and combinations) may repeat itself within a component:

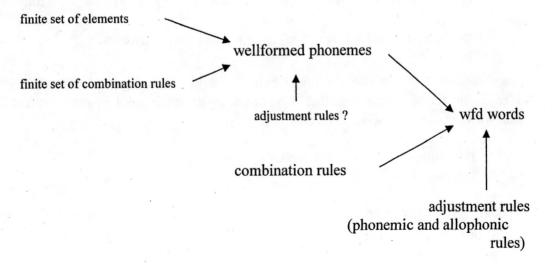

All languages have a fixed set of phonemes. So far one might have thought that these have to be listed. Now that we have elements we can characterize the set of phonemes in terms of constraints on combinations of elements.

Let us assume, for the sake of the argument, that the set of elements is universal. We can then say that in order to characterize the set of segments at either the phonemic or the allophonic level a set of constraints will block certain combinations of elements. For example, at the P-level English does not have a velar glide (see the above chart). We can express this as follows:

A-constraint: ¬ (|gliding| & |velar|)

Note that in this case we do not specify a repair. The reason is that we often do not know what the repair would be. We only need to know which repair corresponds to a segmental constraint if there is another level or representation that has a different segmental inventory.

Imagine the case that the P-inventory differs from the A-inventory. Suppose, for example, that we have reason to say that two phonemes A and B always converge on the same set of allophones:

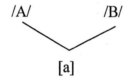

This can be called **complete phonemic overlap** (also called **absolute neutralization**). At this point you might not be able to conceive of cases that would necessitate this kind of but phonologists have frequently proposed analyses in which a given pair of phonemes would end up being pronounced identically in all their occurrences. I give an example. In Dutch, the suffix for the past tense is either [tə] or [də] and the choice depends on the final consonant of the stem much as the plural allomorphy in English:

scho[p] [tə] kick   ze [t][tə] put   la [χ] [tə]   smile

so[b] [də] sob re[d][də] save plaa[ɣ] [də]   tease

There is reason to say that the underlying phonemic form is /də/. The analysis is thus identical to the analysis of the [z] ~ [s] allomorphy of the English plural suffix (except that we state the facts at the P-level:

P-constraint: * ¬ |voice| & |voice|
P-repair: delete |voice|

This analysis is based on the idea that Dutch has /p/, /b/, /t/, /d/, /χ/, and /ɣ/ as separate phonemes. However, the contrast between /χ/ and /ɣ/ does not survive at the A-level where (at least in my pronunciation) we only find [χ]. This means that at the A level we need the following constraint/repair:

> A-constraint: * |velar| & |voice|
> A-repair: delete |voice|

This turns the potential allophone [ɣ] into [χ] in all cases.

Note: [ɣ] only occurs if followed by a voice obstruent, and therefore in forms like plaa[ɣ] [də], but that is another story. Or is it?

Structure Preservation

The rule that turns /d/ into /t/ in the suffix *can* exist at the P-level because /t/ (the result of the rule) is a wellformed phoneme. This illustrates a general point, which is that rules that deliver segments that are wellformed both at the P-level and the A-level *could* end up at either level, depending on the overall analysis. Compare this to the rule that produces aspirated obstruent. This could not be a P-rule because the difference between aspirated and non-aspirated stops is not contrastive in English, which we have taken to mean that there is no phoneme /pʰ/. The aspiration rule cannot be a P-rule because it does not preserve the structure that is wellformed at the P-level.

Redundancy and Minimal Specification

One way of looking at the difference between the P and the A-level is that at the latter level we specify properties (elements) that are **predictable**. If we say that at the A-level segments that have the elements |obstruent| and |stop| must also have the element |aspirated| *in a certain* **sequential context** (namely before a vowel) we *de facto* say that the latter property is predictable from the former properties in that context. Another term for *predictable* is **redundant**. A property Q is redundant if it is predictable.

We will now learn that certain types of segmental constraints can be looked upon as constraints that are associated with an adjustment rule.

Suppose we are dealing with a language that has the following seven vowels at the P-level, here presented in terms of elements that are relevant for vowels:

	|front|	|front| |round|	|back|	|back| |round|
|high|	/i/	/ü/	*/ɨ/	/u/
	/e/	/ö/	*/ɤ/	/o/
|low|	*/æ/	*/œ/	/a/	*/ɒ/

Allowed:

/i/	/ü/	/u/	/e/	/ö/	/o/	/a/
high	high	high				
						low
front	front		front	front		
		back			back	back
	round	round		round	round	

Disallowed:

*/ɨ/	*/ɤ/	*/æ/	*/Œ/	*/ɒ/
high				
		low	low	low
		front	front	
back	back			back
			round	round

As a first analysis, let us propose two constraints that rule out the disallowed vowels:

Constraint: ¬ (|back| & (¬|low| ∨ ¬|round|))   Excludes: /ɨ/ and /ɤ/

Constraint: ¬ (|low| & (|front| ∨ |round|))   Excludes: /æ/, /Œ/ and /ɒ/

The constraints are not associated with adjustment rules because we have no evidence for choosing one in case of violations. Adjustment rules at the P-level come into action if the morphology creates a representation at the P-level that is illformed. But the morphology would typically not introduce illformed phonemes. Rather it creates illformed combinations of phonemes like /t/ + /z/ (in the case of the plural suffix in English).

Note: Illformed segments might be produced when the morphological operation is *non-concatenative*, i.e., when a morpheme is a single element like |nasal| that combines with segments and then could produce illformed. Also, we must consider the case in which a P-rule could produce illformed segments as in vowel harmony cases. Both cases typically lead to "blocking" and not to repair.

I will now argue that this analysis cannot be the right one. The reason for this is that we mentioned that the P-level seems to be governed by a general constraint, which says that it does not contain any *predictable* information. This constraint gives rise to the notion of phoneme in the first place. It forbids non-contrastive properties. This is the defining property of the P-level. It would seem that this general property of the P-level must have consequences for the way in which we specify phonemes in terms of elements because whenever there are constraints on combinations it means that certain things are predictable.

Let us see, then, how we can arrive at a minimal representation for the vowels in question. We have more than one option, depending on whether we do without either the element |back| or |low| or use both:

/i/	/ü/	/u/	/e/	/ö/	/o/	/a/	(11 tokens, 3 types)
high	high	high					
						low	
front	front		front	front			
	round			round	round		

Or:

/i/	/ü/	/u/	/e/	/ö/	/o/	/a/	(11 tokens, 3 types)
high	high	high					
	front		front	front			
		back				back	
	round			round	round		

/i/	/ü/	/u/	/e/	/ö/	/o/	/a/	(11 tokens, 4 types)
high	high	high					
						low	
	front		front	front			
		back				back	
	round			round			

Perhaps the correct representation depends on which vowels group as natural classes at the P-level, and this might be different in different languages.

In any event, certain occurrences of certain elements that *are* present at the A-level can (no, must) be omitted at the P-level. This follows from the requirement that the P-level will not contain predictable information.

Now, in the case of allophony we decided that the predictable elements were blocked at the P-level by a constraint. Recall the analysis of the [p] ~ [pʰ] case:

P-level: */pʰ/

A-level: *[p] word initial before vowel
A-repair: add |aspirated|

Paralleling this analysis we should therefore say that at the P-level certain combinations are excluded:

P-Constraint: ¬ (|back| & (|low| ∨ |round|))   Excludes: /u/ and /o/

P-Constraint: ¬ (|low| & |back| ∨ |round|)   Excludes: /a/, /œ/ and /ɒ/

Paradoxically, instead of saying that this language has /u/ and /o/, we seem to say that it has the forbidden /ɨ/ and /ɤ/. And instead of saying it lacks /æ/, we seem to say that it lacks /a/. This, however, is where the IPA symbols play tricks on us because, after all, these symbols were designed as shorthand for fully specified phones, and not for entities at the phonemic level which are not sound but rather something more abstract (sound intentions). We do not wish to say that [u] is underlyingly an /ɨ/; we merely wish to say that underlyingly it does not have |round| as a contrastive property. In certain phonological theories incomplete representations. which do not, as such, correspond to a specific phoneme that correlates with an actual phone, are called *archiphonemes*, sometimes notated with capital letter version of IPA symbols.

In some sense we have a virtual alternation between [u] and [ɨ] with [u] occurring in all environments, leaving no room at all for [ɨ]. In the allophonic case of [p] and [pʰ] we adopted /p/ as the phoneme and motivated this by saying that the allophone [p] was the more general, elsewhere case, [pʰ] being the more specific allophone. Paradoxically, in the case of [u] and [ɨ] one would want to say that [u] rather than [ɨ] is the general case since [ɨ] is totally lacking. Still, we wish to choose a phonemic representation that lacks the element |round| which, then, is one that would give us [ɨ] at the A-level. This, we must conclude, suggests that the criterion for choosing a specific representation of a phoneme should not be based on how wide the distribution of its potential allophones is, but rather on the degree of complexity of the potential choices at the P-level. The idea is that the *least complex* representation is chosen at the P-level.

Turning now to the A-level we face a different kind of requirement, which is that *all* properties must be present at this level. Why? We haven't really argued why, but the bottom line is that the A-level feeds into the phonetic implementation and for that reason it must be complete. (Full specification is thus an interface requirement for the A-level; in the same vein we could argue that the minimal specification at the P-level is also an interface requirement, namely one that comes from lexical storage which, we must assume, demands maximal simplicity.)

So how do we achieve full specification at the A-level? Firstly, we need to state the relevant constraints:

P-Constraint: ¬ (|back| & (¬|low| ∨ ¬|round|))   Excludes: /ɨ/ and /ɤ/
A-repair: add |round| Turns [ɨ] and [ɤ] into [u] and [o]

P-Constraint: ¬ (|low| & (|front| ∨ |round|)   Excludes: /æ/, /œ/ and /ɒ/
A-repair: ?

/i/	/ü/	/u/	/e/	/ö/	/o/	/a/	(11 tokens, 4 types)
high	high	high					
						low	
	front		front	front			
		back			back		
	round			round			

/i/	/ü/	/u/	/e/	/ö/	/o/	/a/
high	high	high				
						low
	front		front	front		
		back			back	
	round	round			round	round

We are still missing a front or back element for the high and low vowel. Thus, we need a constraint that demands the presence of a *color* element (this could follow from the demand for full specification):

P-Constraint: ¬ (¬|front| ∨ ¬|back| ∨ ¬|round|)
A-repair: add |front| if |high|
               add |back| if |low|

We now arrive at fully specified segments at the P-level:

/i/	/ü/	/u/	/e/	/ö/	/o/	/a/
high	high	high				
						low
front	front		front	front		
		back			back	back
	round	round			round	round

The constraint that blocks /œ/ and /ɒ/ (at both levels) does not appear to have an associated repair rule because this constraint did not allow us to omit an element at the P-level; it merely rules out certain combinations of elements.

Ambiguities in the Analysis?

In the end, with a proper choice of elements we may not encounter ambiguities as we have encountered in the preceding section. Consider an element system that uses the so-called AIU system. Compared to the system used so far we arrive at this kind of system by eliminating |back| and |high|:

/i/	/ü/	/u/	/e/	/ö/	/o/	/a/
front	front		front	front		
	round	round		round	round	
			low	low	low	low

Or:

/i/	/ü/	/u/	/e/	/ö/	/o/	/a/
I	I		I	I		
	U	U		U	U	
			A	A		A

There are no redundancies here.

The only way to achieve greater economy would be to say that one of the phonemes is completely unspecified. Let us say that this phoneme is /i/. We would then adopt a constraint and repair pair at the A-level:

A-constraint: ¬ { }
A-repair: insert I

It has been argued that the complete non-specification of one of the vowels may be useful.

A compromise between the AIU system and the first system is:

/i/	/ü/	/u/	/e/	/ö/	/o/	/a/	(11 tokens, 4 types)
high	high	high					
						low	
	front		front	front			
	round	round		round	round		

This requires a repair rule that adds aperture |low| in case there is no aperture element:

A-Constraint: ¬ (¬|high| ∨ ¬|low|)   All vowels must have aperture
A-repair: add |low|

As well as a rule that adds a color element for high vowels:

A-Constraint: ¬ (|high| & ¬(|front| ∨ |round|) high vowels must have color
A-repair: add |front|

Thus, we arrive at a fully specified system at the A-level:

/i/	/ü/	/u/	/e/	/ö/	/o/	/a/
high	high	high				
			low	low	low	low
front	front		front	front		
	round	round		round	round	

Loan Word Adaptations (Substitutions)

We have independent evidence for the A-repairs coming from the way speakers pronounce words that they have borrowed from another language. Suppose that speakers of a language with the seven vowel system that we have discussed so far try to pronounce a word that has any of the vowels in them that are blocked at the P-level. We predict that such sounds would be unacceptable at the A-level and thus be adapted as follows:

> A-repair: add |round| Turns [ɨ] and [ɤ] into [u] and [o]

We can now even check which repair would be associated with constraints that could not be used to make the P-level more economical:

> P-Constraint: ¬ (|low| & (|front| ∨ |round|))   Excludes: /æ/, /œ/ and /ɒ/
> A-repair: delete |round| & |front| Turn [æ], [ɒ] and [œ] into [a]

If instead [æ] would be turned into [e], we would have evidence for another adjustment rule:

> A-repair: delete |low|

A broad study of loan word adaptation, then, will provide us with insight into possible repairs, especially at the A-level. It remains to be seen whether repairs that are needed for adaptation will always be the same as repairs that can be motivated on language-internal grounds.

Can Repairs be Predicted?

Now that we have elements and a more subtle way of stating constraints and repairs, it would be interesting to explore to what extent adjustments can be predicted from the constraints that trigger them. If we maintain that one and the same constraint can have different repairs in different contexts or in different languages, we cannot expect to find that repairs can be predicted from the constraint. However, it might still be the case that each constraint can be paired with only certain repairs; more than one, but not unlimited. For example, it could be argued that the units that are mentioned in the repair must also be mentioned in the constraint. Consider final devoicing in Dutch. The constraint refers to two elements and to the notion of word final.

P-Constraint: *|voice| & |obstruent| word finally.

Repairs

a.	[hɔndə]	add a schwa at the end	change word final environment
b.	[hɔn]	delete the /d/	
c.	[hɔnn]	assign an allophone [n] to the /d/	delelete |obstruent|
d.	[hɔnt]	assign an allophone [t] to the /d/	delete |voice|

All repairs, except perhaps (b), refer to units in the constraint. Hence we need additional criteria. Let us say that the repair must be *minimal*. Option (a) and (b) involve a whole segment (by inserting a schwa or deleting the final consonant), while (c) and (d) only affect one element. The latter two are thus more minimal. Now we need to decide between (c) and (d). For this we need to appeal to a hierarchy of some kind for the elements. Such hierarchies have been proposed, and it is generally agreed that |obstruent| is a higher, more basic element than |voice|. This, then, provides a basis for saying that the deletion of |voice| is the most minimal operation.

It remains to be seen whether this approach can be developed into a general framework that will allow us to rank constraints according to their likelihood to occur in a grammar.

More than Two Levels?

We have argued in favor of a two-level phonology, with a P-level and a A-level. It is understood that something more is needed beyond the A-level. The A-level interfaces with a module or procedure that I have called **phonetic implementation**. Implementation will be held responsible for changes of the A-level, perhaps those that will be reflected in a narrow transcription, and that would involve co-articulation, i.e., the results of overlapping actions of the articulators.

In some phonological theories that accept the P- and A-level, a level prior to the P-level is proposed, namely the morphemic level (or M-level). At this level constraints would specify the wellformedness of **morphemes** as these are listed in the lexicon. This would be different from P-level constraints, which would hold **words** (simplex words and a subset of the complex words). I have argued in chapter 7 that there is no need for recognizing a morphemic level. It is, in a way, irrelevant whether the morphemes are phonologically wellformed according to some set of criteria. What matters is that expressions that are entered into the syntax, namely words, are phonologically wellformed. If one were to postulate mutant morphemes that would cause the words they enter into to be illformed as words, and no relevant repairs were available, such morphemes would not make it into the next generation of language learners.

This, again, brings us to the issue of loan words. Loan words that eventually make it into the receiving language will end up in the lexicon in a form that will require no repair at the P-level.

Less than Two Levels?

We have already discussed whether we can do phonology by just recognizing one level of representation. If we only recognize one level and we wish this level to be phonemic we will have to assume that all allophonic variation is taken care of in the implementation step from the discrete phonological level to the actual speech event. Alternatively, we could include some allophonic variation in the phonological level, but in that case we abandon the notion of the phoneme (which some phonologists are happy to do). In addition, in that case, we end up having a set if constraints stated for this one level that will be very heterogeneous. On the one hand we will have constraints that are entirely true of all forms at this level, while on the other hand we will have constraints that have exceptions and/or are limited to specific morphological contexts.

Are rules ordered?

A question that has been widely discussed (that is, as we will see, not unrelated to the previous one) is whether the repair rules that apply at any given level need to apply in a stipulated order. Clearly different rules can be related to each other in such a manner that the result is going to be different depending on the order in which the rules are applied. One logical possibility would be that in all such cases there is always one order that is universally chosen. If this were true we could say that ordering is **intrinsic**, meaning that it follows from general principles.

However, it has been argued that rules whose ordering matters are not always ordered in a manner that is predictable from general principles. Rather, the claim is that the ordering in such cases needs to be stipulated. This is called **extrinsic rule ordering**. Here I will not discuss this issue any further, but I will say that the case for extrinsic rule ordering becomes weaker when two levels are recognized.

Cyclicity

Another mechanism that is important when it come to checking wellformedness and doing repair concerns the precise domain that is checked. At the P-level we check words, both simplex and complex. But complex words can be multiple complex, i.e., they can consist of a stem and multiple affixes, or of two or more stems (in the case of compounds). The question now arises whether, in the case of complex words, we check the string of phonemes only once, namely after all morphemes have been put together, or **cyclically**, which means that we check the string at each step in the morphological derivation, beginning with the stem, before any morphology has been applied, and then after each morphological step. This issue is not easy to discuss in a few words, and I will therefore not motivate an answer either way.

At the P-level we will assume that the domains corresponding to each morphological step are no longer visible as such. At this level, then, cyclic application of the checking procedure is not an option.

How are Levels Related?

Let us define a level as an analysis of a linguistic utterance. When we say that there is more than one level we are claiming that one and the same utterance can be analyzed in more than one way. The different ways are not supposed to be contradictory or competing. Rather, they are independent of each other, each telling a different side of the story.

Here I have worked with the idea that there are two phonological levels, the P-level and the A-level. The P-level presents an analysis in terms of units called phonemes, while the A-level presents an analysis in terms of allophones. At each level we define a syntax, i.e., a system that accounts for the manner in which the basic units must be combined into wellformed combinations (this syntax, then, consists of a numeration of the primitives and of the constraints), and then we also have a set of repair rules which come into action if, for whatever reason, a constraint violation is detected.

The question now is whether levels are related in the sense that wellformed representations at one level are passed on to the next level as is, or whether, in this passing on process, certain changes are made. To distinguish such changes from the **intralevel repair rules** we could refer to the rules that perform changes when going from one level to the next as **interlevel correspondence rules**. I have been assuming that the interlevel rules are **identity rules** in that they do not perform any mutations. For example, the phoneme /p/ is passed on as [p] at the A-level. (The difference in brackets around the symbols is merely a reminder of the level we are at.) Then, given that [p] is illformed at the P-level in certain environments, a repair rule will changes [p] into [pʰ] in some of these case and into [p̚] in others, and so on. I will assume that those changes do not change the fact that each of the allophones corresponds to a /p/ at the P-level.

It is crucial to see that repair operations apply within a level and thus do not create new levels.

Levels and Domains

We have to be careful in using the term level. I have just defined it as a particular analysis of a linguistic expression or utterance. We often also find the term level used in the context of hierarchical structure. In fact, I have spoken of the *word level* and the *sentence level*, which clearly are hierarchically related. Henceforth I will avoid such ambiguity in terminology and refer to hierarchical units as **domains**.

Word and Sentence Phonology

In the preceding sections we have discussed the phonological module that accounts for the phonological phenomena at the word level. Obviously, there must also be a system that deals with phonological phenomena at the sentence level. When words are strung together to form phrases and sentences we arrive at a phonological representation that is more than just the linear arrangement of the phonemes that make up words.

Is There a P-level and an A-level in the Sentence Phonology?

When words are strung together into a sentence, do we assume that they are strung together as A-level units? No. The distinction between P- and A-level refers to the distinction between looking at an utterance in two different ways. The utterance can be a single word or a group of words. But there is a noteworthy difference between words and larger units. There is a rich system of P-constraints and P-repairs for words, and much fewer (if any) P-constraints for **domains** larger than words.

   The phonological form of words may sometimes change, depending on other words that they combine with. To account for that we need a system of phonological adjustment rules that operate within domains larger than words:

I want to go	⇒	I wanna go
The idea is …	⇒	The idea **r** is
..get him	⇒	gedim
He is not...	⇒	He isn't....
I can be	⇒	I cam be

There are many changes in the phonological form of words that you are usually not aware of. Some are optional (or rather dependent of your style of speech or register), whereas others simply always happen (i.e., in all registers of your language). These changes, optional or not, are not random, so we need a system of adjustment rules to account for them. The question is whether these adjustments take place at the A-level or the P-level.

   It has been claimed that many of the adjustments that apply at the phrasal or sentence level are conditioned by a set of hierarchically organized domains. The smallest domain is called the **phonological word**. Ph-words are grouped into larger domains called **phonological phrases**, which in turn group into even larger units called **intonational phrases**. Finally, intonational phrases group together into a unit called the **utterance.**

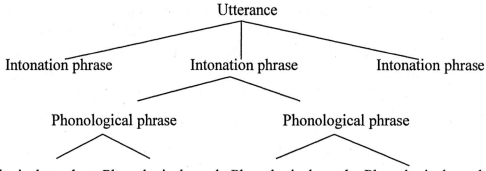

This kind of grouping represents the organization of a sentence *from a phonological point of view*. We will see later that the phonological structure of a sentence is often not the same as the syntactic structure. Hence both are necessary.

The question is whether this grouping reflects the P-level or the A-level. Again, it would take a long exposition to settle this issue. My view is that the organization just presented forms part of the A-level. Whatever domains are relevant at the P-level are, I take it, the domains that are created by the sentential categorial system (the syntax). Of the examples presented earlier, only the change from *want to* to *wanna* would be a P-level change; all the others strike me as A-level changes.

Conclusions

In going from speech to phonology we see two steps, each involving *abstraction*:

     speech $\Rightarrow$ phonetic transcription $\Rightarrow$ phonological representation

       (transcription)   (phonological analysis)

When we make a phonetic **transcription** (in IPA symbols) we go from speech to the **phonetic transcription,** and in doing so we abstract away from minute phonetic detail that is probably never contrastive (including details that are dependent on paralinguistic factors). We then regard the phonetic transcriptions as the representation. which consists of allophones, the A-level. Following that we perform the **phonological analysis,** in which we definitely establish which phonetic properties are contrastive in the language under study (by using the minimal word pair test). This leads to a **phonemic representation** at the P-level, which consists of phonemes.

We assume that linguistic expressions (words and sentences) are mentally represented at two levels, the P-level and the A-level. Both levels are characterized by a set of primitives, constraints, and repairs, which may differ from language to language. I have assumed that the primitives at both levels are drawn from the same universal set of primitives (called **elements**). Both levels are discrete (sometimes called *categorial* or *digital*), and as such they differ from the actual speech signal which is non-discrete, gradient, and continuous (sometimes called *analogue*). The actual speech event is derived from the A-level by a system that is called phonetic implementation.

It is very crucial to see that phonemes and allophones *as such* have no meaning. The phoneme /p/ or allophone [p] does not mean anything, nor does any other consonant or vowel. Phonemes and allophones are one dimension or aspect of morphemes, words, and sentences, and these *are* meaningful units.

Chapter 11

Categorial Structures
(Word Level)

Introduction

We now turn to a different dimension of linguistic expressions, the morphosyntactic dimension. I have divided treatment of this dimension over two chapters, one dealing with categorial structure at the word level (**morphology**) and the other dealing with categorial structure at the sentence level (**syntax**).

Morphological Wellformedness

People have intuitions about the morphological structure of complex words. Consider the following "words":

* reize	re + ize	(cf. re-read, victim-ize)
* sleeping listen	sleep + listen	(cf. sleeping room)
* unchair	un + chair	(cf. un-fair)

Even though *re-, -ize, sleep, work, un-,* and *chair* are all **morphemes** in the English language, the particular combinations given here are not wellformed words. We *can* combine morphemes to form complex words (as we've seen before), but we are not allowed to get away with combining morphemes in any odd way. The "words" are not bad because they contain phonemes or allophones that do not belong to the English language, nor do they violate any phonological wellformedness constraints rules. It is also not obvious that the primary cause for their illformedness has anything to do with semantics.

The "verb" *(to) reize* could mean to do something (anything) again, given that *re-* means "again" and *–ize* simply forms a verb (as in *victim-ize*). There is no reason why *sleeping listen* could not mean "to sleep while you listen" (which is apparently what many people can do). An *unchair* could be something that is anything but a chair.

In this chapter we investigate the system that accounts for morphological wellformedness. We will learn that the illformedness of the preceding words results from the fact that complex words must obey rules (constraints) for combining categories—notated in terms of labels like N(oun), V(erb), "prefix," "suffix," and the like—separate from and in addition to rules that specify their phonological form and meaning.

The Morphological Primitives

Our point of departure is that the morphological-categorial system has the following familiar general design:

set of primitives (morpheme labels)

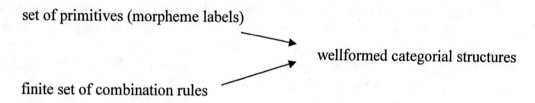

wellformed categorial structures

finite set of combination rules

(In this module, I will not discuss the question as to whether we need adjustment rules in morphology, nor will we explore the possibility that the set of primitives can be further decomposed into a small set of categorial features or elements.)

The primitives of the categorial system are labels like **noun, verb, adjective,** and so on. It is by no means the case that all linguists agree on a fixed set of categories. The most important **categories** for words (also called **word classes**) are:

Noun (*house*)   Preposition (*in, under*)   Pronoun (*he, his, they*)
Verb (*sleep*)   Article/determiner (*the, a*)   Interjection (*gosh, alas*)
Adjective (*warm*)   Conjunction (*and, or*)
Adverb (*slowly*)   Complementizer (*that*)

There are perhaps more categories or **subcategories** (i.e., disinctions *within* the categories just mentioned), like **proper nouns** (*John, Mary*), **transitive verbs** (*give, put*), **possessive pronouns** (*his, her*), and so on.

The categories fall into two classes, depending on the following difference. In a language like English there are, as we will see, morphological rules to form new nouns, new verbs, new adjectives, and to some extent new adverbs. But there are no rules to form new articles, conjunctions, pronouns, and so on. On this basis we call the former group **open categories** (because we can extend the number of words in these classes) and the latter **closed categories**.

Morphemes (as well as words) belong to one of these categories. In addition, as we have already seen, morphemes occur in two basic varieties: **free** and **bound**. A word like *chair* belongs to the free category noun, whereas an ending such as *-er* belongs to the bound category noun. We say that *-er* has this category because when added to a verb it forms a noun; the suffix *-er* is a "noun-maker." It is bound because it cannot occur by itself. The distinction *free–bound* only occurs in the open categories of words. This follows from the fact that there are no means to make new words in the closed categories, hence no bound morphemes for doing that.

Recall that bound morphemes like *-er* are called **affixes**, while the unit that affixes are attached to is referred to as the **base**. For the moment we will assume that the base is always a complete word. I will distinguish bound and free morphemes in terms of a different **superscript** on the category label:

$$\textit{-er } N^{-1} \qquad\qquad \textit{chair } N^{0}$$

The *0* stands for *free*, *-1* for *bound*. Understand the choice of these particular integers as follows. A unit belonging to a zero level category is complete, it is a word, and as such ready for use in the formation of sentences. A minus 1 unit is not complete and cannot be used freely in a sentence.

One might feel that it is not so clear which meanings we can attribute to affixes (like *–s, –ly, -ship, -er, re-, -able*). But with a little bit of practice one can in fact see that these word pieces do have a meaning of their own. These meanings, however, are incomplete in that they have a *variable* in them. This variable will be filled by the meaning of the base with which the affixes will combine:

N-s	More than one N (e.g., *cats*)
Adj-ly	In a A-like manner (e.g., *slowly*)
N-ship	state or condition of being N (e.g., *friendship*)
V-er	person who Vs (e.g., *dreamer*)
Re-V	to V again (e.g., *reanalyze*)
V-able	Can be Ved (e.g., *affordable*)

Thus, even though words are the mininal units with a complete and independent meaning, affixes can still be said to have their own meaning, albeit a meaning with a hole in it. So there is no problem in granting affixes their own status in the lexicon, unless we require for some reason that the lexicon must contain only complete words. But then we wouldn't know where to put the affixes. It makes more sense to regard the lexicon as the place where we store all meaningful units (see Chapter 15).

We need to know two further things about affixes:

- An affix like *re-* *must* be added to verbs: *reread* is fine, but *rechair* or *regood* is not. Thus we need to know the category of the base that the affix attaches to. This implies that each type of affix for making verbs, nouns, and so on falls into a number of types, depending on what kind of base it requires. An affix that makes verbs from nouns (e.g., *ize, victim-ize*) is called a **denomimal** affix. Likewise we have **deadjectival** affixes (that take adjectives as their base) and **deverbal** affixes (that take verbs as their base).

- Affixes must be specified with respect to their position vis-à-vis the base. For example, the affix *-er* comes *after* the base (a verb) not before it. I have already indicated this by a little dash that indicates the position of the base. You will recall from Chapter 2 that *-er* is called a suffix (comes after the base), whereas *re-* (in *reread*) is a prefix.

A convenient notation for indicating the type of base that is required *and* the position of this base is:

$[V^0 \text{-}]$ This means: This morpheme attaches to a verb as a suffix

We will call this a **categorial frame** (also sometimes called an **insertion frame**) of an affix. All affixes must have such a frame listed in the lexicon, together with their word class label. We sometimes see that a word class label is added to the outside of the frame (as a subscript) to indicate the word class label of the word with that particular affix. Thus, if the suffix is question is a noun-maker (N^{-1}), the category N^0 is added to the frame:

$[V^0\text{-}]_{N}{}^{0}$ This means: this morpheme forms a noun by attaching to a verb base as a suffix (e.g., *–er, dreamer*)

Later we will see that there is, in fact, a general principle that states that, if an affix is categorially specified as N^{-1}, it automatically already follows that the complex words will be of the category N^0 (and vice versa). Hence, with that principle in mind the addition of the subscript to the frame is superfluous unless we leave out the N^{-1} label. The point is that either one will imply the other.

A categorial frame and class label together can be regarded as a different notation for a little tree diagram:

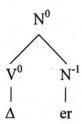

This tree leaves an open slot (indicated by the little triangle) for the position of the base, which must be a verb. So listing *-er* in the lexicon as a partial tree structure would also do the job (although, strictly speaking, mentioning *both* N^{-1} and N^0 is still a bit redundant given that an N^{-1} suffix will always produce an N^0 word, and an N^0 word can only be produced by an N^{-1} affix).

Here is another example of the categorial properties of an affix:

$[\text{- } V^0]_{V0}$ This means: This morpheme forms a verb by attaching to a verb base as a prefix.

This frame is a property of, for example, the morpheme *re-* (as in *reread*), as well as of any other prefix that makes verbs from verbs.

Roots: A Special Category of Bound Morphemes

So far I said that only affixes are bound morphemes, and that bases to which affixes attach are free forms. However, there is a special class of bases that **cannot** occur alone. We call them **roots**. An example in English is *dent* in *dentist* and *dental*. I assume that roots are not capable of occurring by themselves because they do not belong to a word class category. Indeed, by itself *dent* cannot be identified as a noun, verb, or adjective. I will simply assign roots the label *X*:

Note that the anonymous root label indexes as minus one to indicate that roots are not free. In contrast with roots I will henceforth refer to bases for affixation that can occur freely as **stems**.

Roots are peculiar morphological elements whose status is not always clear, at least in the English lexicon. Many words appear to be formed out of two roots:

> phono-gram, tele-phone

If roots have no category it is actually a mystery how these words end up having one. I will not try to solve that mystery here.

A Classification of Morphemes (Take One)

In the following diagram we summarize the categorial primitives at the word level:

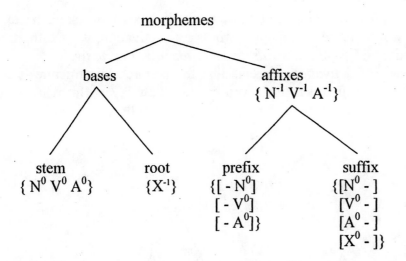

(I left out [- X⁰] among the list of possible bases for prefixes. In English, I believe, roots can be turned into words by suffixes only. If this is true, there is no prefix that makes a root like *dent* into a freestanding word.)

The Morphological Combination Rules: Prefixes and Suffixes

Let us start with an example of a complex word, *activation*, which has several suffixes:

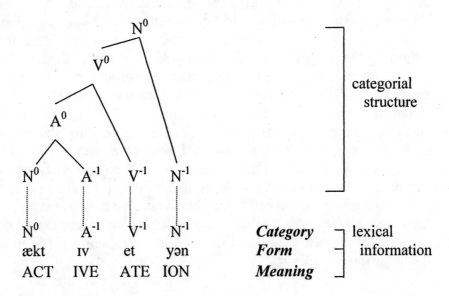

We could even think of adding a suffix *–al* to it (turning it into a possible adjective, *activational*).

In this diagram, we can clearly see how a morpheme has three aspects, three layers of information: a category label, a phoneme sequence, and a meaning (here simply represented as ACT, IVE, etc.). This should be a familiar idea as it was discussed in Part I of this book. It should also not come as a surprise that adding affixes creates a **hierarchical structure**. In other words, complex words are not linear strings of morphemes. Rather morphemes are grouped into **intermediate structures**. Each addition of an affix creates a word. Hence, in complex words like activation, we see the fractal structure that we mention in Chapter 2: *words occur inside words recursively*.

Now. in the case of *activation* it seems that the hierarchical structure is fairly straightforward. Each time you add a suffix you create a new layer. But what about a word like *unfriendly*. How do you know which of the two following structures is the correct one?

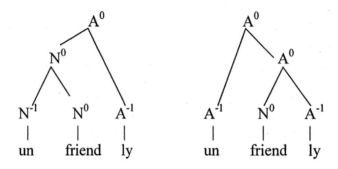

Here's what you can do. Assuming that we add affixes one at a time, the structure on the left contains an intermediate word *unfriend*, supposedly a noun, whereas the structure on the right has the adjective *friendly* as the intermediate step. Do I need to say more? It seems rather obvious that because *unfriend* is not a *possible* word we should prefer the right-hand structure. But does this mean that all the parts of a multiple complex word must be *existing* words? The answer is *no*. As argued before we must make a distinction between existing words and possible words. A possible word is a word that is in accordance with the wellformedness requirements of a language. *Snog* is a possible word, whereas *nsog* is not, even though neither exists. In this case the wellformedness is defined by the phonological wellformedness constraint of the language; we discussed this point in the preceding chapter. *Unfriend* is like *nsog*; it doesn't exist because it could not exist; it is an illformed word. It is not illformed phonologically, nor is it necessarily illformed semantically. I can kind of imagine what an *unfriend* would be, though, an enemy of some sort or a bad friend at least. The illformedness of *unfriend* is, then, categorial (morphological). In English, it seems we *cannot* attach un- to nouns (to form a new noun). We typically attach it to adjectives (to make new adjectives), although we also have a few verbs like *undo, untie,* and *unerase* (to make new verbs).

But even if we know that affixes select bases in accordance with their categorial frame (see above), there are still cases in which we cannot decide on a unique structure. In that case we need to take a closer look at the meaning of the complex word. Consider the following example:

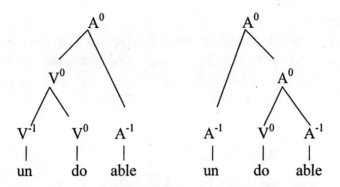

Because *un-* can go with verbs and with adjectives we might assume that there are two *uns*, one that goes with adjectives and makes adjectives, and one that goes with verbs and makes verbs. Now, the meaning of the two words is different, of course:

can be undone   cannot be done

In other words, the morpheme string *undoable* is **ambiguous**. It really can have two different structures that correspond to different meanings. Ambiguity is a general phenomenon in languages. Often what looks like one linguistic expression can have more than one meaning. We see this with simple words like *too, two,* and *to* (which, despite the spelling differences have one phonological form), but, as we now learn, it can also happen with complex expressions (expressions that consist of more than one meaningful unit). In those cases there is one phonological form that corresponds to different categorial structures.

We've just seen that some affixes can take more than one category (roughly with the same meaning) as in *untrue* and *undo*. Do we say, in such cases, that there is one prefix with two frames or two separate affixes? Given the identity in form and meaning for both *uns*, I suggest that it feels more natural to say that there is one prefix with two possible bases.

Let me give you some examples of morphological-categorial combination rules in English.

Categorial Combination Rules: *Suffixation*

$N^0 \Rightarrow N^0 N^{-1}$ *friend - ship, child - hood, host - ess, hand - ful*
$N^0 \Rightarrow A^0 N^{-1}$ *tall – ness, free - dom, loyal - ist, real - ism*
$N^0 \Rightarrow V^0 N^{-1}$ *sing – er, employ - ee, grow - th, inform - ant*

$V^0 \Rightarrow V^0 V^{-1}$ -
$V^0 \Rightarrow N^0 V^{-1}$ *victim – ize, beauti - fy*
$V^0 \Rightarrow A^0 V^{-1}$ *black – en*

$A^0 \Rightarrow A^0 A^{-1}$ *green – ish*
$A^0 \Rightarrow N^0 A^{-1}$ *boy – ish, wood - en, nation - al, pain - ful*
$A^0 \Rightarrow V^0 A^{-1}$ *read – able, help - ful, harm - less, act - ive*

We notice an interesting completeness in this system. It would seem that almost all logical possibilities of relationships among nouns, verbs, and adjectives are used. We can express this in what I call the **morphological (suffixation) triangle**:

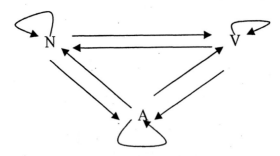

We also note that most, if not all, rules create structures that can be filled by more than one affix. The only case that is missing involves a suffix to make verbs from verbs (perhaps *to chatter* from *to chat* is an example?). English seems to prefer prefixes that can do that: *undo, reread*.

Let us take a closer look at the prefix system. When it comes to prefixes we find many missing cases in English.

Categorial Combination Rules: *Prefixation*

$N^0 \Rightarrow N^{-1} N^0$ *anti - war, ex - president, super - structure*
$N^0 \Rightarrow N^{-1} V^0$ -
$N^0 \Rightarrow N^{-1} A^0$ -

$V^0 \Rightarrow V^{-1} V^0$ *un - do, re - read, mis - align*
$V^0 \Rightarrow V^{-1} N^0$ **en - slave, be - witch**
$V^0 \Rightarrow V^{-1} A^0$ **be - little**

$A^0 \Rightarrow A^{-1} A^0$ *un - fair, dis - loyal*
$A^0 \Rightarrow A^{-1} N^0$ -
$A^0 \Rightarrow A^{-1} V^0$ -

The cases in bold italics are rare. If we ignore them for the moment we face the unexpected fact that prefixes always have the same category as their base. Compared to the suffixation triangle, we only find the following options (hardly a triangle):

There is no apparent reason for why the prefix system is so limited. Thus, we must look for a more principled explanation for the gaps in the class of prefixes. To do this we need to introduce a technical notion, namely the notion of *head* (of a structure).

The Notion "Head of the Word"

Linguists refer to the **category-determining** morpheme of a complex word (i.e., the affix) as the **head of the word**. The head, then, is in some sense the most important unit in a complex word, at least from the categorial perspective (whether it is also central semantically or phonologically for that matter is another question). Later we will see that the notion *head* plays quite an important role in sentence level categorial structure as well.

One approach to the just-mentioned problem is to say that there is a principle that dictates that the head of a complex word must always be on the right:

The Right-Hand Head Principle (RHP)
In a word-level categorial combination, the right-hand unit determines the category of the combination; that is, the right-hand unit is the head

This principle accounts for the fact that prefixes cannot determine the category of a complex word because, by definition, they occur on the left of their base. (Prefixes like *en-* and *be-* would have to be marked as exceptions to this principle.)

But it now becomes questionable whether prefixes have a category of their own. We might just as well say then that prefixes (except for two of them, *en-* and *be-*) do not have a category label. Hence we could mark them as X^{-1}. This proposal requires a slight revision of our classification of morphemes:

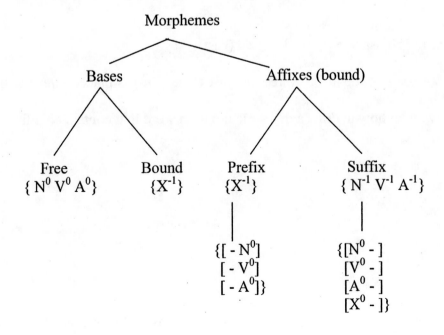

In this connection, it is interesting to notice one further fact about prefixes. Many of them can be attached to more than one type of category.

	N^0	V^0	A^0
dis -	-	disarm	dissimilar
un-	-	untie	untrue
non-	nonsmoker	-	nonexistent
over-	-	overregulate	overanxious

I will leave undecided for the moment whether this tendency is strong enough to warrant trying to find a principled basis for it. There are also suffixes that can go with more than one type of base (*-ish*; as in *green-ish* and *clown-ish*)

Affixes that are Neither Prefixes Nor Suffixes

The discussion so far is largely based on *English* and only on that part of the system for forming new words that uses affixes. I will now discuss two special cases of affixation. The first is special because of the location of the affix, whereas the second case is special because the affix appears to be **phonologically empty**.

Infixes

So far we have assumed that affixes go after the base (suffixes) or before it (prefixes). It will surprise you when I tell you that they can also go **inside** the base. In some languages, such as *Tagalog*, one can insert an affix *after the first consonant of the base*:

bili	binili	buy	bought
basa	binasa	read	read (past)

In this example we see that the affix expressing past tense (*-in-*) is placed *after* the first consonant of the base.

You may wonder how to draw a tree structure for a word that contain an infix:

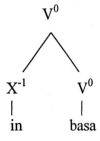

If we want to draw a tree we are almost forced to say that **infixes** (as they are called) are really prefixes (or suffixes, depending perhaps on the word edge that they are closest to), and that there is some phonological reason (involving perhaps a third type of phonological **adjustment rules**) for why the first consonant of the base is swapped to the front of the word. It could be, for example, that in the language at issue words cannot start with a vowel, making *inbili illformed. I will not explore that possibility here, but it seems certain that the normal categorial tree structure of complex words with infixes is at odds with their phonological structure. Perhaps, since the three dimensions of expressions are fairly independent (see Part I), such mismatches are to be expected.

Vertical Morphology

When we form the past tense of verbs, we often do this by adding –*ed*:

walk	walked [t]
miss	missed [t]
mow	mowed [d]
rent	rented [ɪd]

(Note that, in fact, the phonological form varies in a way that reminds us of the allomorphy we have seen for the plural suffix.) What interests us here is that there is a substantial class of verbs that form their past tense in a different way:

sing   sang

If we take the present tense as the base for the past tense (as we do in the –*ed* cases), how do we get the vowel change?

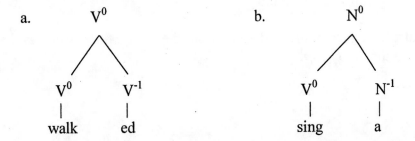

We must (again) assume a phonological repair operation that replaces /ɪ/ with /ɑ/. Alternatively, we say that morphological concatenation does not have to happen in the horizontal dimension, but can also apply in the vertical dimension. Let us say that the base for *sang* is not *sing*, and that both the present and the past form are derived by combining a *verb template* that has an unfilled vowel slot in it:

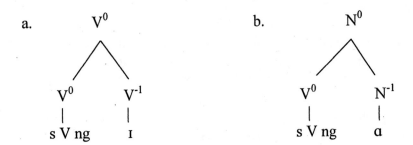

In each case the two morphemes are not combined horizontally (one after the other), but vertically (one on top of the other). Stacked morphemes are then compressed into each other as follows:

$$\begin{array}{c} \text{I} \\ \text{s V ng} \end{array} = \text{sing}$$

Even though in English this kind of morphology is limited to a closed class of irregular verbs (often called *strong* verbs, as opposed to the regular *weak* verbs), there are plenty of other languages (notably most Semitic languages) that use this kind of vertical (sometimes called non-concatenative) morphology on a regular basis.

Affixes Without Phonological Content

Consider the following English word pairs:

	Verb	**Noun**
a.	bottle	bottle
b.	jump	jump

Let us assume that the verb *to bottle* is derived from the noun *bottle*, whereas the noun *jump* is derived from the verb *jump*:

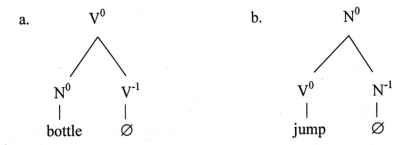

In this case the affix has no phonological content at all. Because the empty affixes appear to change category I have assumed that they *are* suffixes so that we are in agreement with the Right-hand Head Rule, even though this runs against the definition of a morpheme as a category-form-meaning package! Here the form is absent.

This problem (if indeed it is a problem) might lead one to say that the derivations in question should be dealt with by a different type of morphological rule:

a. $N^0 \Rightarrow V^0$
b. $V^0 \Rightarrow N^0$
and so on

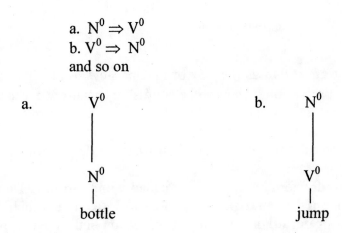

a. V^0 / N^0 / bottle

b. N^0 / V^0 / jump

These rules (sometimes called **conversion** rules) do not look like regular instructions to build a tree diagram since they are in violation of the idea that complex words have heads that determine their category label. It is perhaps better to stick with the idea that affixes can have zero phonological content. This could just be another type of mismatch between the dimensions of expressions.

Now consider the following noun–verb pairs:

Verb	Noun	Verb	Noun
pervért	pérvert	sing	song
protést	prótest	choose	choice

In these cases the addition of phonologically empty affixes triggers phonological adjustment rules that change the stress pattern of the base, or the vowel.

Finally, I will briefly mention a type of affixation that involves affixes that are *almost* phonologically empty. Consider the following example from *Tagalog*:

Tagalog:	lakad	**la**-lakad	walk / will walk
	takbug	**ta**-takbug	run / will run

Here we are dealing with a prefix that is incomplete in the sense that it is pure syllable structure with no phonemic content. The Tagalog prefix is specified as being a consonant-vowel sequence; the phonemic content has to come from the base. Obviously, such prefixes lead to illformed words unless there is an adjustment rule that supplies phonemic content to the syllabic positions of the prefix. A special name for this kind of affixation is **reduplication**.

Again, we can represent this as a normal case of prefixation from the categorial-morphological perspective. What is special here is that the prefixation structure undergoes a phonological operation of copying material from the base. In conclusion, the swapping rule for infixation, the stress-changing rule, and the copying rule for reduplication are all phonological adjustment rules.

Compounding

So far we have talked about **affixation** as *the* way of making new words. This way of forming new words is called **derivation**. (This can be confusing because we also use the term *derivation* in the more general sense of any algorithm that produces a tree structure. In addition, phonologists use the term for the process of applying adjustment rules. I apologize for these terminological ambiguities, although I have little control over these matters.)

There is a second way for forming new words called **compounding**. Derivation and compounding are called **word formation** (as opposed to **inflection**, which doesn't form **words**, but **word forms** or **paradigms;** we discuss inflection in the next chapter). In the case of compounding we combine two zero-level categories. We can make compound nouns, verbs, and adjectives:

Categorial combination rules: *Compounding*

$N^0 \Rightarrow N^0 N^0$	arm - chair
$N^0 \Rightarrow A^0 N^0$	green - house
$N^0 \Rightarrow V^0 N^0$	jump suit
$V^0 \Rightarrow V^0 V^0$	break dance
$V^0 \Rightarrow N^0 V^0$	steam roll
$V^0 \Rightarrow A^0 V^0$	white wash
$A^0 \Rightarrow A^0 A^0$	red hot
$A^0 \Rightarrow N^0 A^0$	nation wide
$A^0 \Rightarrow V^0 A^0$	-

It appears that compounds can also involve prepositions as their first member: *overcoat, undermine, in-depth.* I am not trying to give a complete overview here of all the types of compounding that are found in English.

Given that one case $(A^0 \Rightarrow V^0 A^0)$ is missing, we can say that the system of compounding forms an almost perfect triangle:

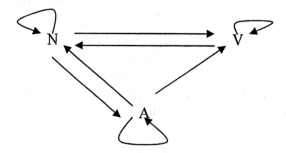

Because both members of a compound are zero-level categories, a legitimate question at this point is, "Which member is the head?" A quick look at the preceding examples suggests that the right-hand member always determines the category of the word that is formed. This suggests that the Right-hand Head Principle (as stated earlier) is correct.

When looking at compounds we see, in fact, that this principle determines more than just the category of the complex word. It also determines the semantics. Semantically speaking, an AB compound is always *a kind of B*; for example, an *armchair* is a kind of *chair*, not a kind of *arm*. But this semantic exponent of headedness can also be found in suffixation: V-er (*dancer*) is a kind of person, not a kind of activity.

There is a type of compounding that appears to violate the semantic implication of the head Principle. A *loudmouth* is not a kind of *mouth*, but somebody *with a loud mouth*. The solution to this problem is to assume that there is a conversion (i.e., a zero affix) that operates on nouns like mouth, changing their semantics from MOUTH into SOMEONE WITH MOUTH. It is this converted noun that is the head of the compound *loudmouth*.

Are there Heads in Phonology Too?

Let us suppose that with reference to the constituent syllable we say that the rhyme is the head (and that within the rhyme the vowel is the head). We might say this because rhymes seem to have greater impact on the nature of the syllable than the onset. For example, when we make pairs of rhyming words we ignore onsets. Also, at least in English, a rhyme can form a syllable by itself, but no onset ever can. In this sense, rhyme (and vowels, too) are free, whereas onset (and consonants in general) are bound.

We now arrive at a puzzling pair of equations:

Phonology: rhymes (being heads of syllables) can occur without onsets, i.e., they are free
Morphology: affixes (being heads of complex words) cannot occur without a base, i.e., they are bound

Why are phonological heads free while morphological heads are bound? This paradox may be apparent. After all, in compounds the morphological head is a free form. The distinction free-bound is independent from the distinction head–nonhead (often called dependent). The crucial property of heads is that they place their *mark* on the resulting structure.

Recursion and the Creativity of the Language System

Some of the morphological rules have an interesting property to which I wish to draw to your attention. This property may look like nothing much, but, in fact, it has extremely far-reaching consequences. Look again at the following compound rule:

$$N^0 \Rightarrow N^0 N^0$$

It allows us to produce the following structure:

$$N^0$$

$$\underset{N^0 \quad\quad N^0}{\diagup\!\!\diagdown}$$

This structure is suitable for *armchair*, *oil well*, and so on. But now note the following. Each of the terminal nodes, being of the category N^0, could itself be rewritten as $N^0\ N^0$, and this could go on forever:

$$N^0$$

oil   well   arm   chair

You've never seen this word, but its meaning is perfectly understandable: *an armchair that has something do with oil wells.*

The point is that we can make compounds as long, and for as long, as we want. There is, in principle, no longest compound, and this implies that the set of possible compounds is **infinite**. *Compounds have a fractal structure.*

A similar point could be made with reference to the derivational rules. There we have seen examples such as:

$$N^0 \Rightarrow N^0\, N^{-1}$$

This rule accounts for forms like *boyhood* and *restless*. In principle, we could also make *boyhoodless* or *restlesshood*. Admittedly, such cases sound odd. We can give better examples with prefixes: *former-pseudo-ex-president*, which shows various applications of the following rule:

$$N^0 \Rightarrow X^{-1}\, N^0$$

What property of the preceding rules causes this fractal infinity? The crucial property would appear to be that we have rules in which the symbol that occurs on the left side of the arrow also occurs on the right side. A rule that has that property is called **recursive**. We can also have recursivity without any rule being recursive by itself; that is, the rule *system* as such can be recursive. In that case we need rule systems like (a) or (b); (c) looks similar but I will explain that (c) is not recursive:

a.	i. $A \Rightarrow B\,C$		b.	i. $A \Rightarrow B\,C$		c.	i. $A \Rightarrow B\,C$
	ii. $C \Rightarrow A\,D$			ii. $C \Rightarrow D\,F$			ii. $C \Rightarrow D\,E$
				iii. $F \Rightarrow A\,F$			

The system in (a) is recursive because we can apply rule (ii) after rule (i), and then we can start over again, because (ii) introduces a symbol that rule (i) can apply to:

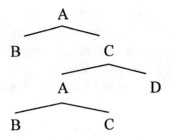

and so on.

The system in (b) also allows a loop because rule (ii) can apply to the output of rule (i), and rule (iii) can apply to the output of rule (ii). Then we can go back to rule (i) and start all over again:

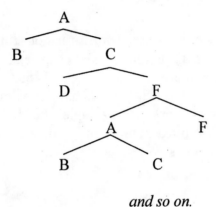

and so on.

The third rule system comes close to being recursive:

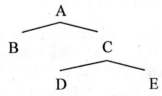

Even though rule (ii) can apply to the output of rule (i), we cannot go back to rule (i) again.

To characterize recursivity in a general way, let us introduce the concept of **feeding**. Let us say that rule R feeds rule P, that is, P can apply to the output of R. If a rule can apply to its own output, it is self-feeding (e.g., A ⇒ A B). Self-feeding leads to recursivity. Recursivity also arises if rule P feeds rule R and R feeds P (option (a) above); this is called direct mutual feeding. Finally, in option (b) we see that rule P feeds R, which feeds Q, which feeds P; this can be called indirect mutual feeding: P feeds Q via R and Q feeds P. (You can construct a case in which Q feeds R indirectly.)

Recursivity ensures that the system characterizes or allows an infinite set of structures using only finite means (i.e., a finite set of building blocks and a finite set of rules). It is sometimes said that recursivity accounts for the creativity of language. Of course, we are not talking about *artistic* creativity here. Rather, we mean that humans can use language to talk about anything they want, about new experiences, things that don't exist, and so on. Everything that we can think of can be expressed. This, of course, can only be so if language is not a closed system, and indeed it isn't. On the one hand there are rules that must be obeyed, but on the other hand those same rules allow us to make new words (and, as we will see, new sentences) all the time. Due to the property of recursivity, the number of words and sentences is infinite. We do not have to have heard a particular compound before we can produce it or understand it. The speakers of a language can create new words (and sentences) on the spot if the need to communicate something arises, or just for the fun of it. In this sense human language is an **open system**. As a result, there is complete **freedom of topic**.

Productivity

There is one apparent difference between word-formation rules and rules for the construction of sentences (which we discuss in the next chapter). It is sometimes said that word-formation rules can be **unproductive**. What is meant is that certain word-formation rules, according to which a number of existing words have been made, are at the present time not used to make new words. Take, for example, the derivation of nouns from adjectives using the suffix *-th*. A limited number of nouns are formed this way, but it doesn't seem possible to make new ones:

> warm - th
> leng - th
> dep - th
> *cool - th
> *big - th

We can contrast this limitation with the way of forming nouns from verbs with *-er*. It seems that we can attach this suffix to all verbs, and, more importantly, it would seem that we can apply *-er* to form words from any verb that might enter the language either as a result of word formation or due to borrowing or any other conceivable means (see Chapter 15).

Productivity is a matter of degree, and it mostly refers to the use of specific affixes rather than to the categorial rules, at least in the case of derivation. In the case of compounding it might be argued that certain types of combination rules are less productive than others. For example, whereas noun–noun compounding is wildly productive, verb–verb compounding seems much less so.

Finally, it will turn out that even rules for sentence formation may be more or less productive.

The Notion of Nonisomorphy

In this chapter we have encountered a few cases in which the categorial morphological structure is at odds with the phonological structure (infixes, zero-affixes, reduplication). This is, in fact, a more general phenomenon and perhaps to be expected if these two dimensions are subjected to their own wellformedness conditions. Given that this is so, the phonological and the categorial structure of words are not necessarily **isomorphic**. We can see that clearly at the level of words. Take a simple word, *worker*: This word consists of two syllables (phonology) as well as two morphemes (morphology). However, the division of the string of phonemes is different in both structures.

Phonological Word Structure

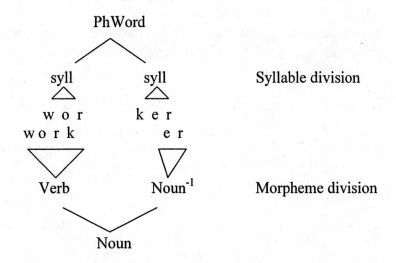

Categorial (**Morphological**) Structure

The fact that words and sentences are structured in two fundamentally different ways is sometimes called **dual patterning**. One pattern is phonological; the other pattern is morphological. However, we should not forget that linguistic expressions really have a **triple patterning,** the third pattern being the semantic structure.

Conclusions

In this chapter, we looked in some detail at the internal categorial structure of words. We have seen a variety of ways in which new words can be made.

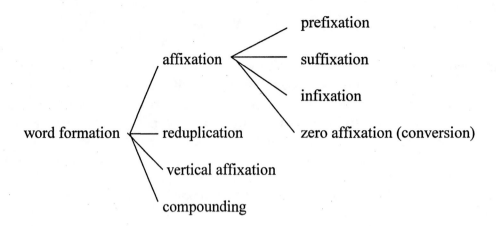

All structures discussed concerns words, specifically complex words. In the next chapter, we will take a detailed look at sentence structure.

Before we continue, let me try to summarize our findings with respect to the word phonological and word categorial (i.e., morphological) modules:

Level: word	Primitives	Combinations rules	Adjustment rules	Special topics
Phonological system	Phonemes (defined as sets of elements)	Phonotactic rules	- Allophony rules - Phoneme substitution rules	Phonological periodic table
Categorial system	Word class labels	Word formation rules	(none discussed)	Right-hand Head Rule

I hope that the reader sees the parallelism in the organization in these two modules. In the next section we will see that the syntactic–categorial system has the same general organization.

Chapter 12

Categorial Structures
(Sentence Level)

Introduction

There are restrictions on how you group words together and on the ordering of words into sentences. As before, we have three systems, each imposing its own set of rules (constraints): the categorial system, the phonological system, and the semantic system. We briefly looked at the sentence-level phonological system in Chapter 10. We will even more briefly look at the sentence-level semantic system in Chapter 13. In this chapter, we will now focus on the categorial side of sentences (what is usually called **syntax**). In most languages, words cannot be combined randomly (like morphemes cannot be combined randomly). Whereas we have not clearly established that there are word-level categorial (morphological) adjustment rules, we will be surprised to learn that the syntactic module can be modeled as having lots of adjustment rules. In fact, like in word-level phonology, there are several types of syntactic adjustment rules.

The syntactic system is a much more complex system of languages than the morphological and phonological systems. Perhaps semantics is even more complex, but you don't need to worry about that so much because I will not deal with the semantic word and sentence systems very extensively. However, you'll see that the syntactic system is quite challenging. Modern Linguistics has been greatly influenced by Noam Chomsky, and he has mainly worked on syntax. As a result, the last four decades have produced a rich literature on the syntactic organization of many different languages. Over the years Chomsky and his followers have often changed course (i.e., formalisms and terminology), and I will not be able to do full justice to this energetic subfield of linguistics, but I will give it more space than was used for the other grammatical modules. Fasten your seat belts!

Syntactic Wellformedness

Consider the following string of words:

The boy throws the ball.

When we say that this sentence is grammatical, we mean that:

- Word categories have been grouped and linearized in the right way (i.e., the sequence is categorially wellformed).
- We can make sense of it (i.e., it is semantically wellformed).
- We can pronounce it (i.e., it is phonologically wellformed).

It thus follows that sentences can be ungrammatical for three reasons. Consider the following sentences:

a.   **The boy the ball throws.*
       *Boy the throws ball the.

b.   **Colorless green ideas sleep furiously.*
       *tomorrow John walked to town.

c.   **He gave up it (He saw it, He gave up his right to vote).*
       *Mary's smarter than John's.

A case can be made for saying that (a) is ungrammatical for categorial reasons, (b) for semantic reasons, and (c) for phonological reasons.

With reference to the first semantic example in (b), it *could* be claimed that this sentence is not semantically illformed, but just semantically *odd* if used in a world in which ideas cannot sleep or have a color. Still, it seems that speaking of something being colorless and green constitutes a semantic and logical contradiction and must thus be bad in whatever world we imagine. A clearer example of semantic illformedness is perhaps: *He is a man and he is not a man.*

The first semantic example in (b) was constructed by Chomsky. He meant to demonstrate that a sentence can be syntactically wellformed while being illformed in semantic terms. The Dutch linguist **Anton Reichling** made this point even more forcefully by constructing the following example:

de vek blakte de mukken

An "English" equivalent would be:

the nog smimmed the plicks

Here we have possible, but nonexisting, Dutch/English words. Still, the sentences can be said to be syntactically wellformed in Dutch/English.

With respect to (c), let us just say that English does not allow these sentences for reasons of phonological wellformedness (the precise constraints are actually not so easy to state and are still under investigation. In any event, it would appear that the sentence-level phonological adjustment rule that turns *is* into *'s* is blocked in certain positions in the sentence).

With respect to (a) the proper reason for its illformedness seems neither semantic nor phonological, and this leaves only categorial ('syntactic') illformedness as an option. There must be a system of constraints that tells a speaker of English that the sentences in (a) are no good.

You might ask how we know that there is a categorial system for constructing sentences? Perhaps we've simply learned all the English sentences that we use in the course of language acquisition. Of course, you could have raised the same point when we discussed the morphological system. But no, this can't be correct because there does not seem to be a limit on the number of sentences (or complex words). Due to recursivity in the system of combination rules (we'll see that sentence structure is also recursive), the number of sentences and words is infinite and you can't learn an infinite number of things by heart no matter how smart you are. I'll demonstrate below how the same property of recursivity accounts for the fact that there is indeed no limit on the number of sentences.

The Syntactic Primitives and Combination Rules

Like the other grammatical systems, the syntactic system consists of three parts:

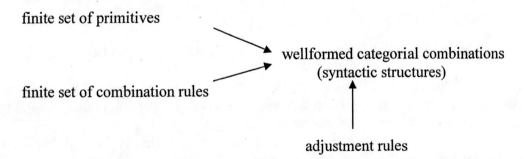

finite set of primitives

wellformed categorial combinations
(syntactic structures)

finite set of combination rules

adjustment rules

We have seen before that the various systems of grammar consist of three things. First, each component contains a list of basic building blocks (primitives). Second, there is a set of rules for combining these basic expressions into complex expressions. Third, there is, or can be, a set of rules operating on the complex expressions to make adjustments. In the case of the syntactic–categorial system we will look at two candidates for adjustment rules: **inflectional rules** and **transformational rules**.

It is important to understand that the syntactic–categorial system is simply a continuation of the morphological–categorial system. The main difference is that the latter produces units of the size *word*, whereas the former system starts with words and produces units of the size *sentence*.

Words and sentences are **significant levels** in language just like the cell and the organism are significant levels in biology. Other smaller, intermediate, and larger levels can be identified, but some levels simply stand out in significance. In biology, the cell can be said to be the smallest autonomous living structure, whereas organisms are living (large) collections of cells that are projected from the DNA information that is contained in the cells. In linguistics, we might say that the equivalent of *being alive* is *having meaning*. Sequences of phonemes that have no meaning are not linguistically alive. Words compare to cells in that they are the smallest freestanding units with meaning, whereas sentences can be regarded as meaningful collections of words that are also in some sense projected from the properties that words have. Not all linguists consider the word-sentence division significant and it is certainly the case that there isn't a lot of difference between the types of structures that are constructed within these two domains. Nor will it always be immediately obvious whether a certain complex expression is a complex word or a sentential construction. Another reason for not maintaining a strict separation between a word and sentence module is that such a separation seems to imply that complex words cannot be formed out of, for example, a phrase (a piece of sentence) and an affix. This raises the question of how to analyze an expression like:

American history teacher

It would seem that the part *American history* is a phrase consisting of an adjective and a noun. But if the whole thing is a compound we have a phrase inside a word. If, on the other hand, we say that the adjective has been added to form a phrase to a compound history teacher, we seem to get a different meaning, namely a history teacher who is an American:

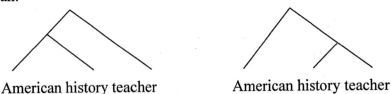

American history teacher   American history teacher

It is indeed the case that this expression is ambiguous and could mean either a teacher of American history or an American teacher of history, but the point is that the first reading presupposes a structure with a phrase inside a word.

We could say that syntactic construction can simply be fed back into the categorial word module, but that would allow for all sorts of constructions that would appear to be absent in the languages of the world. I will not try to solve this problem here, but I maintain that the division into words and sentences is a useful one, and one that captures a significant property of human languages.

The Primitives

The primitives of the syntactic system are the **category labels of words**. I've given you a list of these in the previous chapter. Today, syntacticians use many more labels, and some of those are not so easy to explain. However, we will not worry about that here.

The Combination Rules

Here are some examples of syntactic–categorial combination (rewrite) rules:

Combination rules	Explanation of symbols
a. S ⇒ NP VP	S = Sentence
b. NP ⇒ det N	NP = Noun Phrase
c. VP ⇒ V NP	VP = Verb phrases
d. VP ⇒ V	V = Verb
e. VP ⇒ V S	det = determiner

A special name for these rules is **phrase structure rules**. As before, these rules produce **tree structures**:

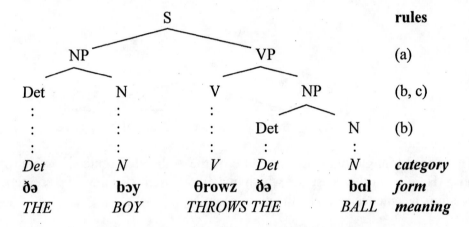

Because there is a one-to-one match between the terminal symbols of the syntactic tree and the category labels of the words, we have now established that the string of words is categorially wellformed. The form (phonological) aspects of the words, as well as their meaning aspects, need to be organized in wellformed structures as well for the sentence to be, as a whole, wellformed. Because the preceding sentence is grammatical, we will conclude that the phonological and semantic structures are, in fact, wellformed.

Now look at the following structure:

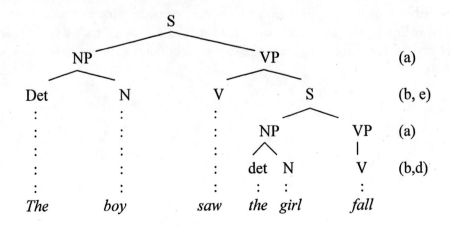

This structure is possible because the rule system above is **recursive**. Rules (a) and (e) are a **recursive pair**: Both rules have a symbol on the left-hand side of the rule that the other rule has on the right-hand side; these rules are mutually feeding. I refer you back to our discussion of recursivity in the previous chapter.

The Unboundedness of Syntax

Let us consider the fact that phrases and sentences can occur inside other phrases and sentences a bit more closely. This nesting is reminiscent of the Russian dolls that fit inside other dolls, except that in the case of syntax the embedded part need not be smaller than the shell:

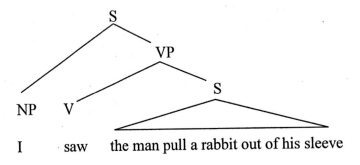

The closed triangle hides the structure of the embedded sentence, which is not relevant now. Here's another case in which we find a sentence inside a sentence. In subject position, a sentence can take the place of an NP:

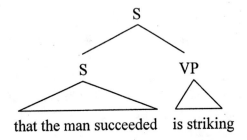

The possibility of nesting phrases and sentences inside phrases and sentences creates an effect of **infinity**. The technical name for this possibility is, as we have seen, **recursion**. Let us review the different types of cases of recursion that we have seen, and then add one more.

a.   S $\Rightarrow$ S   VP

b.   S $\Rightarrow$ NP   VP

c.   VP $\Rightarrow$ V   S

Rule (a) is recursive by itself (self-feeding), while (b) and (c) together introduce recursivity (mutual feeding). In general, we get recursivity if we find the same symbol to the left and right of one arrow (as in rule a), or two symbols repeated in two rules on opposite ends of the arrows (as in the pair b and c).

Recursivity can also be introduced by rules that contain conjunctions:

d.   NP $\Rightarrow$ NP conjunct NP   (the man or the woman)

e.   VP $\Rightarrow$ VP conjunct VP   (eats and sleeps)

f.   AP $\Rightarrow$ AP conjunct AP   (beautiful and rich)

g.   S $\Rightarrow$ S conjunct S   (he drinks and she eats)

Due to recursivity there is no limit on the number of sentences, nor is there a limit on the length of sentences.

We can define recursion as follows. Recursion occurs when:

A unit X is a combination that includes Y where Y is a combination that includes X

or:

A unit X is a combination that includes X

Notice how embedding can easily result when concatenated separate sentences are reanalyzed as one sentence:

Did you see that? Mary fell! $\Rightarrow$ Did you see that Mary fell?

I see a house. The house stands on a hill $\Rightarrow$ I see a house that stands on a hill
                                or: I see a house on a hill

John came. Mary went $\Rightarrow$ John came and Mary went

Thus, recursion is a way to compress different sentences into one sentence, either basically maintaining the sentence structure for the embedded unit (*that stands on a hill*) or shortening it to a phrase (*on a hill*). Note that the mere fact that we can stick phrases inside phrases is a remarkable property of language but does not in itself constitute recursion. Recursion arises when we can stick phrases inside phrases *of the same type*. (e.g., an NP inside an NP, and so on). Recursion is a very specific, simple, yet powerful device that essentially gives language its infinite range of words and sentences.

General Properties of Phrase Structure Rules

Naturally, we need many more phrase structure rules for English than listed thus far. However, rather than enumerating more rules I will turn to a discussion of some important general properties of phrase structure rules, explaining a notation that continues the integer notation that we introduced for morphological–categorial rules.

We have said that words are organized into phrases. Like words, phrases belong to different categories. We have **noun phrases (NPs)**, which are built around a noun, **verb phrases (VPs)**, which are built around a verb, and so on. Thus, words have the power to collect other words around them and form a phrase in which they are the central element. In line with our discussion in the preceding chapter, we will call this central element the **head**, because it is this element that determines the category of the phrase. In other words, this element puts its mark on the phrase as a whole. The reasoning here is thus the same as that which leads us to say that *–er* is the head in *sleeper*. In both cases we refer to a unit as the head of the construction if it determines the category of the complex construction of which it is part.

Extending the integer notation introduced in the previous chapter (*-er* is N^{-1}, *sleep* is V^0), we will now say that a phrase is a +1 (or simply 1) unit. After all, it goes one level **up** from the zero-level for words. Here's an example of a Prepositional Phrase (PP), a phrase that has a preposition (the word *on*) as its head:

$$
\begin{array}{c}
P^1 \\
\diagup\diagdown \\
P^0 \quad N^1 \\
| \quad \diagup| \\
\text{on} \;\; \text{det} \;\; N^0 \\
| \quad | \\
\text{the hill}
\end{array}
$$

I indicate the unit *phrase* by the superscript 1. Thus NP (or Noun Phrase) is the same thing as N^1. (Perhaps you now understand better why I gave the superscript -1 to affixes; these units are one level **below** the zero level for words.)

I just said that a head forms a phrase by combining with other words. There is a better way of putting it: a head word combines with, on the one hand single words (like *the* in *the house*) and, on the other hand, with phrases. Thus *house* in the following example combines with the phrase *on the hill*.

$$
\begin{array}{c}
N^1 \\
\diagup\diagdown \\
N^0 \quad P^1 \\
| \qquad \diagup\diagdown \\
\text{house} \;\; P^0 \quad N^1 \\
| \quad \diagup| \\
\text{on} \;\; \text{det} \;\; N^0 \\
| \quad | \\
\text{the hill}
\end{array}
$$

We now face the question of how we represent the structure of the noun phrase *the house on the hill* in which *house* combines both with *the* and with *on the hill*. Here are two possibilities:

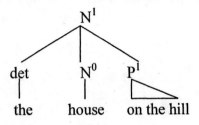

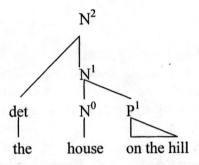

(As before, I use a closed triangle in trees if they want to simplify the structure and leave the structure inside the triangle unspecified.)

In the first structure we have created a **ternary node**: the node has **three** branches. In the second structure we have created an extra layer within the Noun Phrase. Which structure is better? This is not so easy to say. Generally, linguists have claimed that there is a virtue in working with trees in which nodes can only branch in two. I will call this the **Principle of Binary Branching** (PBP). Together with what we might call the **Head Principle** (all complex constructions have a head), the PBP only allows the structure in (a) below, whereas (b) is disallowed:

(As of now, I will adopt the convention to draw a **vertical line** over the head unit. A general term for nonheads is **dependents**, which are below a **slant line** in our tree notation.)

The PBP imposes a significant constraint on the kind of tree structures that can be used in linguistic representations. This principle is in fact compatible with all the structures that we have used previously in our discussion of phonology and morphology. (You might go back and check whether this is correct.)

But we now have to wonder how many layers we can have *within* phrases. Some linguists have claimed that **all** phrases maximally have a **two-layered structure**. Let us refer to this as the **Two Layer Principle** (TLP). They all have a **head** that combines with a phrase (called the **complement**) to form **layer 1**. Layer 1 then combines with another unit (typically a single word) called the **specifier** to form **layer 2.** This creates two layers that we distinguish by our integer superscripts. So the *universal structure for phrases* is claimed to be

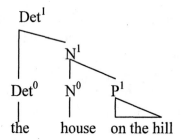

The symbol X here is a variable standing for N, V, A, that is, whatever the category of the head is. Both X^1 and X^2 can be read as XPhrase (Noun Phrase, Verb Phrase, etc.). The head word is a zero-level unit. (Again, note that below the word level we count downward and above the word level we count upward. Thus affixes as heads of words are minus one or X^{-1} units.)

One might now ask whether all word classes can be heads of phrases. Is there a conjunction phrase or a determiner phrase and so on? There is debate about that. One could indeed propose that determiners (or articles) such as *the* project their own phrase, the Determiner Phrase:

$$\text{Det}^1$$

$$\text{Det}^0 \quad \text{N}^1$$

$$\text{N}^0 \quad \text{P}^1$$

the   house   on the hill

Unfortunately, in this book I can't get too deeply involved in these issues. For the remainder of this chapter I will assume that the two-layer hypothesis is correct. This in itself does not entail that there couldn't be a Determiner Phrase, however. That is an independent decision. However, later in this chapter I *will* show that **complementizer** words (like *that* or *whether*) or **auxiliaries** (like *have, be, could*) form two-layer Complementizer Phrases and Auxiliary Phrases, respectively.

I will now show some examples of the more common types of phrases in which the heads are nouns, verbs, adjectives, or prepositions:

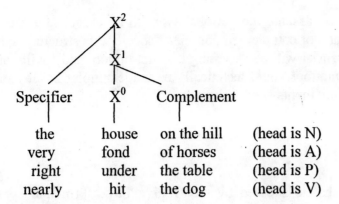

Specifier	X^0	Complement	
the	house	on the hill	(head is N)
very	fond	of horses	(head is A)
right	under	the table	(head is P)
nearly	hit	the dog	(head is V)

In the first two phrases the complements are P^2s; in the other two the complements are N^2s.

In some cases we note that the complement is **obligatory**. You cannot say that someone is *very fond* or that something is *on*. You have to add a phrase to make these expressions complete. Verbs, too, seem to obligatorily come with complements, depending on the verb in question. These things have to be specified in the lexicon for the words that are the heads. Verbs that must come with a complement (that functions as a direct object) are called **transitive** (like *hit*). Verbs that don't take a complement are called **intransitive** (like *sleep*). These two types of verbs are called **subcategories** (or subclasses) of the category (or class) of verbs.

The fact that verbs come in subcategories depending on what they combine with is comparable to the fact that affixes also come in subcategories depending on what they combine with. Go back to Chapter 11 for this property of affixes. Hence, verbs, like affixes, must have an insertion frame. For *hit* and *sleep* these frames are

$$\text{hit} \qquad [\ -\ N^2]v^1$$

$$\text{sleep} \quad [\ -\ ]_{V2}$$

Specifiers, on the other hand, never are obligatory—they are always **optional**—and all heads are supposed to have the option of taking one, which means that no head can be subcategorized as being unable to combine with a specifier.

At this point we need to discuss a point that concerns our use of the superscript integers. Consider the phrase: [mice] (as in *my mother hates mice*). We have three ways of representing this phrase:

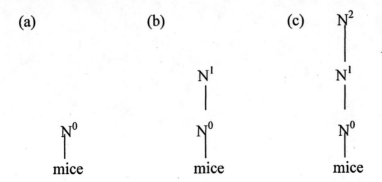

The question is, do we assume the various layers to be universally present even when there is no specifier and/or complement, or do we specify this structure only if these extra units are in fact present? I will be assuming the first option, and I will continue to do so even though representations could technically be made simpler in all those cases where specifiers and/or complements are missing.

Adjuncts

The phrase format that is allowed by the Double Layer Principle appears to be too limited if we consider a wider range of English sentences. For example, suppose we consider noun phrases that contain an adjective phrase in addition to a determiner, like the noun phrase *the beautiful house on the hill*. Are *the* and *beautiful* both specifiers? One approach is to say yes and simply allow a further layer:

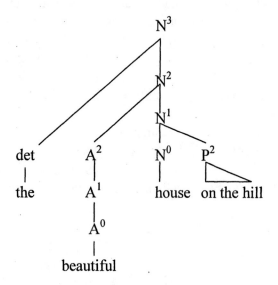

A problem with this idea is that one could add a whole series of adjective phrases before a noun: *a very kind, incredibly rich, shockingly ugly, old man*. Hence, to avoid ending up with an unlimited number of layers, it has been proposed that *modifying* units like Adjective Phrases do not cause the layer **integer** to go up:

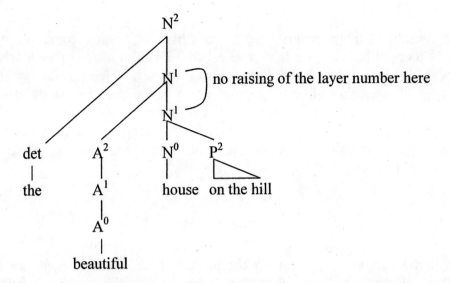

Units that do not cause a rise in the layer integer are often called **adjuncts**.

Turning now to what occurs on the right side of heads, it would appear that nouns can have more than one complement, as in: *The occupation [of France] [by the Germans]*. In fact, we could add *[in the 18th century]* and even more. Only one of those can be a complement; the others must be adjuncts. Or perhaps they are all adjuncts. This raises the question of exactly what is meant by a complement. Many linguists will only refer to a unit as a complement if its occurrence is **obligatory** (i.e., is specified in the insertion frame for the head). If obligatoriness is a necessary property of complements, none of the phrases that may follow occupation counts as a complement since this noun can perfectly well occur by itself (*the occupation lasted 5 years*). Still, one might refer to the first phrase (of France) as a complement because it corresponds to the phrase that would be obligatory if we look at the verb from which occupation is derived. It would seem that occupy as a verb requires a complement (*they occupied France* and not *they occupied*). For this reason *[of France]* could be called a complement while the other phrases would count as phrases. A structure for *The occupation [of France] [by the Germans] [in the 18th century]* would thus display several N^1 layers with the same integer within the N^2:

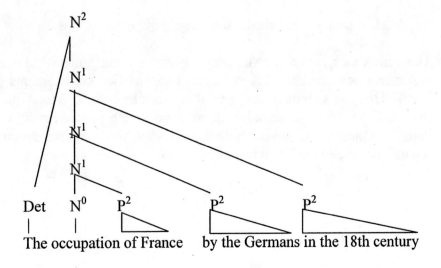

We also get multiple adjunct layers with a verb like *hit*, which combines with a complement on its right but can also have a so-called **adverbial phrase** *(he) hit the ball hard*. Verbs can also be combined with Prepositional Phrases, which play a very similar role to Adverbial Phrases; they all modify the meaning of the Verb Phrase by making it more specific. In fact, verbs can be combined with several nonobligatory modifying phrases: *John went [to town] [by car] [with Mary]*. Clearly such phrases are not complements; they are not obligatory. Hence, an adjunct treatment seems more plausible. (This means, again, that we get multiple V^1 layers.)

True Double Complement Constructions

Recall from Part I that verbs that take a complement (like *hit* or *occupy*) are called transitive. There also appear to be ditransitive verbs, verbs that appear to have two complements:

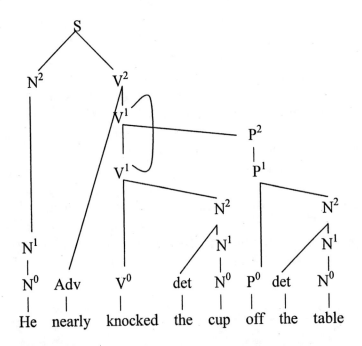

The verb *knock* can take two complements: a noun phrase and a prepositional phrase. Again, we need an extra layer. In this case the two complements are obligatory: *John knocked the cup* sounds incomplete. It may not be correct to treat one of the complements (here *off the table*) as an adjunct, as done in the preceding structure (if adjuncts are defined as phrases that do not raise the integer). An alternative structure would give up on binarity and make the V^1 node a ternary node:

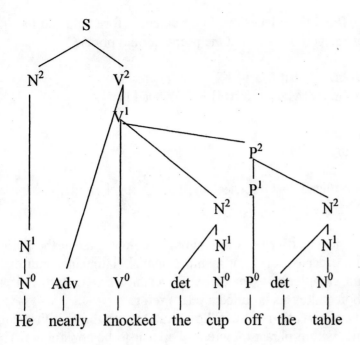

The bottom line is that there are still many questions regarding how or where to attach adjuncts (for nouns and verbs) or extra complements (for verbs).

Word Order Across Languages

An important point that we can make with reference to the preceding examples of phrases is that English appears to choose a fixed order of specifier >> head >> complement *for all phrase types* ("">>"" means *precedes*). Adjuncts complicate the picture, but we'll ignore that for the moment. If all languages worked this way, one might refer to this point as a **language universal**. This universal, if valid, would be a good candidate for a language-specific innate characteristic because there is no apparent reason for why the order would be fixed in this way. Why couldn't English have the following structure:

> The on the hill house big

If all languages would have the same structure for phrases as English, such an apparently contingent (i.e., not logically necessarily) property could only come from an innate trait.

When linguists started collecting data from many different languages they made some very interesting discoveries, which show that phrase structure isn't *that* universal. There are languages that have different phrase structures than those in English. However, it would still appear that there are some interesting restrictions on the variation. Very briefly, let me suggest some important discoveries that bear on phrase structure.

The first observation is that the order *specifier >> head >> complement* is not found in all languages. Again, focusing on the order of head and complement, it was found that in some languages the order is complement >> head, in *Japanese* for example.

It is striking, however, that *Japanese* places the complement before the head *in all phrase types*. I'll illustrate this for the verb phrase and the prepositional phrase:

English: John　　[**hit** Mary]　　VP: head first
Japanese: John-ga [Mary-o **butta**]　VP: head last

English: **by** car　　　　　　PP: head first
Japanese: kuruma **de**　　　　PP: head last

(The terminology head first/head last focuses on the X^1 level, and thus ignores the specifier.)

Although not shown here, the specifier in both languages comes first in the phrase. The difference, then, lies in the order of head and complement. If languages can differ like this, the order of head and complement cannot be universally fixed. Rather, it appears that there is a choice. A choice like this is called a **parameter**.

A second important observation is the following. Despite the fact that languages vary in the ordering of units within phrases, there still appear to be constraints. The most important constraint is that, as we have noted several times, within each language the same ordering is maintained in all phrase types. We do not find cases in which the NP has a complement-head order while the VP has the opposite. If this finding is robust, it is very interesting because there is no clear (logical) reason for why this limitation would exist. And if that is so, it seems likely that this property that languages have must be due to an innate fixation.

The linguist **Joseph Greenberg** (1915 – 2001) was the first to make this observation. He stated that there is a strong *tendency* for different phrase types to have the same ordering *within each language* in terms of the ordering of specifier, head, and complement. Greenberg called this ordering a tendency rather than a law because he thought that there are exceptions. He said that in English (what he called) modifiers precede the noun when they are adjective phrases (*big house*) but they follow nouns when they are prepositional phrases (*house on the hill*). In the terminology that we used earlier we would use the term *adjunct* where Greenberg uses *modifier*. Perhaps it is indeed the case that modifiers/adjuncts are less strict in their ordering properties.

Languages with Free Word Order

In Part I we discussed an Australian language in which the word order within sentences was reported to be rather random (or free). We could still keep track of what goes with what because of the system of (inflectional) endings. It is still a matter of debate how to characterize the phrase structure system for such languages. Some linguists argue that such languages have phrase structure rules that specify grouping but no linear order, but that still does not account for the fact that even words belonging to different groups may be intermixed. Now, as we will see later, a particular type of syntactic adjustment rules, the transformational rules, can move words around and thus change order. It is possible that the languages at issue simply have a rich set of such scrambling rules. Without having at least phrase structure rules that introduce groups (without linear order), it is difficult to see how one could generate sentences at all.

Two Types of Adjustment Rules

We have now concluded our discussion of the phrase structure rules (i.e., the combination rules in the sentence level categorial module). Next, we will discuss the need for adjustment rules in this module. Let's see what it is that we are looking for. What was it again that adjustment rules do? Recall what the adjustment rules in the word phonological system do; they

   (a) Adapt the phonemes to their environment in terms of allophones (*allophony rules*)
   (b) Replace (by other phonemes), delete, or insert phonemes in (*phoneme substitution rules*)

The syntactic theory that has been proposed by Noam Chomsky relies crucially on a class of categorial adjustment rules that are very similar in function to the phonological adjustment rules in (b). Chomsky proposed that we need to have rules that move, insert, and delete words and phrases. He called these rules **transformations**. The theory of syntactic structure also requires a set of adjustment rules that is more like the class in (a). These are called **inflectional rules**. We will first take a close look at inflectional rules.

The Syntactic Adjustment Rules I: Inflection

Here's an example of inflection in English:

   The boy plays outside.

The verb *play* must be provided with the ending *-s* because it occurs in the environment of a third person singular subject (*the boy*). (*The boy* is a Noun Phrase; the term **subject** indicates the **syntactic function** of this NP.) Because inflection involves the addition of affixes (or, more generally, involves the same type of operations that are involved in morphological derivation), it seems necessary to clearly differentiate inflection from the type of word formation that we have called **derivation** in Chapter 11.

The Difference Between Derivation and Inflection

Consider the words *greener* and *greenish*. Both words have complex categorial structure:

$$A^0$$
$$A^0 \quad A^{-1}$$
$$| \quad |$$
$$green \quad er$$

$$A^0$$
$$A^0 \quad A^{-1}$$
$$| \quad |$$
$$green \quad ish$$

more green   somewhat green

Traditionally, despite the fact that both structures seem very similar, a distinction is made between the two cases. The first case (adding comparative –*er*) is called **inflection**, whereas the second case (adding –*ish*) is called **derivation**. What's the difference? I would like to put it as follows:

> **Derivation**: making *new words*
> **Inflection**: making words *ready for use* in a sentence

Consider the following two sentences:

> *John is tall than Pete.
> John is tall**er** than Pete.

When we use a construction containing an adjective followed by the word *than*, we **must** use an adjective ending in –*er*: that is, the sentence position (i.e., environment) *just before than* **requires** an adjective ending in –*er*.

A comparative adjective can be paraphrased as *more A* (i.e., *more tall*). In fact, most adjectives that are monosyllabic or, if bisyllabic and ending in weak syllables like -*ow* or -*y* (as in *shallow* or *happy*), can take the -*er* ending to form a comparative. In other cases the comparative meaning is made by combining the adjective with the adverb *more*:

> That is more important / *importanter than going home.

To make a combination of *more* and an adjective is clearly a syntactic–categorial phenomenon. So the fact that adding -*er* and adding *more* are alternative ways of making comparatives supports the idea that adding -*er* is part of the syntactic system.

Now let's look at adding -*ish*. No matter how long you search, you will not find a sentence position in English that necessarily **requires** an adjective ending in –*ish*. You can find positions that require an adjective, perhaps, but never one in which the adjective must have the suffix –*ish*. Adjectives ending in -*ish* can be used wherever adjectives without -*ish* can be used. *Greenish* is an adjective just like any other adjective, and it occurs in all sentence positions that are appropriate for adjectives, including simplex adjectives (like *green*). *Greener*, although still an adjective, is fit to occur at least in one specific position where *green* is excluded (namely after *than*). Note that *greener* can also occur in positions other than preceding *than*. One can say:

Pete is smart, but John is smarter.

Pete is smart, but John is handsome.

Thus, saying that the comparative form is inflectional does not imply that *all* positions in which it can occur necessarily require a comparative. The criterion to count as inflection is that there must be at least one context in the language that requires the comparative form.

Paradigms

We have a special term for the set of all the inflected forms that come with a particular word. We call that set a **paradigm**. In English, paradigms are very small:

> for adjectives: big, bigg**er**, bigg**est**
> for nouns: boy, boy**s**, boy**'s**
> for verbs: play, play**s**, play**ed**, play**ing**

In other languages (such as Kayardild; see Chapter 4), paradigms can contain hundreds of forms.

Note that the difference between inflection and derivation is usually observed by dictionary makers, who will typically not list all the forms that belong to a paradigm (i.e., the set of inflected varieties of a word), but they will often make a separate entry for a derived word.

A Second Criterion for Inflectional Status

Implicit in the preceding is a second criterion that separates inflection from derivation. Through derivation we make *types of words* that also exist in simplex (**monomorphemic**) form, like adjectives, nouns, or verbs. For example, with *–ish* we make adjectives, but we also have simplex adjectives like *good, important,* and *smart.* Both types occur in exactly the same positions in the sentence. However, there are no monomorphemic words that can take the place of inflected forms. Thus, the lexicon does not contain simplex words that have the meaning of comparatives. Comparatives always have a structure as in (b) following, or they occur with *more*.

The Mechanics of Inflectional Adjustment Rules

For the sake of the discussion, I have made it seem as if the inflectional rule for forming comparatives simply introduces the phonological form *-er* on an adjective that occurs before *than*. However, we have to be a little bit more precise with respect to what it is that an inflectional rule does.

In the case at hand, we postulate an inflectional **adjustment rule** that adds an **inflectional feature** [comparative] to an adjective category that occurs in the relevant categorial structure (i.e., preceding a category of the type comparative conjunction):

(a)   *Inflectional feature assignment*

$$A^0 \quad \Rightarrow \quad A^0 \qquad \text{preceding a comparative conjunction}$$
$$\text{[comparative]}$$

Then we need a second step that provides the structure, which will host the adjective and the inflectional suffix:

(b)   *Inflectional structure assignment*

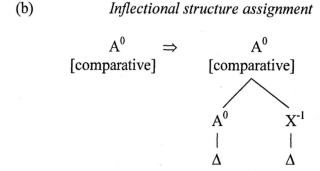

When lexical items are inserted into this structure, the morpheme *–er* fits the bill:

X^{-1} [comparative]	*category*
er	*form*
MORE	*meaning*

Note, in (b), that the inflectional morpheme does not bear a category label, although it does have the label [comparative]. Indeed, inflectional affixes never determine the category label of the word. (This prevents them from determining the word class of the construction that they are part of. We'll leave undecided whether such categoryless morphemes can be heads.)

Other Examples of Inflectional Features

There are various types of inflection, the most important of which I will discuss here.

Government Inflection

A common system of inflection involves the marking of syntactic functions like **subject** and **object**. The relevant inflectional features are called **case features**, and examples are [nominative] for subjects, and [accusative] for objects.

Case features can also be required by prepositions. In English, all transitive verbs and prepositions **govern** the accusative case, which we can only see when we combine them with pronouns:

> We help him / *he
> ...with him / *he

Whereas in English both transitive verbs and propositions always take the same case, in German we have two cases for each category:

Dative Case		Accusative Case	
helfen	to help	sehen	to see
mit	with	ohne	without

Thus, *helfen* and *mit* assign dative case to their complement, whereas *sehen* and *ohne* assign accusative case.

However, for plain nouns English does not seem to make any case distinctions. Do we assume in that case that these nouns have no case feature, or do we say that the case feature is there but that the case affix lacks a phonological form? This would be possible since, as we have seen in Chapter 11, affixes with a zero phonology exist in derivational morphology. In English we would say that inflection (for plain nouns) is covert rather than overt. But English nouns do have one overt case suffix. We also find the so-called genitive ending in cases like *the man's house*. The part that we write as <'s> is an inflectional suffix.

What is expressed in terms of case endings in one language may be expressed in terms of prepositions in other languages. Even in English we can see that these two ways can be in competition. A ditransitive verb such as *give* takes two complements, a direct object (*flowers*) and an indirect object (*(to) the winner*):

> The man gave flowers [to the winner]
>
> The man gave [the winner] flowers

The part in brackets (the indirect object) carries what is called the **dative** case. In the first sentence this case is absorbed by the preposition *to*; in the second example it is covertly unexpressed because English doesn't have a phonological form for the dative case suffix (except in pronouns where it is identical to the accusative form: *him, her*, etc.).

Some languages have many other cases than nominative, genitive, dative, and accusative. For example, there is the locative case, which in English can only be expressed by preposition (the man sits in the chair). In other languages (such as Finnish) there is a locative affix that is attached to the noun.

Agreement Inflection

Case features can be subject to **agreement** such that, for example, the determiner and adjective that goes with a nominative noun must also carry the nominative case feature.

the [NOM] big [NOM] boy [NOM]

We don't *see* this kind of agreement in English, but there are lots of languages that have this kind of overt agreement system. (Again, as with the cases, perhaps English has this kind of agreement covertly, but the point is that the relevant features do not have audible forms.) We do, however, find agreement between subject and verb in **number** ([singular], [plural]):

a.   boy [PLUR] play [PLUR]
b.   boy [SING] play [SING]

The inflectional features do not always have an audible form, however:

a.   the boy-Ø play-S
b.   the boy-S play-Ø

There is no spell-out of the feature [singular] on nouns, nor is there of the feature [plural] on verbs. This may look like DISagreement in terms of the phonological form of the inflectional categories, but the point is that it so happens in English that both the singular and plural morpheme have zero and -*s* as possible phonological forms:

	verbs	nouns
singular	-s	Ø
plural	Ø	-s

In other languages, we often see that the agreement would in fact be expressed by suffixes with the same phonological form, for example:

the boy-**a** play-**a**   (singular)
the boy-**is** play-**is**   (plural)

But, again, the affixes that mark a specific agreement are not necessarily identical in form. We could also have:

the boy-**u** play-**a**
the boy-**is** play-**os**

(In fact, this is precisely what we just saw for English, where -∅ on the noun for singular goes with –s on the verb for singular, and vice versa.)

It may be easier to learn that words ending in the same affix go together, but it *can* also be learned that –*u* goes with –*a* (to mark singular) and –*is* goes with –*os* (to mark plural). Languages can get pretty complicated in this respect. Nouns may differ in the kind of affixes they take for number or case.

Inherent Inflection

Sometimes it would seem that the inflectional feature is not determined by anything in particular outside the inflected word. In that case, it is called **inherent**. Such inherent properties are called inflectional because they often act as the *determinants* in agreement relations. Examples are features like [feminine], [masculine], and [neuter]. In many languages nouns inherently fall into one of these classes (there could be other classes as well), and agreement manifests itself in that adjectives and determiners then agree with these features. The features for number ([singular], [plural]) can also be inherent (in addition to being an agreement feature). For example, if a verb agrees in number with the subject, one might say that the number of the subject NP is inherent, whereas the number of the verb is a form of agreement.

A Direct Phrase Structure Account of Inflection

I mentioned in chapter 7 that we can sometimes circumvent the use of adjustment rules by revising the combination rules, perhaps a move that should be preferred. Well, inflectional adjustment rules *can* be built into the phrase structure rules, as many linguists have argued. Take the very first phrase structure rule that we introduced:

$$S \Rightarrow NP\ VP$$

To express that the inflectional feature for number must be the same for the NP and the VP, that is, to indicate that if the NP is singular the VP (or V in it) must be singular (and likewise for plural), we could revise the rule as follows:

$$S \Rightarrow NP \qquad VP$$
$$[\alpha NUM]\ [\alpha NUM]$$

with α being a variable that ranges over the value "+" and "-."

At this point, I also look back at the language Latin that appears to have a fairly free word order. In these cases inflectional endings provide crucial information to the language user in determining *what goes with what*. It is not obvious that in these languages inflectional features and their affixes can be assigned on the basis of a fixed arrangement in which words occur as dictated by the phrase structure rules (as one can in a language like English), precisely because there doesn't seem to be a fixed arrangement. Earlier, I suggested that free word order languages pose a problem for an approach that starts out with phrase structure rules. It would seem that the inflectional endings in this type of language are fundamental and cannot be derived by adjustment rules.

The Syntactic Adjustment Rules II: Transformations

So far we have discussed the syntactic–categorial system, focusing on the phrase structure rules and a first class of adjustment rules, namely, inflectional rules. This section deals with transformational rules, that is, adjustment rules that make more dramatic changes in the structures that are generated by the phrase structure rules:

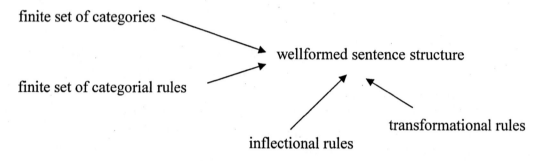

The diagram suggests that transformational rules apply before inflectional rules. Because transformation influences the positions of words in the sentence, inflection should not apply until the positions of all words and phrases have been fixed. (This is analogous to our finding that in the phonological component, phoneme substitution rules must precede allophony rules.)

Question Sentences

We start the discussion about transformational rules with an examination of normal statement sentences and corresponding question sentences. Compare the following two sentences:

(1)　　a.　　John will buy flowers.
　　　　b.　　What will John buy?

(In this section, I have numbered all examples because there will be considerable reference to examples in the text.)

In both sentences we have the verb *buy*, which takes a subject (*John*) and an obligatory object—*flowers* in (1a), *what* in (1b). Also, in both cases, *buy* is accompanied by an auxiliary verb *will*. You may find it strange to think of the word *what* in (1b) as being the object of *buy*. However, you will agree, I hope, that *what* in some sense stands for the thing that will be bought, just like *flowers* in (1a) is the thing that will be bought.

What we have here, then, is a pair of sentences that are highly similar, except for the fact that one is a **statement**, whereas the other is a **question**. Both sentences have the same parts (i.e., subject, object, verb, auxiliary), but they occur in different orders:

(2)   John   will   buy   flowers

                       What   will   John   buy?

The subject *John* and the auxiliary *will* occur in opposite orders, and it would seem that the object *what* in the question occurs all the way at the beginning of the sentence, whereas in the statement the object *flowers* immediately follows the verb. It seems reasonable to suppose that being a statement or being a question is what causes these differences in word order.

We might now suppose that both sentences are derived from one basic structure and that when that structure occurs in the environment of a *question marker*, adjustment rules (transformations) apply. This is the basic idea that Chomsky had in the 1950s.

Perhaps this approach reminds you of a phenomenon that we discussed in Chapter 10 (on phonology). We noticed there that a particular morpheme sometimes has two different shapes depending on its context, that is, on morphemes that it is combined with. We discussed the following example:

(3)   electri[k] - electri[s]ity

In that case, we analyzed the alternation between *electri*[k] and *electri*[s] by formulating an adjustment rule that changes *k* into *s* before *-ity*. It would seem that the different shapes of statements and questions can also be regarded as alternations of the notion of *sentence*, which suggests that the alternation between the two sentences can be handled in a similar way. Noting the analogue between allomorphy (different surface shape of a morpheme) and the variation between the structure of statements and question sentences brings out that phonological adjustment rules (in this case a rule replacing /k/ by /s/) are very similar to the class of transformational rules that we are now ready to introduce. We have to decide which of the two variants is basic (*electrik* or *electris* in the case of allomorphy; statement order or question order in the case of sentence structure variation). Instead of putting you through the exercise of trying out both options, I'll make what I know to be the correct choice and say that the statement order is basic. If that is so, we need two adjustment rules:

(4)   a.   *Subject-Aux inversion*: Subject Aux $\Rightarrow$ Aux Subject in a Q-sentence

         b.   *Q-movement*: Move a Q-word to the beginning in a Q-sentence

Rule (4a) switches the linear order of the subject NP and the auxiliary verb, whereas rule (4b) moves the question word *what* to the beginning of the sentence.

Before we see how this works, I must introduce what we will take to be the overall structure of a sentence. Earlier, we adopted something as in (5a), but now we will use (5b). The motivation is, first, that the sentence must have a head (like all constituents) and, second, the auxiliary must have a place in the sentence:

(5)   a.

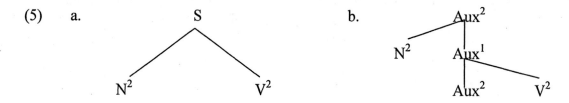

When we introduced (5a) we did not consider sentences that, next to the main verb, have a so-called auxiliary verb (John *will* come). These auxiliary verbs need a place too, and the proposal in (5b) is, in fact, that these verbs constitute the head of the sentence (a rather fancy spot for verbs that are called *auxiliary*). In other words, we treat the sentence as a two-layer phrase with the auxiliary as the head, the subject NP as the specifier, and the object NP as the complement. Thus Aux^2 is equivalent to the symbols S.

Let's now look at the application of the two transformational rules:

(6) **Phrase Structure Rules**

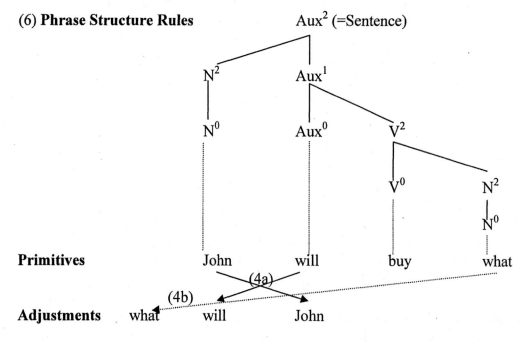

There are two problems here regarding the adjustments. What is the structure after the transformations have been applied? Specifically, are we saying that *John* ends up in the Auxiliary spot and *will* in the Noun Phrase spot? That would be rather odd because that would create a mismatch between the labeling of the terminal nodes in the tree and the word class properties of the words involved. Secondly, when we move *what* to the front, where does it end up? It doesn't seem to be part of the sentence structure anymore. That doesn't seem right either. If we compare this to the phonological adjustment rules that substitutes /s/ for /k/, we have assumed the /s/ is integrated into the syllable structure of the word by occupying an onset position in fourth syllable of the word. Analogously, we want to make sure that the word *what* will be somehow integrated into the sentence structure.

To solve the first problem, let us say that *John* does not go anywhere and that instead *will* moves to a position in front of John. This, of course, only solves half of the problem because we now need to determine how *will* can be integrated into the sentence structure. By moving both *will* and *what* to the front of the sentence we seem to have two words hanging in midair, as shown in (7):

(7)

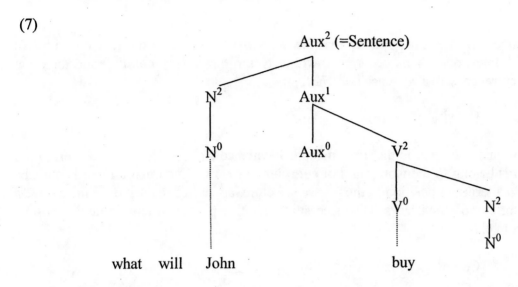

So let us see whether we can arrange things in such a way that both *what* and *will* end up being incorporated into the phrase structure of the sentence. It would seem that we need to formulate our phrase structure rules in such a way that two extra positions at the beginning of the sentence will be present, but the question is how to motivate these positions independently. By this I mean: Is there any independent evidence for having these extra positions? Yes, there is. The evidence will come from comparing so-called **main sentences** with **embedded sentences**. This means that we need to make a little detour here and look at the structure of embedded sentences. The difference between a main sentence and an embedded sentence is shown in the following sentence:

(8)   Harry said [that John will buy flowers].

What we have here are actually *two* sentences:

(9)   **Main sentence**   [Harry said X]
             Embedded sentence   X = [that John will buy flowers]

[Harry said X] is a sentence comparable to [Harry said nothing]. But instead of the object NP *nothing*, we fill the object slot by a whole sentence [that John will buy flowers]. (We can do that, i.e., have a sentence inside a sentence, because of recursion.) In other words, the verb *to say* can take as its complement either a noun phrase or a whole sentence. Let us see which phrase structure rules we need now. (10a) and (10c) are the equivalent of some of the rules that I introduced on page 219. Rule (10b) is needed to know that we have an auxiliary phrase. Note that (10c) allows the verb to take a sentence as its complement:

(10)   a. $Aux^2 \Rightarrow N^2 \, Aux^2$ (cf. $S \Rightarrow NP \; VP$)
                     b. $Aux^1 \Rightarrow Aux^0 \, V^2$
                     c. $V^1 \Rightarrow V^0 \, Aux^2$ (cf. $VP \Rightarrow V \; S$)

(Observe that rules (a) and (c) are mutually feeding and thus make the rule system recursive.)

At the same time we must assume that the verb *to say* occurs in the lexicon with two insertion frames, one for its occurrence with a Noun Phrase (*say nothing*) and the other for its occurrence with a sentence (*say that...*):

   (a) $[- N^2]_V{}^1$ (b) $[- Aux^2]_V{}^1$

Now, the point to notice is that the embedded sentence starts with a special word, *that*. Such words belong to the word class of **complementizers**. Given that all words must be inserted in a terminal position in the phrase structure, an embedded sentence must have a position for **complementizers**. This necessitates another phrase structure rule that will be written as in (11):

(11) $Comp^1 \Rightarrow Comp^0 \, Aux^2$

(By the way, the term **complementizer** is distinct from the term **complement**. Both terms are related in as far as complementizers *introduce* sentences that are complements of a verb.)

With the rule in (11), and the other rules that we already used, we can generate the following structure for an embedded sentence where we have added an extra shell to the sentence. This shell is headed by the complementizer position $Comp^0$. The sentence (Aux^2) is thus the complement of this complementizer:

(12)

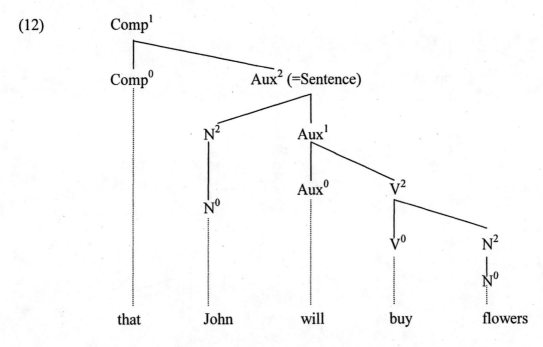

that   John   will   buy   flowers

In a way, we can say that the word *that* has an insertion frame that indicates that this word can take a sentence as a complement: $[- Aux^2]_{Comp}{}^1$.

Given that embedded sentences start with a complementizer such as *that*, it would seem that embedded sentences show us yet another shape of sentence structure, which means that we now have a three-way variation in sentence structure:

(13)   a.   John will buy flowers.   statements
          b.   What will John buy?   questions
          c.   that John will buy flowers   embedded sentence

Still pursuing the idea that the different shapes that sentences can take must *all* be derived from one common structure, I will show that we can solve the problems raised by (7) if we adopt the idea that something like the structure in (12) underlies all three sentence types in (13).

At first sight it would seem that the Comp shell provides only *one* extra position, the position that is occupied by *that* in an embedded sentence. However, if we regard this shell as a phrase in its own right (a Comp phrase), we expect its head to not only have a complement (i.e., the sentence or Aux^2), but also a specifier. With two extra positions we can now say that *what* moves to the specifier of Comp, whereas the auxiliary moves to the head of Comp:

(14)

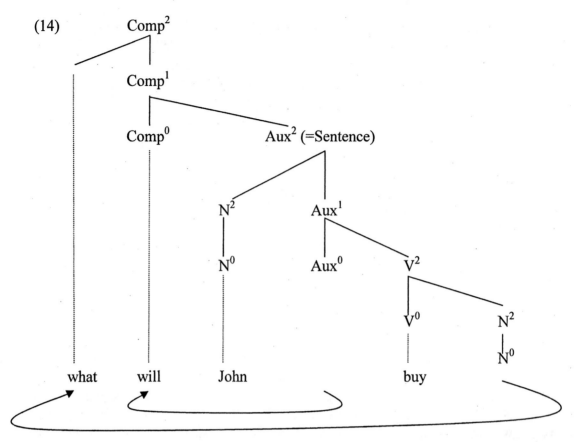

We have now shown that both what and will can be moved to a position in the tree structure so that they no longer have to float in mid air. Notice that both movements leave a gap in the structure, namely at the original site of these two words, but we will say that it is acceptable that not all terminal positions in a sentence structure are occupied by an actual word. (I'll come back to this point below.) The basic form of a sentence is usually called its **deep structure** and the surface form (which results from applying the transformations) its **surface structure**.

Let me finally update the phrase structure rules:

(15)   a. $Comp^2 \Rightarrow Spec\ Comp^1$
              b. $Comp^1 \Rightarrow Comp^0\ Aux^2$
              c. $Aux^2 \Rightarrow N^2\ Aux^2$
              d. $Aux^1 \Rightarrow Aux^0\ V^2$
              e. $V^1 \Rightarrow V^0\ Comp^2$

So far I've talked about transformations as if they move **words**, which are terminal elements in the tree. However, in the following sentence Q-movement has moved a **phrase** rather than a single word:

(16)   [What kind of flowers] did John buy?

Thus, transformations must be able to make reference to structure (i.e., groups of words). We refer to this as **the Principle of Structure Dependency.** Transformations are structure dependent. They don't operate on linear strings of words; they take into account how these words are organized into phrases. This means that they can target non-terminal nodes as well. This principle, in fact, supports the idea that sentences are not just linear arrangements of words, but are instead grouped into phrases.

We have now demonstrated the basic idea behind the need for syntactic–categorial adjustment rules that move things around (called transformations). When this theory had just been proposed, syntacticians also formulated transformations that would insert phrases or delete them. Later, they decided that only movement transformations are needed, so I will not bother to discuss data that at first appeared to motivate these other kinds of operations.

To repeat: the essential motivation for postulating transformational rules comes from the desire to derive the various types of sentences (statements, questions, embedded sentences) from a common underlying source. This desire, as we have seen, also motivated the postulation of adjustment rules in phonology. Indeed, transformations and phonological adjustment rules (those that perform phoneme substitutions) are completely analogous in their roles. In fact, inflectional rules can be seen as analogous to allophony rules in as far as both perform additive operations on the building blocks in each module. Inflectional rules perform additive operations on words (they add inflectional affixes), while allophony rules add non-contrastive features to phonemes. These analogies support our point that the various components of the grammar are organized in very similar ways.

It might be argued that the parallelism is undermined by the facts that the phonological adjustment rules that are analogous to transformation do not move around phonemes. However, besides rules like the one that changes /k/ into /s/, we did see other examples of repair rules that perform more dramatic changes. We can think back to the case of reduplication. Recall the example from *Tagalog* reduplication in chapter 11:

(17)   C V – C V C V C   [la-lakad]

                 l a   k a d

For the reduplicative prefix to copy phonemes from the base, we need a copying operation. Copying isn't movement, but it comes close. Then, when we discussed infixes, it was suggested that the phonological form of the infix could be regarded as being moved inside the base. Additionally, we could mention the fact that there are, in fact, rules that change the order of phonemes, and such cases do in fact occur. The phenomenon is called **metathesis**. Think of the pair *central* and *center*. In the first word we find the /r/ before the vowel, while in the second word the /r/ occurs after the vowel..

It has, in fact, been suggested that that transformational rules do not move units either, but instead also **copy** them. This leads to two occurrences of the units that are copied, which means that one of them must be deleted, or left unpronounced. Differences among languages could then lie in whether the original or the copy is pronounced.

(18)   Deep structure: John will buy what
                 Copying   **what will** John will buy what
                 Deletion   **what will** John will
                 Deletion   John will buy what
                 Deletion   **what**   John will buy
                 Deletion   **will** John will buy what

The various deletions are options that make languages different. Here I cannot discuss the merits or problems for this copying-plus-deletion theory of movement.

An Alternative to the Complimentizer Phrase Hypothesis?

We might consider an alternative to solve the problem in (7). Let us say that we move phrases while preserving their affiliation to the original positions in the sentence structure. We could represent that idea along the following lines:

(19)

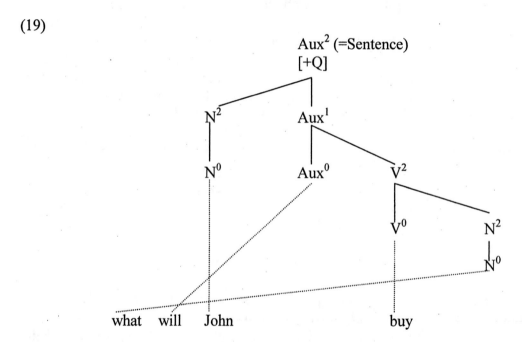

That is a very interesting idea, but it doesn't address the issue that we do need a position for complementizers in embedded sentences. Hence, this idea does not relate all three sentence types.

Why Moves Things Around?

One might wonder *why* it is that words have to be moved (or copied) in a Q-sentence. Why should the Q-word come at the beginning, and why should the Aux-element move to the comp-position in questions but not in statements?

Some languages other than English (such as Chinese languages) do *not* move question words to the front of the sentence, and in languages that do move them, we do not always find the movement of the Aux-element to the beginning. Apparently, languages can differ in terms of the transformational rules that they have, just as they can differ in terms of their phonological repair rules.

Note, by the way, that even in English one *can* leave the question word in its original position (syntacticians say: *in situ*, which is Latin for *in its position*):

(20)   You bought what?

Such questions are called *echo questions*. In English you can only use these expressions in response to someone saying what he bought. So, in fact, an echo question is not a question because you already know the answer. A regular question (What did you buy?), on the contrary, is used when someone has not yet informed you what he bought.

Stepwise (Cyclic) Movement

Finally, let me mention one remarkable property of the movement of question words. Consider the following sentence:

(21)   [When did the boy say [he fell from the tree]]

This sentence is ambiguous because the *when* could inquire about the time of saying or the time of falling. This means that there are two underlying structures:

(22)   a.   [The boy said *when* [he fell from the tree]]

            b.   [The boy said [he fell from the tree *when*]]

To derive the question from underlying structure (a), *when* moves from a position within the matrix sentence to the front of the matrix sentence. To derive the question from underlying structure (b), *when* moves from a position within the embedded sentence to the front of the matrix sentence.

It is interesting in its own right that a question word can move from within an embedded sentence up to the beginning of the matrix sentence. This shows that this kind of movement can cross sentence boundaries. In fact, it can cross more than one boundary:

(23)   [When did the boy say [he saw [Mary fall from the tree]]]

The underlying structure for this sentence is:

(24)   [The boy said [he saw [Mary fall from the tree *when*]]]

But the following are also possible underlying structures:

(25)   a.   [The boy said [he saw *when* [Mary fall from the tree]]]

        b.   [The boy said *when* [he saw [Mary fall from the tree]]]

This means that the sentence has three meanings.

       One might wonder whether the movement from an embedded sentence moves the *when* word in one big step, or in smaller steps:

(26)   [-   The boy said [he saw [Mary fall from the tree *when*]]]

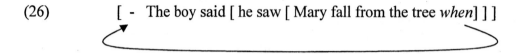

(27)   [-   The boy said [- he saw [- Mary fall from the tree *when*]]]

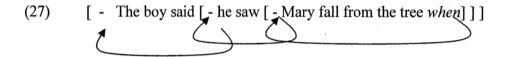

The stepwise movement method may seem more complicated, but there is evidence that this is how things work.

       It seems reasonable to expect that a movement cannot take place in cases where the landing site of the moved entity (the specifier of the complementizer node; see 14) is already occupied so that the presence of a word in that position would block movement. Consider the following sentence:

(28)   [When did the boy say [*how* he fell from the tree]]

In this sentence *how* occupies the position for question words. This means that *when* cannot have come from within the embedded sentence, as we can see in (29):

(29)

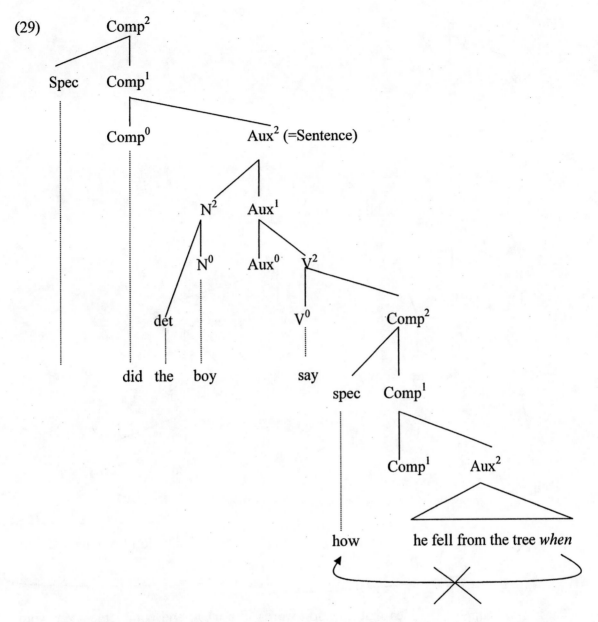

If the *when* in the embedded sentence cannot move to the front within its own sentence, it cannot move further to the front of the matrix sentence either. We can make this even more interesting. Consider the sentence:

(30)   [When did the boy say [that he fell from the tree]]

At first sight you would think that the word *that* must block the reading with *when* coming from the embedded sentence, just like the word *how* in (28) did. But there is a subtle difference between (28) and (30): the word *that* does not occupy the specifier positions of the embedded sentence, it stands in the Comp^0 position:

(31)

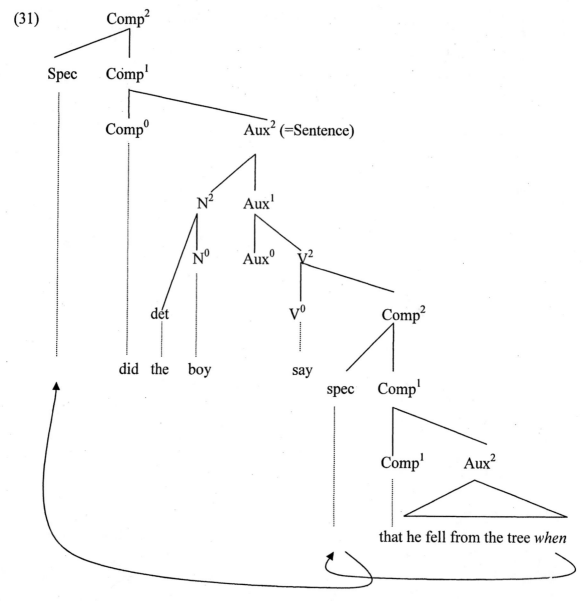

These facts support the idea that question words like *when* and complementizer words like *that* indeed occupy different positions. At the same time, this array of facts supports the idea that the movement of questions words takes place in a step-wise manner.

An Extra Argument for Transformations

Let us assume for a moment that questions and statements are *not* derived from a common phrase structure but instead are produced independently from each other. This could be motivated by the preference to do away with adjustment rules. If we make that move we do not even have to add any phrase structure rules because we could continue to assume that all sentences have the same general Comp shell structure and simply allow positions to remain empty. We will see later that we need to allow for that anyway. In this approach we would produce the sentence *What will John buy?* directly, without any transformations.

(32)   Phrase structure rules & primitives:

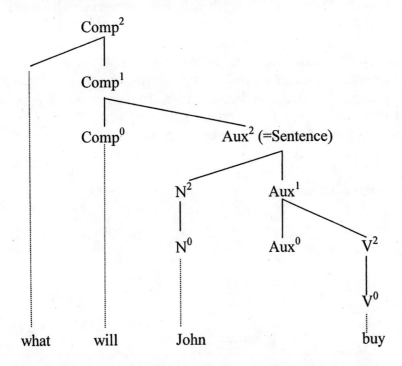

Fair enough, but now consider the needs of the verb *buy*. *Buy* is a transitive verb, and that means that its insertion in a sentence structure is controlled by a **subcategorization property** expressed in its insertion frame that says that this verb **must** be followed by a direct object: $[- N^2]$. It would seem that this property is not satisfied in the structure in (32) because there is no direct object immediately following *buy*. In other words, as far as the grammar is concerned, the preceding sentence should be ruled out in the same way that the following sentence is ruled out:

(33)   *John will buy

We know that the question word *what* in (32), which is all the way in the front of the sentence, acts as the direct object of *buy*! But if we generate the sentence with the question word in the front we will have a hard time explaining how the grammar knows that *what* functions as the object of *buy*. We can't just say, "Look for a Q-word at the beginning, because the following sentence is not grammatical either:

(34)   *what buys?

In fact, another problem that we have when we insert the primitive *what* directly in front (rather than moving it there) is that we can then also make sentences like this one:

(35)   *what will John buy flowers?

You will start to see, I hope, that it is going to be very difficult to come up with a precise procedure that will ensure that *buy* has one, and not more than one, object. We don't have that problem if we follow the analysis that we provided earlier. We insert the question word to the right of the verb. Then we check whether everything is wellformed, in particular whether *buy* has a direct object. This will be so; the direct object will be *what*. Then we move *what* to the specifier of Comp^2 and all is well.

I will add that some linguists have come up with systems of phrase structure rules that avoid all these problems and still can do without transformations. In one variety of this approach we would generate the elements that are moved in the movement approach directly in the position where they are in the surface structure, while we generate an abstract **silent echo** (italicized in 24) of these elements in the position that they have moved from (in the movement analysis).

(36)   Phrase structure rules & primitives:

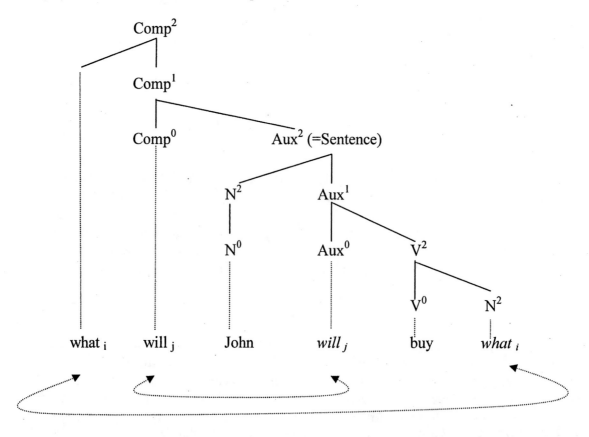

We then say that the silent echoes are not realized in the phonological structure of the sentence (which is why we call them *silent*), even though they are present in the mental representation of the sentence. In addition, we assume that echoes and the real words are **linked** (or **coindexed**) to guarantee that they are semantically identical (and not too far away from each other). This linking or coindexing is indicated by the dotted bidirectional arrow and by subscript letters in (36).

Conclusions

The syntactic–categorial system has the same general design as the phonological and morphological–categorial system (primitives, combination rules, and adjustment rules). The combination rules have the property of recursion, as in the morphological system. (Let us make explicit here that we have not encountered recursivity in the phonological system.)

We have come to the important conclusion that all major sentence types that we have looked at (embedded, questions, or statements) can be derived from one common phrase structure:

(37)

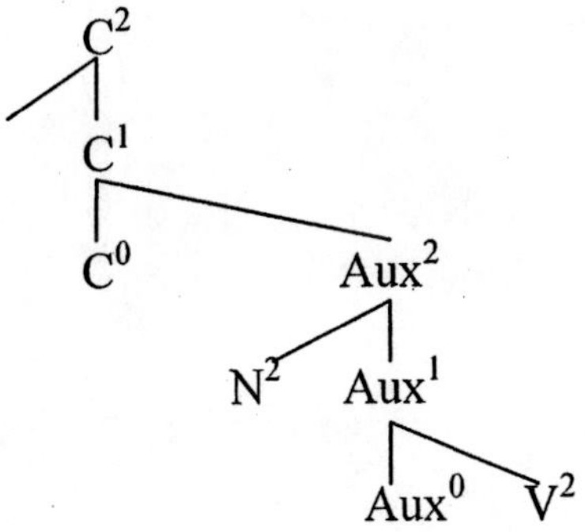

$$
\begin{array}{c}
C^2 \\
C^1 \\
C^0 \quad Aux^2 \\
N^2 \quad Aux^1 \\
Aux^0 \quad V^2
\end{array}
$$

We then discussed two types of syntactic adjustment rules: inflection rules, and transformational rules. Syntactic rules apply first and derive the various sentence types (statements, questions, embedded sentences) from the common underlying structure in (37). Inflectional rules then apply to supply words with endings that are required given the syntactic positions that words are in.

Adding what we have learned in this chapter to the diagram at the end of the previous chapter, we now arrive at the following picture:

Level: word	*Primitives*	*Combinations rules*	*Adjustment rules*		*Special topics*
Phonological system	Phonemes (defined as sets of elements)	Phonotactic rules	- Allophony rules - Phoneme substitution rules		Phonological periodic table
Categorial system	Morpheme and word class labels	Word formation rules	(none discussed)		Right-hand Head Rule
Level: sentence					
Categorial system	Word class labels	Phrase structure rule	- Inflectional rules - Transformational rules		X-bar organization

You will recall that at the sentence level we have only briefly touched on the phonological side (in Chapter 10). In the next chapter, we will take a look at the semantic side of both words and sentences. As promised, when all these aspects are added up, we end up with a total of six grammatical modules, three at the word level and three at the sentence level.

Chapter 13

Semantic Structures
(Word and Sentence Level)

Introduction

I will spend less time on meaning in this book than I did on phonology, morphology, and syntax. This should not be taken to imply that the semantic system is not important. On the contrary. Someone once said:

> Language without meaning is meaningless.

Indeed, with reference to a comparison I made earlier between cells and words, and organisms and sentences, one could say that language without meaning is lifeless. No matter how bonding it can be to listen to someone else's voice, if the noises had no meaning we would sooner or later lose interest in listening and engage in other activities.

Meanings as Concepts

The question *What is meaning?* has caused linguists, philosophers, and many other people to write many books and articles. In this chapter we will see that any answers that one might come up with are likely to be controversial.

Perhaps the most obvious answer is that a meaning is something mental. You might say that knowing the meaning of the word *dog* boils down to having a mental representation or mental description of a certain type of animal. Let us call such a representation or description a **concept**. We would now like to be more precise about this representation or description. Do we envisage a concept as a mental picture, an image of some kind, or rather as a list of necessary properties? If we go the latter way, we face the question of what we mean by *property*. One might answer by listing properties such as having a tail, being furry, making a barking sound, or, more technically, being a mammal, and so. It would seem that these properties must themselves be understood as concepts (the concept of *tail*, of *fur* or *barking sound*), which means that we end up saying that a concept is defined in terms of other, more basic concepts. Clearly, this kind of reduction to smaller, more basic things has to stop at some point, and therefore there must be a point at which we can speak of the most basic concepts, concepts that can no longer be reduced to more basic concepts. Such concepts, one might say, are the primitives of meaning. Note that this still does not answer the question of what a concept *is*, and it would seem that no one has really been able to come up with a good definition or understanding of these mental entities.

Homeless Concepts

Whatever concepts are precisely, let us agree on the idea that the meaning of a word is a concept (or collection of concepts, a conceptual structure). We can also say that a linguistic expression (let us confine the discussion to words for the moment) is made up by three types of mental or cognitive structures: a conceptual structure, a phonological structure, and a categorial structure. These are of course the three dimensions that we talked about extensively in Part I of this book.

To demonstrate that semantic structure exists independently of the two other structures, we can construe conceptual structures that (at present) are not expressed in words, *homeless concepts*, so to speak. There are, in fact, lots of meanings for which we do not have words in English. For example, the little dented area between the nose and the upper lip is a "body part" that English has no word for. (I'm not aware of any other language having a word for it, but that doesn't mean that there *could not* be a word for it.) However, that fact does not prohibit us from thinking about this part of the face, or understanding it as a concept. Concepts that do not correspond to words are like lost souls wandering around in an eternal space looking for bodies to inhabit. We can perhaps always describe these concepts in terms of phrases ("the little dented areas between the nose and the upper lip"), but, when such concepts are of high importance and are frequently in need of being referred to, the best thing is to have a single word for them.

Two people with a sense of humor, **Douglas Adams** and **John Lloyd**, wanted to be helpful and provide word forms for homeless concepts that seem useful. The forms that they used were English place names, the reasoning being that place names (and proper names) are forms without a meaning. Here are some of their "new" words:

> **abilene** (Adj.)—Descriptive of the pleasing coolness on the reverse side of the pillow.

> **ahenny** (Adj.)—The way people stand when examining other people's bookshelves.

> **banff** (Adj.)—Pertaining to, or descriptive of, that kind of facial expression that is impossible to achieve except when having a passport photograph taken.

> **bodmin** (Adj.)—The irrational and inevitable discrepancy between the amount pooled and the amount needed when a large group of people try to pay a bill together after a meal.

> **goole** (N.)—The puddle on the bar into which the barman puts your change.

It would appear that there are many (apparently shared) concepts for which there are no words in English. Many of the proposals that Adams and Lloyd make in their book are highly useful, indeed. Whether they will make it into the English language is another matter. I know very few people who have seen this little funny book.

Again, we must realize that concepts for which there is no single word can still be talked about; we can always describe such a concept. For example, *English* has a word, *pith*, which *Dutch* does not have. The word refers to the white stuff on the inside of an orange peel. Dutch people can talk about it by describing it, much in the same way that I just described it in English.

It is, as we have seen, quite easy to construe meaningless phonological words (recall: *the nog smimmed the plicks*). Likewise, we now realize, we can also construe "phonology-less" meanings.

Are all Linguistic Concepts Thought Concepts?

According to some scholars, concepts (i.e., the meaning side of words) are the same "stuff" that our thoughts are composed of (assuming that thoughts are indeed *compositional*, i.e., constructed out of smaller units). If this is so, it follows that conceptual structures are not specifically linguistic. We have just seen that this is indeed true because there are many wordless concepts that float around in our minds. We can also refer to the fact that we can have thoughts without (silently) making sentences. The claim that you can have thought processes that do not rely on language, i.e., on silently thinking in terms of words, is not easy to prove. It also depends on how broadly you define the notion of thought. It is probably the case that when you are very much aware of your thoughts (because you try to solve a problem in your mind, or concoct a plan) silent language plays a big part. But our minds are roaming around all day and night, and include feelings, emotions, and associations, and you perhaps you will agree that language is not a necessary part of all that is going on.

The view that the semantic side of language draws on an independently given "system of thought" would reduce the grammar *in a strict sense* to just two dimensions: phonology and morphosyntax. *Meaning* in this view arises by linking linguistic expressions (i.e., phonological forms associated with a category label) to a conceptual structure/thought:

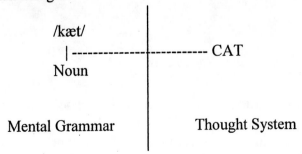

In this view a concept is considered to be a word meaning if, indeed, it associates to a phonological form and word class label. (It is customary to represent concept in terms of English words in capitals.)

Others argue, however, that there *is* a distinction between thoughts on the one hand and a specifically linguistic meaning structure on the other hand. In this view, the two systems (thought and linguistic meaning) are related but not identical. This view holds that of all the concepts that are floating around in our head, a subset has the special status of being part of words, whereas others, well, are just concepts. The latter group of concepts can be described in terms of words, but they are not expressed in terms of a single simplex word.

```
/kæt/
   | -------------------------------- CAT-------------------------CAT
  Noun


Mental Grammar       linguistic concepts          thought concepts
```

If linguistic concepts are a proper subset of thought concepts, it may not be easy to differentiate between the two views just discussed. It would be worthwhile to explore whether there are linguistic concepts that are not possible as thought concepts per se, concepts in other words that can only exist by virtue of being part of a linguistic system. We could call such concepts **grammatical concepts** (meaning: grammar-specific concepts). I will leave undecided here whether such grammar-specific concepts exist. Their existence will be hard to prove because it would involve showing that people whose language lacks a certain grammatical property, which, allegedly, is necessary to have a certain concept, truly do not have that concept, which means that they really cannot grasp it. Things get even more complicated if one would like to argue in favor of grammar specific concepts that exist in *all* languages, because then we would have to turn to people who do not have any language to see whether they can grasp the concept in question. One can think of very young infants or adults who for some reason have grown up without language input. Needless to say that it will be very difficult to test whether such individuals possess or lack a certain concept. *If* grammar-specific concepts exist, one could rightly say that humans would be unable to think certain things if they did not have language. This, however, is a somewhat controversial and indeed difficult to prove claim.

The Sapir-Whorf Hypothesis

A related issue regards the notorious question as to whether the language(s) that we grow up with end up controlling our thought processes to the extent that one could say that people who speak a different language in some sense think differently or have different ways of looking at the world. The view that this is indeed so has a long history in linguistics and anthropology and is known as the **Sapir-Whorf Hypothesis** (after two linguists–anthropologists, Edward Sapir and Benjamin Lee Whorf). This hypothesis is still a matter of controversy, although a case can be made for adopting a weak version of this hypothesis. Language may not be able to control our thoughts, but it can certainly influence our thoughts.

Concepts are considered to be mental entities in their own right, and their potential basis in experience is considered irrelevant. Such extreme conceptualists will point to concepts that do not correspond to existing entities in the real world such as the concept UNICORN and practically all non-human creatures in the worlds of *Star Trek*. They might furthermore claim that the most basic concepts, out of which more complex concepts can be constructed at will, are perhaps innate properties of the human mind.

A Strict Non-Referential View of Meaning

We have thus far implied perhaps that concepts necessarily correspond to things in the real world. If this were so, one might believe that concepts arise in the mind by generalizing over many exposures to things in the world. We can also imagine someone having the view that the existence of real word entities that concepts refer to is irrelevant to a theory of word meaning or semantics in general. Thus, proponents of a strict-non-referential semantics are not committed to the idea that concepts derive from exposure to the world and thus not to the necessity of there being an actual referent for each concept.

A Strict Referential View of Meaning

Accepting the difficulty in defining precisely what concepts are, most people assume that entities of this sort exist in our minds. We might now ask the question of whether concepts/conceptual structures exist in their own right (as units of thought and word meanings) and are as such independent from the outside world, or whether concepts must **refer** to things and events in the real, mind-external world.

In accordance with this question we find two types of semanticists, namely those who treat semantics as an autonomous (non-sensory-based) system of concepts (**non-referential** or **internalist semantics**) and those who treat semantics as a system of correspondence rules between linguistic expressions (words and sentences) and the mind-external world (**referential** or **externalist semantics**). In referential semantics, at the level of *words*, concepts refer to (or stand for) things in the world; these things could be called **referents**. Note that the externalist and internalist view of *concept* applies to concepts in general and not just to those that are used within the linguistic system. The preceding diagram, in fact, depicts the internalist view. The externalist view would add referents:

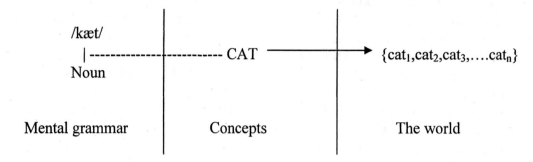

The referent of the concept CAT is of course not one specific cat. Rather, the concept can be used to refer to any cat, or, as semanticists like to say: the **set** of all cats (past, present, and future). Instead of the term *set*, one also often uses the term **category**. A category, then, is the set of entities to which a specific concept refers. Clearly, most categories are open-ended. This means that a concept must allow us to identify entities that have never been encountered as belonging to the relevant category.

So who is right, the internalist or the externalist? At first sight you might be inclined to say that the referential approach simply adds an extra dimension to the internalist view. Both approaches agree on there being concepts, which are mind-internal entities. The externalist simply adds to this that these mind-internal concepts are related to mind-external entities, and that hardly seems a controversial point to make. The two views can be made more extreme and polarizing, however.

Cutting Out the Middle Man

In an extreme externalist view it is claimed that we can even skip the notion of concept altogether and say that the meaning of a word simply *is* the set of things that the word refers to (or denotes). For example, we would say that the meaning of *cat is* the set of all (possible) cats:

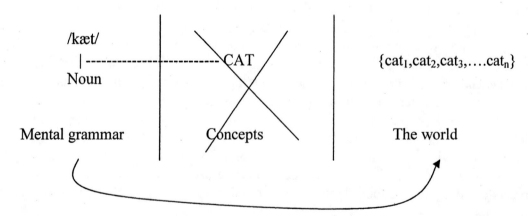

We could refer to this view as the non-mental externalist approach, i.e., in this approach no mental entity called *concept* forms part of what we call *meaning*.

An apparent obvious problem for this approach is that many words have meanings that do not seem to correspond to anything in the real world. Think of the word *unicorn*, for example. To this, the non-mental externalist answers that the referents of words do not have to exist in the present-day real world. The referent must be something that could potentially exist, if not in our world, then in some **possible world**. This could be yesterday's world, the world 100.000 years ago, some future world, or, indeed, a fantasy world. Each such world can be represented as a (set-theoretic) model consisting of entities, relations between entities, and actions of entities, and words could then be said to refer to entities, relations, and actions in some model. This approach is called **model-theoretic semantics**.

Is There an Outside World?

Another objection to the non-mental externalist view is that according to many people we cannot really know what is in the (or an) external world. According to this view, we can only know our sensory experiences of the outside world. To put this differently, we can only know the way that we represent the outside world in or mind. This view, in fact, makes it easier to speak of non-existing possible worlds because such worlds necessarily only exist in our mind. In fact, it would seem that all these possible mind-internal worlds (one of which allegedly corresponds to the actual world) are not too different from the models that a model-theoretic semanticist works with if we are willing to assign a psychological status to these models.

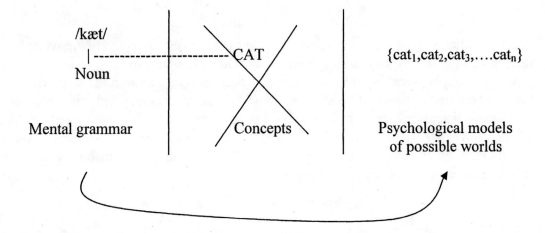

The objection that we cannot truly know the outside world can thus be countered by saying that we know mental representations of this world, and this view has as a bonus that we can make more sense of possible worlds because these would be mental constructs in the first place.

Bringing Both Approaches Closer Together

One might argue that the strict non-referential semanticist cannot explain how it is possible that we use language to talk about (our mental representation of) the outside world. In fact, strictly speaking, such a semanticist is committed to the view that we can only talk about concepts. What the relationship is between these concepts and our perception of the outside world is left undefined. The strict referential semanticist, on the other hand, overlooks the fact that conceptual structure is independently needed if it is the case that linguistic expressions catch only a part of the conceptual representations that make up our thought.

Looking back at the last diagram, you might wonder, as I do, how much difference there really is between mental concepts (that may or may not correspond to things in the real world) and psychological models (that may or may not correspond to things in the real world). However, let us grant that a distinction of this sort can be made and that concepts are different from psychological models of possible worlds. Concepts, one might argue, are more abstract as they generalize over many instances of all the members that belong to categories in our psychological models of possible worlds.

The question is now whether a proper theory of semantics should deal only with concepts, only with referents (now understand as the ingredients of our psychological world models), or with both. We can represent all the relationships that we have been discussing in the following triangle, often called the **semiotic triangle**:

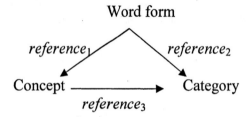

A strict conceptualist will only deal with the arrow labeled *reference₁*, while a strict referentialist will only deal with the arrow labeled *reference₂*. In both cases, the package of word form plus what is referred to can be understood as a sign in the semiotic sense. It seems to me that a theory of semantics should primarily be concerned with *reference₃*, in those cases where *reference₁* in fact holds, that is in those case in which a concept is used linguistically by being linked to (referred to by) a (phonological) word form. This raises the question of whether there is any need at all for a direct relationship between forms and categories.

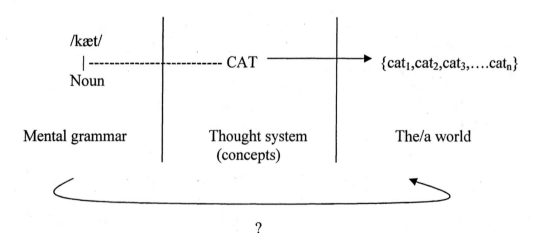

There are several classes of words in all languages that either have no conceptual contents at all, or whose conceptual content, if taken to be the meaning by itself, seems to miss something important. The first category consists of **proper names,** and the second category consists of **pronouns** (like *he, I, they, mine,* etc.), **determiners** (like *a, the, this, that*). and adverbs (like *here, there,* etc.).

Proper names seem to have no conceptual content at all. All proper names are only meaningful in a specific context in which they are used to refer to a specific entity. (At best, proper names might contain information about the type of entity that they refer to. For example, Peter is most likely a name of a male.)

The other examples of semantically near-empty words are pronouns. A pronoun does have some semantic content. The pronoun *she,* for example, has the concepts FEMALE and SINGULAR. But beyond that there is nothing. I can say *I saw a dog watching a movie,* and that would be a contentful and thus surprising bit of information. But if I say *I saw him watching a movie,* the response is most likely *Who is him*? So, even though in the first case we don't know which specific dog was doing this remarkable thing, we still know a lot more than when we hear the sentence with *him*. Similar remarks could be made about determiners. If I say, out of the blue, *Can you buy me that book?,* you will have no idea what to buy. If, on the other hand, I point to a specific book while uttering the sentence, or if we have just been discussing a specific book, you will understand which book I'm referring to. Likewise, if I say *Let us go there,* you will have no clue where to go unless I point to a place or refer back to a place we've been talking about. What do we make of all this? It would seem that some words more than others get their specific meaning only when uttered in a specific context.

Expression Meaning and Utterance Meaning

To address the issues just discussed, semanticists will tell us that we have to distinguish several layers of meaning. The following three-way distinction is sometimes made:

Expression meaning
The meaning of a linguistic expression, when considered in isolation, i.e., out of any context

Utterance meaning
The meaning of a linguistic expression when used in a specific context

Communicative meaning
The meaning of a linguistic expression as a communicative act

So far we have been talking about what we will henceforth call **expression meaning,** the meaning proper, so to speak, i.e., the meaning that a linguistic expression has by itself in the mental lexicon. Normal nouns, verbs, adjectives, and adverbs have lots of expression meaning, but words belonging other classes often have very little expression meaning. Proper nouns, one might argue, have no expression meaning at all. The expression meaning of linguistic expressions is a conceptual structure (about which more below).

We now turn to the **utterance meaning**. Linguistic expressions are meant to be used, and we use them in actual situations. When used in an actual situation we **fix the reference** of the conceptual structure of a linguistic expression. Coming back to our last diagram, one might argue that fixing the reference comes about by relating the word form-plus-conceptual structure to entities and events in the situation in which the utterance is used. This means we do *not* really need the *direct link* from word form to referent, but we do crucially need the arrow going from the conceptual structure to the referent. It is this relationship that establishes the utterance meaning.

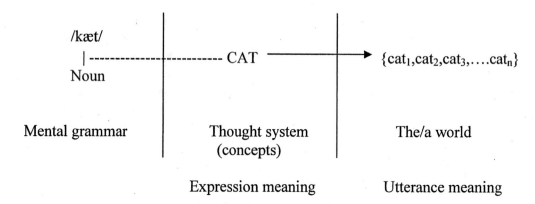

Through fixation, all words acquire a fixed referent or class of referents. When used in a specific situation, it is clear (or at least it should be) what the referents are of pronouns, adverbs, or expressions like *that dog* or *the dog*.

We have now discovered that *conceptual semantics*, which studies meaning as conceptual structure (expression meaning), and model-theoretical semantics are not at all in conflict with each other. Both are, so it would seem, necessary parts of the study of linguistic meaning.

And there is more. The perhaps most important dimension of meaning is that when we produce linguistic expressions, we usually have the intention to change the behavior and/or state of mind of other people. We wish to make a **statement**, ask a **question**, issue a **command** or a **warning**, and so on. In other words, when we make an utterance we often perform a communicative act, or, as the specialists say, a **speech act**. This dimension of meaning is called **communicative meaning**.

Semantics and Pragmatics

In addition to semantics, we also have what is called **pragmatics,** which studies everything beyond the literal, i.e., expression meaning. Thus, what was called communicative meaning would certainly, in most linguists' understanding, be part of pragmatics. As for the utterance meaning, one might find some who make this part of pragmatics, while others consider it semantics. These definitional differences are not of any deep importance, however.

Layers of Meaning Within Expression Meaning

Things are never simple, especially not when we try to understand what meaning is. We have established that there are three layers of meaning for any linguistic expression that is used in a specific situation. Before we continue with issues that regard the meaning of linguistic expressions that are morphologically or syntactically complex, let us take a closer look at expression meaning, as before mostly focusing on the meaning of words. Again we can distinguish three layers:

> Descriptive meaning
> Expression meaning that defines potential referents
>
> Social meaning
> Expression meaning that correlates with rules of social conduct
>
> Emotive meaning
> Expression meaning that conveys subjective attitudes

I will give some examples of each dimension of expression meaning. Bear in mind that we speak of expression meaning in each case because the meaning aspects we consider are part and parcel of a linguistic expression when taken in isolation, i.e., outside of any specific context.

A word like *dog* has a clear **descriptive meaning** because the conceptual structure of dog is such that it defines a set of potential referents, i.e., the set of all dogs. Dog has no social or emotive meaning. In many languages we find different pronouns, the choice of which depends on what your social relation is to the person that you are addressing. Corresponding to English *you*, Dutch has three pronouns *jij*, *jullie* and *U*. The difference between *jij* and *jullie* is that between singular and plural, which is part of their descriptive meaning. The third pronoun *U* can be used for singular and plural, but, and this is what we focus on here, you would use it when addressing a person older than you or a person who somehow has a higher status. So you would say *U* to your parents, a police officer, and the queen. The difference between *jij/jullie* and *U* is one of **social meaning**. These pronouns, then, have both descriptive meaning (although little because they are pronouns) and social meaning. In other languages, like Japanese, there are lots of words or parts of words (affixes) that have a social meaning dimension. In fact, in English (and probably all other languages), we have many word pairs that are alike in descriptive meaning but would not be used in the same social context. You can probably easily think of examples from the domain of many body parts and activities that are used in the semantic domain of sexual reproduction.

Any linguistic expression can be uttered with various emotions that depend on a variety of factors, but some words have the specific function of expressing emotions. Examples of such words are **interjections** and **exclamations** (like *wow*, *ouch*, *ajaja*i, and so on), and curses or swear words (like *godammit*). We say that such words have **emotive meaning**. In fact, often such words have very little other meaning.

Encyclopedic Information and Connotations

When I use the word dog in your presence, we presumably both activate the same conceptual structure (DOG). In addition, however, we will both experience a host of dog-related associations that could be but are not necessarily the same. Any given person might have all sorts of knowledge about dogs, from books or personal experience, e.g., that they are a man's best friend, that you have to walk them, that they can bark annoyingly or poop on your doorstep, and so on. Some of that knowledge is often called **encyclopedic knowledge** (if it concerns fairly objective facts that are or could be generally known), while other associations are referred to as **connotations**. Connotations can be positive or negative and are more subjective and personal than encyclopedic knowledge. When we say that *he eats like a lion*, we draw on a connotation of the word *lion* such as *eats ferociously*.

It is generally accepted that encyclopedic information and connotations fall outside the domain of meaning (whether expressive, with its three subdivisisions, utterance, or social meaning). However, if connotations, especially negative connotations, become very strong and generally held within a speech community this might affect the use of a word in that people will avoid it in most situations, except when they wish to be rude. Often in those cases a word with a near equivalent descriptive meaning will take its place, and that then leads to a both words having acquired a dimension of social meaning.

Double Talk

Related to the previous avoidance of words with negative connotations is what is often called *double speak* (or *double talk*), which refers to a situation of language use in which the speaker avoids the use of a word that has negative connotations and replaces it by a word or expression that is new and thus neutral (or even overly loaded with misplaced positive connotations).

> *pass away* for *die*
> *air support* for *bombing*
> *lay off* for *fire*

The more friendly sounding word or phrase is also called a *euphemism*. The linguist William Lutz has published widely about this phenomenon and other related misleading uses of words and phrases, which are especially popular among governmental bodies.

Compositionality

When we speak about the meaning of a linguistic expression we generalize over the meaning of simplex expressions (i.e., monomorphemic words, or affixes; **morphemes** in essence) and the meaning of expressions that are complex. An expression is complex if it consists of several morphemes (forming a complex word) or of several words (forming a sentence). However, the meaning of complex expressions raises a specific question, which is how their meaning can be known.

We know the meaning of morphemes because morphemes are listed in the lexicon as combinations of phonological form, meaning, and category label. Thus, the meaning of a morpheme is, in a sense, given, namely in the lexicon. We have memorized it, so to speak. When someone uses a (monomorphemic) word that we have never heard before, we do not know its meaning and we have to ask the person about it.

Complex words may also be entirely new to us, but when exposed to those we often do know what they mean. How is that possible? How can we know the meaning of a word that we have never heard or seen before? For example, after we have just discussed that some people have been contacted to hand in their work, while others have not, I might say to you, *Why don't you talk to the contactees*? Then I will go after the people I haven't talked to yet. Presumably *contactee* is a word you have never heard before. Yet you understand that it means *people who have been contacted*, just as *employee* means *people that have been or are employed*. You know the meaning of *contactee* because you know the meaning of *contact* and you know the meaning of the suffix *–ee*. You simply put these two meanings together and, *voilá*, you know the meaning of the whole thing. You *compose* the meaning of the whole thing from the meaning of its parts.

This kind of semantic composition is something you do all the time, especially when listening to sentences. During each waking hour, while listening to others or reading things, you digest sentences that you probably have never heard or seen before. (I bet that this book is full of them.)

We have learned in the preceding chapters that there are an infinite number of complex words and sentences, which means that it could never be true that we know and understand languages because we have memorized all the expressions.

The inescapable fact that we can compute the meaning of complex expressions is referred to as **compositionality**. In computing the meaning of complex expressions we take into account what the parts mean, but, and this must be added, also how those parts have been combined. We already discussed this in Part I. *Lover boy* means something different from *boy lover*, and this means that the order of the parts is important. But not just the order. Also the grouping. *I saw the man with binoculars* can mean two things depending on whether *with binoculars* is grouped together with *man* or with *saw the man*. All this leads to the following formulation of what is called:

<u>The Principle of Compositionality</u>
The meaning of a complex expression can be derived from the meaning of its parts, and how these parts have been combined.

Now, complex expressions, having come into general use, can acquire meaning aspects that are unpredictable in terms of this principle. For example, the meaning of *sleeper* as *foreign undercover agent who has blended in as a regular citizen* cannot be predicted from the meaning of *sleep* and *–er* in that order. This means that the word *sleeper* must be listed in the lexicon with that meaning. Likewise, fixed expressions such as *he kicked* *the bucket*, meaning *he died*, must be listed in the lexicon, which thus contains more than just words (see Chapter 14).

The Semantic Word System

With all these preliminary matters out of the way (although we will return to some of them), let us now discuss some more specific issues at the level of the semantic word and sentence system, starting with the *fomer*.

The area of semantics at the word level is often call **lexical semantics**. Lexical semantics has five main goals. First, focusing on what we have called **descriptive expression meaning**, it tries to decompose these meanings into smaller pieces; these pieces do not have generally accepted terms because there are various approaches. Terms like *semantic features*, *semantic properties*, and *(basic) concepts* are often found. As stated in Part 1, we can think of these primitives as primitives of human thought, perhaps in part innately given.

The second goal is to catalogue and explain meaning-specific relationships between words such as the relation between *flower* and *tulip* (subset relation) or between *good* and *bad* (opposites), etc. We will see that analyses of such relationships typically presuppose some form of lexical decomposition.

The third goal is to study the phenomenon that most words have more than one, in fact, multiple meanings. Open a dictionary and you realize immediately that is it highly unusual to find just one meaning listed under each **lemma** (i.e., dictionary entry).

The fourth goal is to account for different ways in which words can be creatively used to express thoughts, or to refer to things and events that do seem to be in the scope of their (descriptive expression) meaning. The latter point is nontrivial in view of the fact that one can use, for example, the word *foot* not only to refer to a certain body part of many animal species, but also to the lower part of a mountain, as well as other things like a certain unit of measurement. It would appear that the semantic structure of words is highly flexible, such that words can be used in novel circumstances all the time.

Finally, we will turn to the meaning of complex words.

The Primitives

One can think of the semantic system as being organized in the same way that the other grammatical systems are organized:

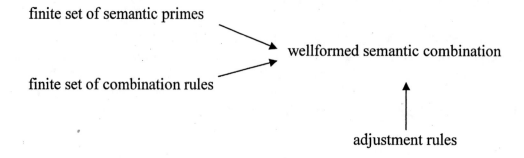

268

The primitives of semantic structure are atomic **concepts**, that is, basic concepts that do not seem to be divisible into smaller concepts. The big question is: What are these basic concepts? This question, as it turns out, is not so easy to answer; in fact, some semanticists consider the quest for the ultimate semantic building blocks fruitless.

An argument for saying that word meanings consist of smaller semantic units comes from the fact that we can group them into "natural classes" (as we could do with phonemes on different grounds):

> *girl, woman, lady, aunt, widow, mistress*

All seem to fall into the class of *females*. In fact, they also all fall into the class of *humans*. We can show that FEMALE and HUMAN are distinct semantic properties, because both, taken by themselves, form classes that exclude the other:

> FEMALE: all the above and *doe, hen, mare*, etc.
> HUMAN: all the above and *human, baby, parent, child, man, boy, actor, uncle*, etc.

(As before, we will use capitals to represent semantic units, either whole word meanings or meaning ingredients.)

Labels like FEMALE and HUMAN stand for properties of *things*; that is, all the above are things, making THING also a candidate as a semantic property. Another special semantic property of nouns is involved in the following difference:

> man, flower, game   vs.   rice, water, gold

The former can be counted and, accordingly, put in a plural form, whereas the latter cannot. There thus is a semantic property, let us say MASS, that the former three lack. We can then say that the presence of the property MASS prevents the addition of PLURAL (which indeed can itself be thought of as a semantic property).

Recall that **proper names** are special in that they have very little meaning. They are almost purely referring. Take a name like *John*. At best it contains the semantic property MALE.

Now consider the conceptual structure of some other types of words, starting with verbs. The verbs *kill, trip, frighten* all share a meaning element, CAUSE:

> kill   CAUSE TO DIE
> trip   CAUSE TO FALL
> frighten   CAUSE TO BE FRIGHTENED

Other semantic properties of verbs can be seen in the following verbs:

fall, walk, fly	MOTION
touch, smash, push	CONTACT
burn, melt, grow	CHANGE OF STATE
all the above	EVENT

Many basic adjectives correspond to basic semantic concepts that express properties:

big	BIG
small	SMALL
big, small, etc.	PROPERTY

Whereas others belong to classes:

red, blue, black	COLOR

Prepositions seem to correspond to relational concepts:

in	IN
before	BEFORE
in, before, …	RELATION (IN TIME OR PLACE)

While conjunctions seem to correspond to logical concepts:

and	AND
or	OR
and, or	LOGICAL RELATION

Many words—especially nouns, verbs, and adjectives—correspond to sets of semantic properties, whereas other word categories typically correspond to one semantic property.

It is not always easy to decide whether a given concept is basic or can still be further divided into smaller (more) basic concepts. For example, one might argue that the concept BIG is not basic as it involves the more basic notion SIZE. It is not exactly clear (at least to me) what the criteria are for recognizing a concept as basic. This, in part, has to do with the distinction we made earlier between meaning and encyclopedic knowledge. We know that the *thing* water consists of two hydrogen atoms and one oxygen atom, but these properties do not qualify as semantic properties of the *word meaning* WATER. In this case that may be clear, but in many other cases the distinction is not so clear.

Finally, note that the semantic properties are not all of the same rank. For example, the properties THING and EVENT seem to be higher-order properties that embrace whole sets of lower-order properties:

THING $\Rightarrow$ FEMALE, MALE, HUMAN, etc.

EVENT⇒ CAUSE, CONTACT, CHANGE

Thus, there is some sort of hierarchical network that holds concepts together. Related to this idea of a network of concepts is the idea that the concepts that make up the meaning of a word also form a network, with some concepts being more central (or prototypical) and others being more peripheral.

The preceding overview has been very haphazard. This was not a systematic overview of semantic properties (what they are, and how you can establish them). As I said, some semanticists believe that the idea of analyzing word meanings in terms of basic concepts is the wrong way to go. I do not share this view, however. I believe that we can maintain the general idea that word-level semantics has the same architecture as the other components, namely of having a finite set of primes and a finite set of combination rules.

Thematic Roles

The semantic analysis of verbs calls for a special category of semantic concepts called **roles**. Each verb meaning involves some kind of event in which we find **participants** and **circumstances**. For example, many verbs involve an AGENT, that is, someone "doing the doing" as in the verb *(to) kill*, where someone is doing the killing. This verb also has a second role, referring to the entity that is being killed; this role is called the THEME. We should not confuse the term AGENT with **subject**, which is a syntactic notion. The phrase that is the subject of a sentence is not always, semantically, an AGENT. In the sentence *John saw the door*, John is not an AGENT, because John is not actively doing anything. Rather, *John* is now called an EXPERIENCER. Another role is LOCATION, as in *He put the car in the garage*, where *in the garage* has the role of LOCATION.

We find different lists of roles in different books and studies, and I will not try to come up here with a definite survey. However, the point remains that the roles are part and parcel of the conceptual structure of verbs.

Intuitions About Relationships Between Words

Assuming that we have listed all our semantic primitives (a job that is not finished yet, in part because of methodological problems), we can account for the fact that speakers have intuitions about all sorts of relationships among the meanings of words. Important **semantic relations** among word meanings other than identity are:

- **Synonymy**: words having the same descriptive expression meaning
- **Hyponymy**: including relation (*flower* includes *rose*)
- **Hyperonymy**: included relation (*rose* is included in *flower*)

In addition, there is a whole array of cases that involve **opposition:**

- **Antonymy**: word meanings express opposite poles on a scale (*large, small*)
- **Direct opposites**: two words divide a scale (above, below)
- **Complementaries**: two words are logical opposites within a domain (*aunt, uncle*)
- **Heteronymy**: several words cut op a domain (color words, days of the week)
- **Converses**: words that indicate reversible relations (*husband, wife*)

Not all these types are mutually exclusive. *Above/below* is both an example of direct opposites and of converses.

Clearly, we can account for all these relations (rather than just listing them with examples) if we analyze words into smaller building blocks. Synonyms, for example, would be words that share all conceptual building blocks. A hyperonym would have a component that is the main component of its hyponym, and so on.

Homonymy and Polysemy

A big problem in lexical semantics is the fact that most words seem to have more than one meaning. Here we have to be careful in distinguishing between the case in which two words happen to have the same phonological form and those cases in which we want to say that one word form has several (related) meanings. In the first case we speak of homonymy:

- **homonymy**: two words have the same form
  if *form* is phonological form we speak of: **homophony** (*new, knew*)
  if *form* is written form we speak of **homography** (*read*, present tense, and *read*, past tense)

Homonymy is not so widespread in languages. However, almost every word has more than one meaning such that these meanings are related. In that case we speak of polysemy:

- **polysemy**: one word has more than one (related) meaning

The form *light* is interesting for our purposes. On the one hand we have two words *light*, one meaning *visible radiation*, the other meaning *not heavy*. This is a case of homonymy (and indeed both homophony as well as homography). When we then focus on the *radiation* light and look it up in a dictionary we find a wide variety of meanings as exemplified in sentences such as:

> When the sun comes up it will be light
> In the distance we can see a light
> Can you give me a light
> We need to change the light
> And so on

Thus the word *light* (as a noun) can mean: visible radiation, a flame to light a cigarette, a light bulb, and so on. Clearly all these meanings are related, yet the word can be used in all these ways and the context of use will make it clear which meaning is being used.

Here is another example involving the verb *run*:

> He runs a mile every day.
> The water runs trough the pipe.
> His nose runs.
> He runs a business.

We are usually totally unaware of the fact that we use words in a variety of circumstances that seem to evoke different (yet related) meanings, assuming indeed that there is some commonality in all the different uses.

How do we account for this **polysemy**? In almost all cases, we seem to have a sense that one of the meanings is more central than the others (visible radiation, running as a fast form of human locomotion) and it would seem that the other meanings are somehow derivable from this central meaning. Perhaps, indeed, we can think of the semantic structure of words as involving central concepts and peripheral concepts while saying that the semantic context that words appear in may determine which of the concepts are actualized.

Another question is: How does polysemy arise? It is reasonable to suppose that the more central meaning is the original or oldest meaning and that the other meanings came into existence through a diachronic process of semantic change. How do such diachronic changes come about? In the next section, we'll have something to say about that question.

Metonymy and Metaphor

People play with the semantic properties of words by sometimes using words in novel or at least unexpected ways. If someone says:

> There were only 20 heads present

while referring to a meeting, he doesn't **literally** mean that there were 20 *heads* in the meeting room. Rather he implies that there were 20 *people*. Thus *head* (part of a person) is used for the whole thing. This phenomenon is called **metonymy** (or **synecdoche**), a word use in which we refer to something by using another word that either has a broader or narrower meaning. In the previous example *heads* has a narrower meaning than persons. (This is also called **pars pro toto**, a Latin phrase that says precisely that.) If, as I regularly do, we say *we* where we mean *I*, we use a term that is broader (*we*) to refer to a narrower concept (*I*). Here are some more examples: I wear wool (for a sweater made of wool), or I read Kafka (a book by Kafka). In the last example it isn't even clear whether a book is part of the totality of the person Kafka, but still there is a relationship of some sort between the person Kafka and the books that he wrote.

Often cases metonymy are "frozen" and well known, but people can certainly be creative and come up with new ones:

I had five baseball caps in my classroom today.

When I say this, I mean that there were five people wearing a baseball cap.

Metonymic use of words creates the seeds for semantic change. If a particular case is used frequently, it could happen that the extended usage starts to be seen as a simple and independent, yet related, meaning of the word. Consider the word *chip* in the context of computer technology, and compare that to the original *chip* (of wood).

There is a second way in which extended use comes about, namely **metaphoric usage**. Take the following two sentences:

a.   When it comes to eating, my child is *like* a giant.
b.   When it comes to eating, my child is a giant.

When I use the (a) sentence, I am comparing my child to a giant; that is, I am comparing his appetite to that of a giant (and I am assuming that giants have big appetites). In the (b) sentence I do the same thing, but now I say that my child *is* a giant, which, of course I do not mean **literally**. This is a different kind of non-literal usage from synecdoche and metonyms. In metaphoric usage we place a word meaning in a context in which we are forced to select only one particular semantic property while suppressing the others. Metaphors, then, are based on a partial similarity between the entity that we wish to refer to and the referent of the word that we are using.

The linguist George Lakoff (1941) has constructed an extensive theory of human cognition on the basis of metaphors. In his view, the metaphors we use in language reveal how we think about the world, how we represent relationships. The use of metaphors, says Lakoff, "is pervasive in everyday life, not just in language but in thought and action. Our ordinary conceptual system, in terms of which we both think and act, is fundamentally metaphorical in nature." (Lakoff and Johnson 1980, 3). The evidence for this claim comes from examining the way in which metaphor influences the use of words. Here is an example that Lakoff and Johnson give to show that our use of words reveals that we think about argumentation as a form of war (on their page 4):

> Your claims are *indefensible.*
> He *attacked every weak point* in my arguments.
> His criticisms were *right on target.*
> I *demolished* his arguments.
> I've never *won* an argument with him.
> You disagree? Okay, *shoot!*
> If you use that *strategy,* he'll *wipe you out.*
> He *shot down* all my arguments.

It would seem that all the italicized words are perfectly normal and ordinary words to use, and you don't have to feel very poetic when you use these words. However, this clearly shows how our use of words is heavily based on making implicit comparisons between physical events (like fighting, shooting) and more abstract nonphysical events (like arguing).

Semantic Combination Rules

Semantic primitives must be combined to form complex concepts or word meanings. What are the properties of this combinatorial system? In some approaches, word meanings may simply be a list of concepts (perhaps ordered from more central to less central). This list view was a hallmark of many early theories of word meaning, which see word meanings as a list of semantic features (where each feature stands for a primitive concept). An example of this approach would be to represent the meaning of the word *dog* as a list of semantic features, e.g., [animal], [mammal], [four-legged], [furry], etc.

In other cases, the meaning of a word will take the form of a **complex conceptual expression,** which can be characterized in the form of a formulae with brackets or a tree structure. So, for example, it might be argued that the verb *(to) kill* has the following conceptual structure:

a.   CAUSE (y, BECOME (DEAD (x)))

b.

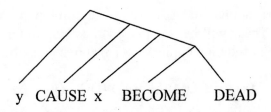

y CAUSE x   BECOME   DEAD

In this approach, we still have semantic primitives (like CAUSE, BECOME, DEAD), but rather than just listing them we organize them in a hierarchical structure that reflects how they "hang together." When we write these expressions, they look like paraphrases of the word, but of course they aren't. The idea is that the meaning of *(to) kill* is represented in the mind of the speaker in terms of the semantic primitives CAUSE, BECOME, DEAD organized in a manner that reflects how they go together. The *y* and *x* are variables that can be filled in by the meaning of the *agent* of the verb *to kill* and the *them* (or target) of this verb. Having two such variables, the meaning structure of *to kill* is, what we call, a two-place predicate. To become a complete expression a two-place predicate must be combined with two arguments. The term *argument* is apt because a two-place predicate is like a (complex) function that will be satisfied by being applied to two arguments:

> function application (the underlined part that is placed between square brackets is the function, the bold part is the argument, the part behind the = is the value that the function returns when applied to its argument:

> a. [CAUSE (y, BECOME (DEAD(x)))] **MAN** =
> > CAUSE (MAN, BECOME (DEAD (x)))

> b. [CAUSE (MAN, BECOME (DEAD (x)))] **DOG** =
> > CAUSE (MAN, BECOME (DEAD (DOG)))

The meanings that results can be paraphrases, as:

> "(the) man kill(s) (the) dog"

(We haven't really dealt with the semantics of the parts between parentheses though.)

All transitive verbs (like *kill*) are two-place predicates (whether or not they can be decomposed into smaller concepts), while intransitive verbs (like *sleep*) are one place predicates:

> SLEEP (x) MAN = SLEEP (MAN)   (the) man sleep(s)

It is common to view not only verbs but also nouns (like *man*, *dog*) and adjectives (*small*) as predicates that need an argument:

> MAN (x), DOG (x), SMALL (x), etc.

This means that when verbs, nouns, and adjectives are combined some variables will remain in the final formula. These will be satisfied by the actual referent of these words. This means that the outcome of function application (b) above is really:

> CAUSE (MAN (x), BECOME (DEAD (DOG (y))))

In the formula view of word meaning (as opposed to just having a list of semantic features), it is almost as if the conceptual system forms a language in its own right, often called **the language of thought** or **mentalese**. In this language of thought, the basic concepts are the words, while the way of combining them is the syntax. In other words, mentalese has the by now familiar structure:

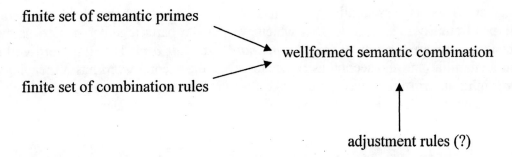

If this is the correct way of viewing things, then we can say that linguistic expressions (sets of categorial and phonological structures) get their meaning by being paired with expressions from the language of thought.

The Semantic Structure of Complex Words

So far we have discussed the meaning side of simplex words or single free morphemes, making the point that the meaning of such morphemes is most likely a formula consisting of basic concepts and variables. Now I briefly turn to the meaning side of (morphologically) complex words. Because we are capable of interpreting complex words that we have never heard before, there must be a mechanism that accounts for that.

For starters, we need to reflect on the meaning structure of affixes. We have said several times that affixes have meanings. The suffix *–er* means, roughly, "SOMEONE WHO Vs," where V stands for any verb. Given what we have said about free morphemes, it seems reasonable to expect that the meaning of affixes can also be analyzed in terms of basic semantic primitives and formulae. Accordingly, we can group affixes in classes based on their semantic structure. The suffix *–er* and the suffix *–ee* (in *employee*) both have the semantic element, PERSON, for example. The suffix *–en* (in *blacken*) has the semantic element CAUSE, and its full semantic representation is something like this:

$$-en : \text{CAUSE (y, BECOME (A (x)))}$$

We can apply this function to an actual adjective, black:

$$black: \text{BLACK(x)}$$

function application:

$$[\underline{\text{CAUSE (y, BECOME (A (x)))}}] \text{ (BLACK(x))} =$$

$$[\text{CAUSE (y, BECOME (BLACK(x)))}]$$

The value of the semantic function of the morpheme *–en*, when applied to the semantics of the adjective *black*, returns the meaning of the verb *to blacken*.

We have now explained how it can be that the meaning of a complex word *as a whole* can be derived from the meaning of its parts and the way that they have been put together. This is essentially what has been called **the principle of semantic compositionality**. That the way in which we put the parts together matters is evident when we compare these two words: *arm chair* and *chair arm*. The first word will strike you as familiar and the second as new. However, the second word has a meaning in its own right: an arm that feels/like/etc. like a chair. The precise meaning, in other words, depends on which element is the function and which is the argument.

The Meaning of So-Called Functional Morphemes

While it seems intuitively clear what the meaning is of nouns, verbs, adjectives and prepositions (although less with the last one than with the first three), the meaning of many other words is not so clear at all. Firstly, we have already mentioned that words like pronouns (*I, me, you, she, his,* etc.) and words like *here, there,* etc. have a very minimal expression meaning. The use of these words is especially dependent on the context of use, which will give them their utterance meaning. But there are many other words that seem to depend rather heavily on context such as:

and, or, not, because, if, all, some, every, most, etc.

As opposed to words that have a clear independent expression meaning, these severely context dependent words are sometimes called **syncategorematic words**. Accordingly, the words that have clear expression meaning are called **categorematic words**.

To put it in denotational terms, categorematic words refers directly to entities and events in the world, while syncategorematic words do not seem to refer to independent parts of the world. Syncategorematic words seem to modify the way that categorematic words refer to the world.

Among the bound morphemes we find the same distinction because morphemes that we have called *inflectional* (like *–ed* for past tense, or *–s* for plural) also seem to modify the way that the units that they are part of refer to the world.

Semantic Adjustment Rules

As in the case of the other systems, we might wonder whether there is a set of semantic rules that perform adjustments on conceptual expressions, that is, on combinations of primitive concepts. I am not aware of good examples of such adjustment rules, but that doesn't have to mean that the notion of adjustment is irrelevant in this domain.

The Semantic Sentence System

In the introductory sections of this chapter we have discussed two approaches to meaning, which can best be understood by considering the semiotic triangle:

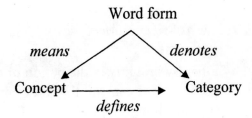

The left-hand arrow represents the idea that the primary task of semantics is to specify the relation between word form and a conceptual structure (the non-referential or non-denotational view). The right-hand arrow focuses on the relation between the word form and the referent, the entity in the world to which the word refers. A diehard denotational semanticist will not pay much attention to the right-hand arrow and thus not to the bottom arrow either, while a diehard conceptual semanticist will ignore the right-hand (and thus also bottom) arrow. I argued that there is no reason to ignore either relation since both seem to form a part of the idea of meaning. We followed the terminology, which refers to the conceptual meaning as the descriptive expression meaning, while the denotational meaning was called the utterance meaning.

We can easily imagine how the meaning of sentences can be represented in a non-denotational approach, which, as one might expect, would be quite the same as how we derived the meaning of complex words. The meaning of *the man sleeps* would be derived by combining the meanings of *the man* and *sleep*:

sleep: SLEEP (x)
man: MAN (x)

[SLEEP (x)] MAN (x)] = SLEEP (MAN(x))

The resulting x variable would be *bound* by linking it to an actual referent, which in itself indicates, at least if we represent all nouns, etc., as predicates with a variable, that a strictly conceptual representation is not entirely complete. This, however, is a matter of debate, and non-denotational semanticists will probably say that nouns and adjectives do not have an x-variable in their conceptual representation.

The Denotational Approach to Sentence Meaning

Just like the meaning of a words is seen as the set of entities or events to which the word refers, the meaning of a *sentence*, in denotational semantics, is a set of **situations** in the (or a), namely the set that makes the sentence **a true statement**. To precisely characterize the relationship between linguistic expressions and situations in the/a world, the denotational semanticist constructs a **model** of the world (using sets and relations between sets). Often, there is an intermediate step in which the expression is *translated* into an expression of a well-defined logical language (using predicate and propositional logic), and the ingredients of these expressions are then said to be *interpreted* by linking them to sets in the model.

Truth Values as Sentence Meanings

Denotational semantics goes one step further by bringing in the notion of *truth*, which is a property of sentences rather than words. First, we can say that the sentence *The cow sleeps* refers to the intersection of the set containing a specific cow (which is derived from the cow set in terms of an operation that is triggered by combining *the* and *cow*) and the set of sleeping things. Viewed somewhat differently, one might say that uttering the sentence in question is an assertion that this specific cow is, in fact, in the set of sleeping things. If she is in that set, the sentence is true, but if she is not in that set, the sentence is false. We can now say that the meaning of a sentence S is equal to the situation in the world (modeled in the form of sets) that makes this sentence a true statement, and this is often formulated by saying that the meaning of S is its **truth conditions** (i.e., the conditions that make it true).

Fixing the Flexible Symbolization.

We already touched on one aspect of the sentence-level semantic system when we said that the semantic context in which a word is placed determines the suppression of certain semantic properties of a given word. I will call this **fixing the flexible symbolization**.

A more specific interaction is involved when certain words require specific semantic properties of the words that they are combined with. Take the following sentence:

The table eats an apple.

This sentence is odd because, apparently, the semantic structure of *eat* specifies that its AGENT must have the semantic property ANIMATE. This is called **(semantic) selection**.

Another way of thinking about semantic selection is to say that a verb like *eat* attributes a semantic property to its agent. If this attribution clashes with what we know about the world that we live in (where tables do not eat things), we regard a sentence as odd. There are two alternatives, however. We might also suspect that the sentence is made in the context of a fairy tale in which all sorts of things (that are "dead" in our world) are living creatures. A second alternative is that the speaker is using the word *eat* in a metaphorical way because, for example, there are such wide cracks in the table that whole pieces of apple disappear in it.

Idioms

Idioms are sentences or phrases that have a meaning that we cannot derive from the parts. Thus, their meaning is not compositional. Take the expression *kick the bucket*. This means *to die*. (Of course, there is also a compositional reading for this phrase.) The meaning *to die* cannot be predicted from the parts. This means that such phrases have to be listed in the lexicon with their special meaning.

Long-Distance Dependencies

We have seen in the chapter on syntax that words that go together semantically do not always form a constituent:

> *What* does the boy *buy*?

What and *buy* go together semantically; that is, *what* is the THEME of *buy*. The surface syntax of this sentence has the two words separated. So how do we figure out that these two words belong together? Well, we have seen that the syntax provides a representation (the deep structure) where *what* and *buy* do form a constituent. There are two basic strategies. We can complicate the syntax and say that there is a level of representation for sentences of this sort where *what* is in the right place:

> The boy buys what

At this level we compute the meaning compositionally so that *what* is incorporated in the meaning of the sentence as the argument of *buy*.

The approach to syntax that we discussed in Chapter 12 is of exactly this sort, and if we say that in this approach meaning is computed at deep structure, we do not have to worry about the fact that the surface structure has words that belong together semantically that are separated.

Another approach would be to complicate the semantic computation and make it somehow possible for semantic rules to relate words that occur at a considerable distance from each other. Here I will not discuss how such an approach might work, but such approaches certainly have been developed.

The Interpretation of Pronouns

Pronouns like *he* refer to very big sets, i.e., the set of *all* things (possible with the restriction that the things have to be male or at least not specifically female). In conceptual terms, one might think of the HE concept as consisting of more basic concepts like THING, MALE, etc.

Consider the following sentences:

*I love me	I love myself
*You love you	You love yourself
*He loves him	He loves himself

If two pronouns have the same referent and they occur within one sentence, the second must be a reflexive pronoun (i.e., end in *-self*). This is why the sentences on the left are ungrammatical.

To make it clear that two pronouns refer to the same person, let us use indices:

*I_i love me_i	I_i love $myself_i$
*You_i love you_i	You_i love $yourself_i$
*He_i loves him_i	He_i loves $himself_i$

Third person pronouns, however, can refer to all other persons (that are not the speaker or the spoken to). Since there are always many other persons around, two occurrences of a third person pronoun can refer to two different people:

He_i loves him_j

Now consider the following sentences:

I_i said [that she loves me_i]	*I_i said [that she loves $myself_i$]
You_i said [that she loves you_i]	*You_i said [that she loves $yourself_i$]

All of a sudden it is alright that we use the non-reflexive pronoun *me* or *you* to refer back to *I* or *you*, whereas the use of *myself* or *yourself* renders the sentence ungrammatical. The clue to our mystery is that the requirement to use the reflexive form holds if both occurrences of the first or second person pronoun belong to **the same sentence** (or, as linguists usually say, the same **clause**). With third person pronouns there is only one difference, which is, as we have seen, that the *him* in the embedded clause can refer to some other person than the *he* in the main clause:

He_i said [that she loves $him_{i/j}$]	*He_i [said that she loves $himself_i$]

In summary:

- A non-reflexive pronoun refers back to an entity outside the clause
- A reflexive pronoun refers back to an entity inside the clause

Linguists have called such rules **interpretive rules**—in other words, rules that play a role in determining what a sentence means. Depending on which linguist you talk to, these interpretive rules are said to belong to the syntactic or the semantic system.

Conclusions

We have explored the field of semantics, perhaps the most difficult aspect of language to grasp. We have discussed the organization of the semantic component at the word level and at the sentence level. In both cases, I've tried to maintain the idea that grammatical components contain primitives and rules for combination. In semantics, at the word level, the primitives are basic concepts about which we need to find out a lot more. At the sentence level, the primitives are word meanings.

As in the cases of phonology and morphosyntax, we need to come up with an account that will do justice to the intuitions that speakers have, in these cases, concerning semantic wellformedness of sentences, paraphrases (different sentences with the same meaning), ambiguity (sentences that seem to have more than one meaning), matters of "inference" (i.e., knowing about "logical reasoning"), and so on. Semantics is a rich and complex field of inquiry to which I cannot do justice here. I will briefly mention some salient issues.

In the computations of the meaning of complex words (at the word level) and the meaning of sentences, the principle of semantic compositionality plays a fundamental role. An important part of this principle is that it has an eye not only for the meaning of the parts that we put together, but also for the constructions that these parts enter into; that is, constructions as such have meaning.

Chapter 14

The Lexicon

Introduction

We have mentioned the lexicon numerous times. We've said that it contains all the morphemes of the language (free morphemes, roots, affixes), but in the previous chapter I mentioned the fact that idiomatic expressions also need to be listed in this module. It is therefore appropriate to take a closer look at this storage component.

Ways of Getting New Morphemes

The list of morphemes comprises affixes, roots, and free morphemes (simplex words). These must all be listed because they constitute unpredictable combinations of form, meaning, and category.

A primary aspect of learning a language is memorizing the list of morphemes, which, for the most part, are arbitrary associations of forms and meanings combined with a category label.

The list of **morphemes** (which forms an important part of the lexicon) is pretty much fixed at any given point in time. However, the list can be extended in a number of ways. In Chapter 12 we spent quite some time on discussing how new words can be formed by combining morphemes. We called this **word formation**. The question now arises as to whether newly formed words are entered into the lexicon. I will return to this question below. First, I want to ask whether there is a way of getting new morphemes. It turns out that there are two mechanisms to do that, which I call **borrowing** and **word (morheme) invention**.

The Cheap Way

The first way (borrowing), which I will call **the cheap way**, for getting new words is to "borrow" them from other languages. Such words are called **loan words**. It might be better to call this form **copying**, because the language that delivers the original of course keeps the word as well.

In general, all languages that are in **contact** with other languages will have loan words. Often these words need some adaptation because the donor language may have phonemes or phoneme combinations that the receiving language does not have.

Adaptations of loan words are a result of the fact that all words in the lexicon must be checked for phonological wellformedness. Sometimes the adaptation is only partial; in this way, new phonemes or phoneme combinations may enter the language, for example, the cluster /km/ in Khmer (Rouge). Through loans, a language may acquire new phonemes. *Dutch*, for example, has acquired the phoneme /g/ via English, such as *goal*. Thus, through loan words a change can occur in the phonological word system.

Word copying is part of a larger topic that we refer to as **language contact**. Contact arises when two populations with different languages exchange material goods or cultural products. Contact can also exist within the individual, when a person knows and uses more than one language (bi- or multilingualism).

The Case of English

English has many words that were once borrowed from French or Latin, but that today are felt as completely English:

Loan word in English
tax, royal, jury, crime, sermon, art, fur, army, captain

These words are not morphologically complex, at least not as they appear in English. Hence, these words are (single) morphemes.

English is closely related to languages such as Dutch and German, as well as Icelandic, Swedish, Danish and Norwegian. All these languages belong to a language family called Germanic. French, on the other hand, falls within the group of Romance, which also comprises languages such as Italian, Spanish, Portuguese, and Romanian (among others). All languages in the Romance family are developments of Latin, which some 2,000 years ago came to be spoken in a wide area due to the Roman occupations; its wide distribution lead to the development of many local dialects, and some of these developed into the national languages like Spanish, Italian, etc. Meanwhile, within the western world Latin remained in use in its old form as the language of the Catholic Church, the law, and science. Because of this latter fact many languages that were used in western countries adopted words from Latin. As of the seventeenth century, French also become a prestige language that many educated people in various western countries liked to use, and this resulted in many French loanwords in other languages. When all this is taken into account, we quickly note that English really stands out as having an unusually large number of words that were originally borrowed from French, and the reason for this is simple. French speaking people from Normandy (a part of France) occupied England for a considerable amount of time, and during that time French was the dominant language among the English upperclass, which consisted of many nobleman of Norman origin. As a result, English soaked up an incredible number of French words, almost making the lexicon of the language a blend of words of Germanic and Romance origin.

Borrowing From the World

Languages can also borrow words from the real world. That may sound strange because the real world is not a language. But there are many noises out there that can be used as a model for the form of a word that refers to the source of the sound. The word *cuckoo* refers to a bird that makes a sound that sounds somewhat like this word form. Words that come about in this way are called **onomatopoeia** or **onomatopoeic** or **iconic words**.

Sometimes onomatopoeic words violate the phonological wellformedness in order to stay as close as possible to the real world model.

Examples of iconic words in English:

cock-a-doodle-doo (the name for the sound made by a rooster)
bang (activity or event that involves a lot of noise)
meow (children's word for cat)

The Phonological Way

The "cheap way" introduces new words (morphemes) into the language on a case-by-case basis, but that doesn't mean that borrowing is a marginal phenomenon. In this day and age, due to the dominance of English as a world language, many languages all over the world are adopting English words into their lexicons.

The second way of extending the list of morphemes I will call **word invention**, or **the phonological way** of making new words. Here we find several different cases. There is no conclusive classification; the data is a bit messy. People are very creative in making new words, and they come up with new ways all the time.

Coinage

Sometimes we consciously combine phonemes to produce a new word form when we need, for example, a new technical term or a brand name. This happens a lot in the context of computer, information, and Internet technology, and in commercial business when people need new names for products or companies (think of words like *Kleenex*). This is sometimes also called word **manufacture** or **coinage**. We could also call it the *free scrabble* way if we would think of this as a variant of the Scrabble game in which we can make non-existing words on the condition that they sound like English words.

snig, blomp, penk, strolp

All these "words" are possible English words, even though they don't (yet) exist.

Blending

A second phonological way is to blend the phonological form of two words into one word (called **blending**):

smog	smoke *and* fog
brunch	breakfast *and* lunch
spork	spoon *and* fork
motel	motor *and* hotel

There is a certain pattern here in that we seem to take the onset of one word and the rhyme of the second word. Again, the condition is that the words sound like English words, i.e., are phonologically possible English word forms.

Acronyms

A third phonological way is the making of **acronyms**, that is, forming a new word by taking the initial letters of a group of words. Here we have two subtypes (*UCLA, URL* = pronouncing the letters separately; *AIDS, NATO* = pronouncing the letters as one form). Names for organizations and recurrent principles often emerge in this way.

Clipping

A fourth phonological way is to shorten a word and thus produce a variant of the longer version. We see this in proper names (*Pam(ela)*) and current items (*fax < facsimile*). We call this **clipping**. It is debatable whether, in these cases, new words are made. It would seem that the speaker makes a *new form* of a word, not really a new word with a new meaning (although the shortened form of proper names may be more endearing). We also apply clipping in cases like *ad, flu, telly, sitcom,* and so on.

Again there seem to be certain regularities in the way in which clippings are formed. In clippings, we might also argue that the speaker uses a subconscious rule because there are regularities in the manner that clipping occurs. *Profess* is not a wellformed clipping of *professor*; *prof*, however, is. Apparently we take the first syllable and the immediately following consonant (unless the first syllable ends in a consonant, as in *ad*).

The World Wide Web

Frequent users of the Internet and World Wide Web are familiar with the emergence of new words based on all these four methods, as well as with websites that actually catalogue these new words, providing their meaning and proper ways to use them.

Lexicalization of Complex Words

Is there anything else in the lexicon besides the list of morphemes? What about the products of morphology, the complex words? One might think that it is not necessary to list all of them in the lexicon. For starters, there is no such thing as "all of them," because the set of possible words is, as we learned in Chapter 12, infinite. However, even words that *are* made need not be listed because if we've made them once, we can make them again. This being so, we still cannot exclude the possibility of existing complex words being incorporated into the lexicon. For one thing, we often seem to have an awareness of having heard or seen certain complex words before. How can we have that sensation if we do not list words we hear or read? Perhaps this happens in particular to complex words that are very frequent or that have been around for a long time.

However, certain complex words *must* end up in the lexicon because the words in question acquire properties that cannot be deduced from their parts and the relevant morphological rules. For example, the word *opener* doesn't just mean anybody or anything that opens; it refers to a specific instrument to open bottles. This aspect of its meaning is unpredictable, and therefore *opener*, even though it is formed in accordance with morphological rules, must be listed in the lexicon. Another example is the form *length*. On the one hand, one might say that this is regularly derived from *long* (compare *warm–warmth*); on the other hand, it contains the vowel /e/ instead of /o/. This is an unpredictable property; hence, *length* must be listed in the lexicon, whereas we do not have to assume this for *warmth*.

Compounds have a peculiar property of their own. Take noun + noun compounds. The precise semantic relation between the two nouns is not fixed. Here are some examples of semantic relations between the head and dependent member of the noun compound. In each case, we specify the semantic function of the first member of the compound:

purpose of head (as instrument)	magnifying glass, search engine
purpose of head (as location)	fruit market, battle field
how head *works*	air gun, vacuum cleaner
location of head	polar bear, space station
what is *caused by* head	tear gas, sneeze weed
cause of the head	emergency stop, hunger strike
source of the head	goat cheese
possessor of head	dogs' home, student loan
content of head	fruit cake, film festival,
topic of head	border dispute, tax law
resemblance to head	zebra crossing, box kite

Which interpretation is relevant depends on a variety of factors. An *air gun* could be a gun that is made of air, or one that causes air, or one that resembles air, or one that is owned by the air—but given the world that we live in these are not the most likely interpretations. In other words, the meaning of a compound is heavily determined by the nonlinguistic context. As a result, we must list each compound in the lexicon because the precise meaning is not predictable on linguistic grounds.

Word forms that are made by inflectional rules are generally fully regular, so listing these in the lexicon is unnecessary. However, in some cases we encounter irregular forms like *better* and *best* as the comparative and superlative of *good*. Such irregular forms are called **suppletive**, and they must be listed in the lexicon.

Finally, what about the product of the syntactic system? One might at first be inclined to say that the lexicon is no place for phrases and sentences, but that would be a mistake. The lexicon must also contain sentences, specifically so-called **idiomatic expressions**:

> Let the cat out of the bag.
> Kick the bucket.

Such sentences may be regular in terms of their syntactic structure and their phonology, but they are not regular in terms of their semantics. We already mentioned idioms in Chapter 13, where we noted that their meaning is not compositional, that is, not predictable from the parts and their combination.

Somewhat to our surprise, then, we must conclude that the lexicon contains not only morphemes and complex words, but also phrases and sentences.

Conclusions

Concluding, the lexicon is a list containing:

- a. all simplex words
- b. all affixes
- c. all roots
- d. all derived words that have unpredictable properties
- e. all compounds
- f. all inflectional suppletive forms
- g. all sentences and phrases that have unpredictable properties

At this point, let us introduce a term for units that are, or can go in the lexicon: **lexeme**.

Chapter 15

The Linguistic Structure of Sign Languages

Introduction

The importance of the study of sign languages to the field of linguistics in general can hardly be overestimated. Sign languages and spoken languages are produced and perceived in different physical modalities: the manual–visual modality and oral–auditory modality, respectively. Until recently the emphasis in linguistic research has been on spoken languages and, in fact, on a rather limited number of these. The proposals that have been made about universal properties of languages and typologies have therefore been based on a rather small subset of human languages. Recent research on languages other than English, especially on languages from language families other than the Indo-European family, have often challenged the postulated universals, suggesting modifications or complete reconsideration. This, in itself, illustrates the importance of the investigation of languages other than the ones that have been used to formulate the hypotheses in the first place.

In this respect, sign languages form a very important testing ground for language universals and typologies, and for differentiating between those universals and typological features that depend on the effects of the modality of production and perception and those that depend on the innate, cognitive capacity for language.

Sign languages started to attract the attention of linguists only a few decades ago. In the early 1950s, **Ben Tervoort** from Amsterdam in The Netherlands observed the communication of some young deaf children and recorded properties of that communication system that indicated an independent linguistic system in a different modality. For example, he observed that signs had a constant form with a constant meaning, and that these were not derived from the spoken language. In this respect, Tervoort placed himself in the tradition of the French priest L'Épée (1712-1789), a pioneer in the recognition of French sign language.

Tervoort's important work was, unfortunately, not widely noticed. The real breakthrough came when American researcher **William Stokoe** realized in 1960 that simplex signed words can be decomposed into smaller (formal, meaningless, hence: phonological) units.

His initial goal was to develop a notation system for signs because he was planning to make a dictionary that would move beyond a book with pictures associated with an English gloss. He wanted to organize the lexicon in a way that he believed would reflect the phonological structure of the signs, and he also simply wanted to move away from having pictures or drawings only. Hence, he developed a system for describing signs at the level of form or, in other words, the **handshape**, the **movement**, and the **place of articulation** (Stokoe, 1960). Together with Casterline and Cronenberg, he produced a dictionary of American Sign Language, published in 1965. This work attracted the attention of researchers both in the United States and in many other countries and helped to raise sign languages to the status of natural languages worthy of linguistic interest.

Work in the 1970s expanded the knowledge of ASL structure greatly (see Klima & Bellugi, 1979), and gradually other sign languages became the objects of serious description and analysis as well. The then commonly held views that sign language was really a limited form of pantomime, or that there was one universal sign language used by deaf people all over the world, began to make way for consideration of these languages as full-fledged separate linguistic systems. This had an effect on the deaf communities in various countries, which began to become aware of the status of their languages and of their own status as a cultural group.

A particularly important effect was that deaf education policy changed from the oral approach, which had been dominant since the banning of the use of signs during a conference in Milan in 1880, to the policy of **Total Communication**, involving the use of all means of communication to promote the communicative abilities of deaf children. Here, linguistic research contributed to making an important distinction, namely, between the **natural sign languages** of the deaf community and the **artificial sign systems** that were most frequently used in schools for the deaf under the new Total Communication policy. Signed systems, as we have discussed, are a combination of the spoken language of the hearing community and the sign language of the deaf community. It is clear that the use of the Total Communication policy, even though it promoted the use of sign systems (rather than true sign languages only), has nonetheless formed an important bridge between the oral approach and full recognition of sign languages as the means of communication and education.

A considerable amount of work in this early period was at the level of dictionary making and the description of basic grammatical rules. This, in turn, led to the development of practical tools that were of immediate use to the educational system. Such practical and descriptive projects necessarily had to precede the more theoretically oriented work that was to follow. Even today, however, much too little is known about a sufficiently large number of individual sign languages at the descriptive level to facilitate broad comparative research.

In the 1970s, 1980s, and early 1990s, the interest in sign linguistics increased rapidly, and gradually a shift in emphasis revealed itself. Early work often had the goal of establishing sign languages as **true languages**, worthy objects of linguistic research. As a result, a lot of energy was spent on showing the parallels between sign languages and spoken languages. Gradually, however, some researchers began to pay more attention to those properties of sign languages that seem to differ significantly from those of spoken languages.

Addressing modality-specific aspects of signed and spoken languages, as well as formulating more abstract principles of language structure in order to properly generalize over both modalities, was often seen as a daring step, but also as a sign of maturity of the field, only possible once sign languages had been established as respectable linguistic objects.

Meanwhile, **sign linguistics** remained a specialized field. However, the linguistic community in general (although still rather naive about sign language) no longer classifies this specialization as peripheral to linguistic inquiry. In addition to the specialized journals and conferences that have been in existence for nearly two decades, today we regularly find sign language contributions in general linguistic events, and the debate around the issue of the contribution of sign linguistics to linguistic theory has become more open.

Phonology

The study of the form (i.e., phonetics and phonology) of both spoken languages and sign languages is perhaps the least likely area to reveal formal equivalences between signed and spoken languages because the languages use totally different channels for production and perception. Nonetheless, as mentioned earlier, signed words, as well as spoken words, can be decomposed into meaningless, yet distinctive, chunks. As in spoken languages, we can study the "phonological" wellformedness of signs in terms of possible combinations of the various form units, and we can establish the variation in phonetic realization of these units.

By breaking down the signs into form-chunks (handshape, etc.), Stokoe showed that sign language has a level of structure that is comparable to what we call phonology in spoken language. Phonology is about the fact that words have an organization below the smallest meaningful units, an organization in terms of elements, phonemes, and syllables. When Stokoe showed that, for practical purposes, signs *can* be analyzed in terms of handshapes, movements, and so on, he open the door to a linguistic level of analysis that recognizes these units as building blocks in the mental organization of signs:

1. The handshape
2. The location of the hand
3. The movement of the hand

Each of these three units, Stokoe argued, has a fixed number of "values." To avoid underestimating the difference between spoken language and sign language, Stokoe referred to the parameters Handshape, Location, and Movement as **cheremes**, and to the study of their combinations as **cherology**. Other researchers, however, and Stokoe himself as well, in a later edition of his study (published in 1978), started using the terms **phoneme** and **phonology**. The idea then became prevalent that the aspects Handshape, Location, and Movement are the formal analogues to phonemes, which make up syllables in spoken languages.

We have seen that in spoken language we can establish a hierarchy of units: Elements make up **vowels** (|HIGH| and |FRONT| makes /i/) and **consonants** (such as |STOP|, |LABIAL|, |VOICELESS|, which make /p/), and phonemes are sequentially grouped into syllables (pa, ta, bri), which, together, form the words. In sign, we likewise have a hierarchical organization of units: Elements characterize **handshapes** (|EXTENDED INDEX FINGER|), **locations** (|FOREHEAD|), and **movements** (|STRAIGHT|, |HORIZONTAL|), and these units together are simultaneously grouped into a smallest unit that can make up a sign; there is no generally accepted label for this unit, and, in fact, we could label it either as *segment* or *syllable*. Here I will use the label **syllable**, as is commonly done:

a. Spoken language   b. Sign language

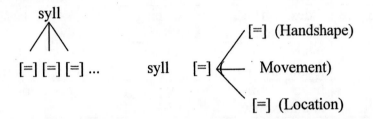

("[=]" = a set of elements representing a particular Handshape, Movement, or Location.)

Making a parallel between parts of signs and parts of words was essentially due to the fact that the units seemed to be used in building morphemes in the way phonemes in spoken languages are used to build up morphemes. The main difference, then, between spoken languages and sign languages was claimed to involve the presence of linear order among phonemes in the spoken language and the absence thereof in sign language. This point has been expressed in the above diagrams by arranging the units of spoken language syllables next to each other (to indicate sequential organization), while the units from of the sign language syllables have been stacked on top of each other (to indicate simultaneity).

   Just as in spoken language, we can find minimal pairs (i.e., signs that differ in just one feature).

   The examples VERKLIKKEN (to fink), TANDARTS (dentist), and INSTITUUT (institute) from Sign Language of the Netherlands (SLN) show that the handshape feature can be distinctive. The three signs show the same features for place and (type of) movement and thus only differ in handshape. The examples ONSCHULDIG (not-guilty), WONEN (to live (somewhere)), and LEREN (to learn) illustrate the distinctive use of location.

   In the following table these six signs have been analyzed in terms of their handshape, movement, and location:

	Handshape	Movement	Location
VERKLIKKEN	index and middle finger extended – bent	tapping	left side of the mouth
TANDARTS	fist with thumb extended	tapping	left side of the mouth
INSTITUUT	Index finger extended	tapping	left side of the mouth
ONSCHULDIG	Index finger – thumb contact	tapping	Chest
WONEN	Index finger – thumb contact	tapping	left side of the mouth
LEREN	Index finger – thumb contact	tapping	Forehead

Clearly, the logic of phonological analysis is no different from that applied to spoken languages. If, for example, two handshapes appear to be never strictly contrastive, they are possibly phonetic variants of a single phonological handshape unit. And, indeed, Stokoe discussed examples of allophonic variation.

One Hand – Two hands

The six examples just discussed all use one hand. It does actually not matter which hand the signer uses. People will generally use their preference hand, but they can easily switch to the other hand if, while signing, they pick something up from the table, or if they are holding a bag.

There are also many signs that are made with two hands. In those cases either both hands do the same thing (they mirror each other), or one hand, generally the non-preference hand, functions as the location for the *active* hand.

Morphology

As with most natural languages, there are a number of ways to make words out of other words or parts of words. As discussed in Chapter 13, we distinguish inflectional morphology from word formation. In **inflectional morphology**, affixes are added to make a word fit into a sentence, whereas in **word formation** new words are made. The two types of word formation are **derivation** and **compounding**. Although compounding is clearly set apart from inflection because it combines free words, derivational and inflectional morphology share the use of affixes that are added to bases. We say that inflectional affixes do not change the **core meaning** of bases, whereas derivational affixes do.

The second type of word formation (**compounding**) takes two words and puts them together to make a new word whose meaning may not be just the sum of its parts.

One example of a compound in English is *greenhouse*, which is not simply a house that is green, but rather a house in which green things are grown. It is common in compounds not only for the meaning to change but also the phonology. For example, in *greenhouse* the primary stress is on *green*, whereas in the phrase *green house*, the primary stress is on *house*.

The Trade-Off Between Syntax and Inflection

Languages differ in terms of what they express with syntactic and lexical means (word order, choice of words) and what is expressed through inflectional affixes. For example, *English* has a past tense *{-ed}* and a present tense (realized as *{-s}* for third person singular, zero otherwise). It lacks an affix for future tense, however, instead using the auxiliary verb *will*. Compare a language like *Latin*, where verbs agree with their subjects in number (which is only the case for third person singular in English) and gender (i.e., nouns are masculine, feminine, or neuter, as in Old English, and the ending of verbs shows what the gender is of the subject noun.) Latin verbs also have inflectional affixes that show *tense* (more than just present and past, including future) and *mood* (passive or active). Adjectives also agree in number and gender with the nouns that they modify. We discussed such differences in Chapter 4, where we compared *English* and *Kayardild*. We learned that agreement can make word order superfluous, or at least less crucial. Also, with the marking of subject properties on the verb, we can even leave the subject unmentioned. Latin *veni, vidi, vici* must be translated as *HE came, HE saw, HE conquered*.

English, therefore, has a relatively impoverished inflectional system, which has consequences elsewhere in the grammar. For example, *English* word order is more fixed than *Latin* (or *Kayardild*), and subjects are required in English but not in Latin, because the subject in Latin can be inferred from the verb.

Thus, what one language expresses through an inflectional affix requires a separate word in another (an overt pronoun, or a word to indicate future tense), or it calls for a fixed word order (to indicate SUBJECT vs. OBJECT). Where does ASL stand in this respect when compared to English, for example?

Tense (Time) Marking

ASL uses adverbs, often at the beginning of a sentence, to mark tense (or time). For example:

LONG-TIME-AGO ME SMALL ME GO-TO [ASPECT: HABITUAL] FISH WITH GRAND FATHER

When I was a child, I often went fishing with my grandfather.

The capital words here represent signs of ASL in terms of their meaning indicated by an English gloss. Dashes between glosses indicate that they stand for one sign. So there is one ASL sign that means LONG-TIME-AGO. The adverb LONG-TIME-AGO is used to set the time frame (i.e., to indicate past). (ASL does not have an affix on the verb; the verb GO-TO has a modifying feature represented by the gloss [ASPECT: HABITUAL], which we will explain later.)

There are also spoken languages (notably languages that have very little morphology) that indicate tense by using separate words. The past time is assumed until and unless another time is indicated. This can occur with either another time adverbial (e.g., LATER or TOMORROW, meaning the next day in a past context) or a shift of the body forward to indicate a more future time or backward to indicate a more past time. Thus, tense sign can be manual as LONG-TIME-AGO (a backward waving over the shoulder) or nonmanual (a change in body posture).

Another way of expressing past time is to use the verb FINISH in ASL.

YOU EAT **FINISH**?
Have you eaten yet?/Did you eat?

Such an independent verb may develop into an inflectional suffix by becoming a tight unit with the verb (EAT in this case). It is not clear whether this has already happened in ASL.

Most other western sign languages express time in the same way as ASL. However, there appear to be true past tense suffixes in *NihonSyuwa* (*NS*), the sign language of Japan, which uses a sign meaning *past* that is distinct from the NS sign OWARU (finish). This sign cannot be separated from the verb, it never occurs except after a verb, and it is accompanied by the mouthing [ta], which is how the past tense morpheme is pronounced in spoken Japanese. The similarities between the western languages may be due to a global (mutual) influence between these languages.

Pronouns

We first need to discuss how pronouns are expressed in ASL. As was discussed earlier, sign languages are in a modality, which, in production and perception, is very different from that of spoken languages. One of the most salient properties of sign languages is the use of **space**. Signs are articulated in a space next to and in front of the signer's body. This space, which is referred to as the **signing space**, can be used for a variety of functions. An important function is identifying roles in the sentence (such as SUBJECT, OBJECT).

If the signer wishes to sign a sentence involving his father, the family dog, and the truck in the backyard, for example, then these referents are SITUATED (linguists say: LOCALIZED) in the signing space. Crucially, these locations are unrelated to the actual whereabouts of the relevant referents. Father may be at work, the dog may be in the house, and the truck may be in the garage. Hence, the signer is not literally pointing at these referents. He is simple painting a picture, much like a person might do when he arranges some arbitrary things on the table in order to explain what happened in a particular situation. A person might say: "Okay, this (putting a cup to his left) is my father, that (putting a spoon in the middle) is the truck, and that (putting a piece of bread to his right) is the tree. Now, on that day my father (pointing to the cup) walked over to the tree (moving the cup to the spoon), and then he stood there looking at the truck (pointing to the piece of bread).

Signers do this kind of painting the picture all the time, and they do not need an actual table or surface with objects on it.

It has often been commented that localization is a typical modality-specific property because there is no apparent analogue in spoken languages, but as we have just seen, speakers do in fact use actual spaces (tables and so on) to do something very similar. It is fair to say, though, that the signing space plays a much more prominent role in sign languages, and its use is more abstract. In a way, a location can function much like a pronoun (such as *he, she*) in spoken language. Once referents have been localized, the location can be referred to by means of a pointing gesture. Thus, the pointing sign and the location that it identifies together take on the function of a pronoun. Different locations that have been set up by the signer are associated with different persons.

In fact, this use of the sign space has been conventionalized to such an extent that it is a rule of grammar that pointing to one's chest means *I* (first person), pointing forward means *you* (second person) and pointing sideways means *he* or *she* (third person).

Thus, pronouns are represented as signs that point to locations in the signing space. (These signs are called **indexes**.)

Person Marking

I will now show that the person locations can be also used as affixes that mark person (1st, 2nd, or 3rd person) *on* the verb. This marking can be expressed in the movement of the verb, whereby the beginning of the movement often indicates the SUBJECT (or agent) of the verb and the end point the INDIRECT OBJECT (or benefactor). The verb GIVE (to give) in ASL can be modified in its movement to indicate first the subject and then the indirect object. The OBJECT (or theme) of GIVE is represented by the moving hand itself, which is shaped as if it were holding the thing being given.

Where the agent is first person and the receiver is a third person, the movement is from the signer to the location of the third person referent.

Aspect Marking

Another way in which sign languages have rich inflectional systems is in the area of marking **aspect**, which pays attention to things like beginning points or endpoints of an action or state, or the frequency of an action, irrespective of time. Take the example GO-TO. We can inflect GO-TO for habitual aspect by repeating (linguists say **reduplicating**) the sign rapidly. This reduplication changes the meaning of the sign in a predictable way; in this case, the sign means *to go to a place on a regular basis*. If the same sign is repeated with a slower, circular movement, the result is *continuous* aspect (meaning *on and on*), and the sign means to *go to a place over and over again (but not necessarily on* *a regular basis) for a long time.* If one begins to sign GO-TO but abruptly stops before the sign is completed, this is **unrealized aspect**: *He started going, but then he held back.*

Adjectives can also undergo aspect marking; for example, the sign SICK can be inflected for habitual aspect, resulting in the meaning *sickly*. The sign SAME can be inflected for continuous aspect to yield the meaning *monotonous*.

English doesn't have much in the order of **aspectual affixes**, being low on inflection in general. But many other spoken languages do have aspectual affixes. Thus ASL, while being different from English, uses formal grammatical rules that are clearly within the pool of grammatical mechanisms that languages can use.

Plural Marking

Many signs can form plurals with a type of reduplication accompanied by a horizontal (in the case of verbs) sweep of the hands. This is one regular way to form plurals. If we go back to our old friend GO-TO and repeat the sign while moving the hands in a horizontal arc, the resulting meaning is *go to many places.*

There are other ways of forming plurals as well, depending partly on the phonological form of the sign. The sign LOOK in ASL normally is made with two fingers extended, but if one extends all the fingers except the thumb and uses both hands, the resulting sign means *many people look.*

Word Formation

We have looked at **inflection**, which modifies words to make them fit into sentences without changing their core meaning. We now turn to how sign languages make new words with new or different content.

Compounding

As mentioned earlier, a compound is a word that consists of two words in a special semantic relationship. On the phonological side, usually the first member of the compound has the stress. In ASL, when two words combine to form a compound, we also see that certain phonological processes occur. For example, if the first member of the compound has repeated movement when it occurs as an isolated word, the repetition of that movement is lost. This is analogous to the weakening of the vowel of the second member of a compound in English examples like *chairman*. When a compound is reduplicated for plural or habitual, in ASL only the *second* member of the compound repeats.

Compounding is a very robust and often productive process in the sign languages of the world. Consider the following compounds in ASL:

NAKED + ESCAPE = streaker
ELECTRIC + M-A-I-L = e-mail (the second part is fingerspelled)

(ELECTRIC is usually signed with repeated movement, but in the compound, only one movement occurs.)

Incorporation

In ASL, the handshape that is used to represent the grammatical object of verbs like GIVE can indicate the object's shape. It is as if the object shape is incorporated in the verb. In the example below, the handshape that symbolizes the book thus functions at the same time like the pronoun *it* and as an indication of the *shape if it*. Generally it is required that the specific referent (called here **antecedent**) of the pronoun is first mentioned.

BOOK, HE-GIVES-IT-HIM

The signer makes the sign for BOOK and then signs HE-GIVES-IT-HIM, making a handshape that looks at if the hand is holding a book.

Handshapes that thus represent object, subject, and their typical shape are called **classifiers**.

Derivation

A number of verbs have corresponding nouns whose movements are different from those of verbs. They suggest a derivational process for deriving nouns and verbs from one underlying form, adding the different types of movement. Typically, verbs have one continuous motion, whereas nouns have repeated restrained movement. (Compare the ASL signs TO-SIT and CHAIR.)

It has also been claimed that ASL has affixing signs that are placed after the stem, such as a suffix that means *one who V's* (like English *-er*).

Syntax

The basic word order of ASL is SVO; the basic word order of Japanese Sign Language is SOV. However, just as in spoken languages, events may conspire to change that basic word order. Consider, for example, the use of classifiers, discussed earlier. For such classifiers, as we mentioned, an antecedent is required. This antecedent typically will precede the classifier. Assuming the classifier is incorporated in the verb, this will mean that the verb will occur last. Similarly, if we have a verb with person affixes, the referential points in the signing space must be set up first by pointing at them. The resulting sentence will have the order: noun phrase, noun phrase, verb. A concrete example is:

COW INDEX$_a$ HORSE INDEX$_b$ $_a$KICK$_b$

The cow kicked the horse.

Let me spell out how this sentence is articulated, bearing in mind that this set of instructions is by no means meant to be the syntactic analysis. As in the case of spoken languages, syntactic analyses of sign sentences use tree structures. Here, however, I did not supply this formal level of analysis:

1. Make the sign COW.
2. Point to a spot in the signing space where you position the cow.
3. Make a sign HORSE.
4. Point to another spot in the signing space where you position the horse.
5. Make a kicking sign with your hand from point **a** to point **b** (i.e., the back of the hand faces point **a** and you act out that **a** kicks **b**).

If we reverse the subscripts on KICK (i.e., if we reverse the direction of the verb movement), the meaning will be *The horse kicked the cow*.

Hence, the use of classifiers and person affixes on verbs necessitates a deviation from the basic word order of ASL from SVO to SOV. In short ASL uses both SVO and SOV; it depends, as in this example, on the kind of verb.

Most sign languages also have a process called **topicalization**, whereby a noun phrase that the sentence (or whole discourse) is in some sense *about* moves to the beginning of the utterance. The topic occurs with a special **nonmanual behavior** (**NMB**), here indicated by a horizontal line over the topicalized sign BOOK; the little *t* stands for *topic*:

t _____
BOOK, WHERE BUY?

As for the book, where did [you] buy it?

The topicalized constituent can even come from an embedded sentence, as in:

t _____
BOOK, WHO YOU THINK WANT BUY?

As for the book, who do you think wants to buy it?

English, as most other languages, of course, also has topicalization rules (which, technically can be seen as transformational rules). You can say: "Beans, I like." In all languages, such rules create varieties of word orders.

Simple and Complex Structures

In spoken languages, sentences can be complex, containing a sentence within a sentence (due to recursion). We find this in ASL too:

> ME SEARCH MAN SELF HELP WASHING-MACHINE.
>
> I'm looking for a man who can help me with the laundry.

> RAIN WILL, ME FEEL
>
> I have a feeling it's going to rain.

However, the expression of complex ideas in complex sentences is an area of sign language structure that clearly warrants more research. It is, of course, quite crucial to demonstrate that the syntax of sign language is recursive because recursion has been taken as a hallmark of human language.

Non-Manual Behaviors

As said before, sign language is not just a matter of hands. It is a matter of the whole upper body, or perhaps we should say the part of the body that is normally visible. A few signs exist which do not even have a manual part, consisting solely of some non-manual aspect. These are often "taboo" signs. Female ASL speakers use such a sign for *having your period*, and it involves pushing your tongue against the inside of one of your cheeks.

Word Pictures and Mouthing

Frequently, especially when signers address hearing people whose signing is poor, they will produce (reduced forms of) spoken words (silently); such mouth gestures are called **word pictures**. They do this especially for nouns, and especially for words containing labials, which are easy to speech read. Thus, for example, the sign glossed as FINISH is accompanied by the **mouth picture** [fI] in the North American states of the United States. However, in the state of Hawaii, where the spoken word commonly used to mean *finish* is *pau*, the sign FINISH is accompanied by the mouthing [paw]. There is controversy about the question as to whether mouthing is an inherent part of sign language or should be looked at as **pollution** of the sign language by the spoken language. In many cases the mouthing is optional and depends on the signer's willingness to accommodate his conversational partners who don't know sign language so well. But there are also signs in which the word picture seems to be obligatory. For example, in Japanese Sign Language past tense affix must be accompanied by a mouth gesture [ta]. In any event, mouthing is a form of influence from the spoken language on the sign language. There is also mouth activity that is not based on spoken words, involving all kinds of lip, tongue, and cheek postures. This is called **mouthing**. Mouthing is typically obligatory.

Facial Expression and Body Posture

In sign languages, the face and the position of the body can also serve a function that is very similar to the function of intonation (sentence melody) in spoken languages. It is certainly true that deaf people find sign language without facial expression boring, much as someone speaking in a monotone can put the user of a spoken language to sleep. Such **intonational** use of nonmanuals falls within the domain of syntax, and I will now discuss some examples of such nonmanual behaviors (NMB).

A specific way in which NMB (in particular, facial expression) is used is for indicating the negated part of a sentence, as well as questions. The NMB for negation is either a headshake or a frown. The NMB for *affirmative* is a head nod. Consider the following sentences:

<u>Neg (head shake)</u>_____   <u>Pos (head nod)</u>_
ME UNDERSTAND PHYSICS, MATHEMATICS

I don't understand physics, but I do understand mathematics.

<u>t(opic)</u>_____ <u>Neg</u>____ <u>Pos</u>_____
ME UNDERSTAND PHYSICS, MATHEMATICS

What I understand is not physics, but mathematics.

As before, the lines above the sentences indicate how far the NMBs extend. Although the words of the two sentences are identical (i.e., the manual part of the signs is the same), what is negated or affirmed differs. Note that in these sentences no negative manual sign such as NOT is present. The negative facial expression serves as the only negator in the sentence.

The NMB for a yes–no question (YNQ) is a raising of eyebrows and widening of the eyes.

<u>YNQ</u>_____
YOU READ BOOK

Are you reading a book?

The NMB for a wh-question involves partial eye closure and furrowing of the brows. In the following examples there are no wh-words such as WHO, WHERE, HOW, and so on; rather, we get a wh-facial expression:

Wh_____
BOOK YOU READ

Which book are you reading?

Wh____
NAME

What's your name?

Wh____
WRONG

What's wrong?

Wh_____
HAPPEN

What happened?

In addition, ASL (an other sign languages) also has question words (WHO, WHERE, etc.) which can then also be used to form questions, typically accompanied by the NMB for questions.

Conclusions

I have shown here that sign languages have complex phonological, morphological, and syntactic structures that are distinct from but often parallel to those structures found in spoken languages. The serious linguistic study of sign languages is still relatively young; it can be traced back only about 45 years, compared with the study of spoken language that goes back a couple of millennia. An important lesson to come away with is that sign languages are indeed languages that deserve serious study and consideration by the linguistic community.

Sources and Further Reading

Part I: Linguistic Matters

1   Everything You Always Wanted To Know About Linguistics (But Were Afraid To Ask)

The Most General Sources

Crystal, D. 1997. *The Cambridge encyclopedia of language*. 2nd ed. Cambridge: Cambridge University Press.
Crystal, D. 2007. *How Language Works: How babies babble, words change meaning, and languages live or die*. New York: Avery Publishing Group.

Popular Overviews of Linguistics and Language Issues

Fischer, S. R. 1999. *A history of language*. London: Reaktion Books.
Ingram, J. 1992. *Talk, talk, talk: An investigation into the mystery of speech*. London: Viking.
Janson, T. 2002. *Speak: A short history of languages*. Oxford: Oxford University Press.
Matthews, P. H. 2003. *Linguistics: A very short introduction*. Oxford: Oxford University Press.
McWhorther, J. H. 2001. *The power of Babel: A natural history of language*. New York: Holt.
Miller, G. A. 1996. *The science of words*. New York: Scientific American Library.
Napoli, D. J. 2003. *Language matters*. Oxford: Oxford University Press.
Smith, Neil. 2005. *Language, frogs & savants: More linguistic problems, puzzles and polemics*. Malden, MA: Blackwell Publishing.

Articles in the Press about Languages and Linguistics

Wade, N., ed. 2003. *The Science Times book of language and linguistics*. Rev. exp. ed. Guilford, CT: The Lyons Press.

Misunderstandings about Language

Bauer, L., and P. Trudgill, eds. 1998. *Language myths*. London: Penguin.
Evans, N. 1998. Aborigines speak a primitive language. In *Language myths*, ed. L. Bauer and P. Trudgill, 159–168. London: Penguin.

A General Work about Everything from Thought to Speaking

Levelt, W. J. M. 1989. *Speaking: From intention to articulation*. Cambridge, MA: MIT Press.

A General Work about Different Forms of Human Communication

Finnegan, R. 2002. *Communicating: The multiple modes of human interconnection*. London: Routledge.

Semiotics

Keller, R. 1998. *A theory of linguistic signs*. Oxford: Oxford University Press.
Nöth, Winfried. 1990. *Handbook of Semiotics*. Bloomington and Indianapolis: Indiana University Press.

Facial Expression and Gesturing

Darwin, C. 1872. *The expression of the emotions in man and animals*. Repr., Chicago: University of Chicago Press, 1965.
Ekman, P. 2003. *Emotions revealed: Recognizing faces and feelings to improve communication and emotional life*. New York: Times Books.
McNeill, D. 1992. *Hand and mind: What gestures reveal about thought*. Chicago: University of Chicago Press.
Kendon, A. 2004. *Gesture: Visible action as utterance*. Cambridge: Cambridge University Press.

History of the English Language

Crystal, D. 2004. *The stories of English*. London: Allan Lane.

Varieties of English

Bailey, R. W., and J. L. Robinson. 1973. *Varieties of present-day English*. New York: Macmillan.

Dillard, J. L. 1973. *Black English: Its history and usage in the United States*. New York: Vintage.

Kachru, Braj B., Yamuna Kachru, and Cecil L. Nelson, eds. 2006. *The Handbook of World Englishes*. Malden, MA: Wiley-Blackwell Publishing.

Mair, Christian. 2006. *Twentieth-Century English: History, Variation and Standardization*. Cambridge: Cambridge University Press.

Mugglestone, Lynda, ed. 2006. *The Oxford History of English*. Oxford: Oxford University Press.

Schneider, Edgar W. 2007. *Postcolonial English: Varieties Around the World*. Cambridge: Cambridge University Press.

Wolfram, W., and E. R. Thomas. 2002. *The development of African American English*. Oxford: Blackwell.

A Popular Work about Prescriptivism

McWhorter, J. 1998. *Word on the street: Debunking the myth of a "pure" standard English*. Cambridge, MA: Perseus.

Overviews of the Languages of the World

Aitchison, J., B. Comrie, M. Polinsky, and S. Matthews. 2003. *The atlas of languages*. New York: Facts on File.

Garry, J., C. Rubino, A. Faber, and R. French, eds. 2001. *Facts about the world's languages: An encyclopedia of the world's major languages*. New York: H. W. Wilson.

Grimes, B. F., ed. 1996. *Ethnologue: Languages of the world*. 13th ed. Dallas, TX: Summer Institute of Linguistics, Inc.

Lyovin, A. V. 1997. *An introduction to the languages of the world*. Oxford: Oxford University Press.

Ostler, Nicholas. 2005. *Empires of the word: A language history of the world*. New York: Harper Collins Publishers.

Ruhlen, M. 1987. *A guide to the world's languages*. Vol. 1, *Classification*. Palo Alto, CA: Stanford University Press.

Woodward, R. D., ed. 2004. *The Cambridge encyclopedia of the world's ancient languages*. Cambridge: Cambridge University Press.

Writing

Coulmas, F. 1996. *The Blackwell encyclopedia of writing systems*. Oxford: Blackwell.

Coulmas, F. 2003. *Writing systems: An introduction to their linguistic analysis*. Cambridge: Cambridge University Press.

Rogers, H. 2005. *Writing systems: A linguistic approach*. Malden, MA: Blackwell Publishing.

Sampson, G. 1985. *Writing systems*. Palo Alto, CA: Stanford University Press.

Spelling Issues

Sebba, Mark. 2007. *Spelling and Society*. Cambridge: Cambridge University Press.

Language Death

Crystal, D. 2000. *Language death*. Cambridge: Cambridge University Press.

Crystal, D. 2003. *English as a global language*. 2nd ed. Cambridge: Cambridge University Press.

Dalby, A. 2003. *Language in danger: The loss of linguistic diversity and the threat to our future*. New York: Columbia University Press.

Grenoble, Lenore A., and Lindsay J. Whaley. 2006. *Saving languages: An introduction to language revitalization*. Cambridge: Cambridge University Press.

Miyaoka, Osahito, Osamu Sakiyama, and Michael E. Krauss, eds. 2007. *The vanishing languages of the Pacific Rim*. Oxford: Oxford University Press.

Nettle, D., and S. Romaine. 2000. *Vanishing voices: The extinction of the world languages*. Oxford: Oxford University Press.

Ancient Languages

Kiss, K. E., ed. 2005. *Universal grammar in the reconstruction of ancient languages*. Berlin and New York: Mouton de Gruyter.

Woodward, R. D., ed. 2004. *The Cambridge encyclopedia of the world's ancient languages*. Cambridge: Cambridge University Press.

Sociolinguistics

Coulmas, Florian. 2005. *Sociolinguistics: The study of speakers' choices*. Cambridge: Cambridge University Press.

Labov, William. 2006. *The social stratification of English in New York City*. 2nd ed. Cambridge: Cambridge University Press.

Language Change

Aitchison, J. 2001. *Language change: Progress or decay?* 3rd ed. Cambridge: Cambridge University Press.
Campbell, L. 2004. *Historical linguistics: An introduction.* 2nd ed. Cambridge, MA: MIT Press.
Hopper, Paul J., and Elizabeth Closs Traugott. 2003. *Grammaticalization.* 2nd ed. Cambridge: Cambridge University Press.
Kiss, Katalin E., ed. 2005. *Universal grammar in the reconstruction of ancient languages.* Berlin and New York: Mouton de Gruyter.
McMahon, A. M. S. 1994. *Understanding language change.* Cambridge: Cambridge University Press.
McMahon, April, and Robert McMahon. 2005. *Language classification by numbers.* Oxford: Clarendon Press.
Traugott, Elizabeth, and Richard B. Dasher. 2003. *Regularity in semantic change.* Cambridge: Cambridge University Press.

Language Evolution

Aitchison, J. 1996. *The seeds of speech: Language origin and evolution.* Cambridge: Cambridge University Press.
Bickerton, D. 1990. *Language and species.* Chicago: Chicago University Press.
Burling, R. 2005. *The talking ape: How language evolved.* Oxford: Oxford University Press.
Deacon, T. 1997. *The symbolic species: The co-evolution of language and the human brain.* New York: Norton.
Lock, A., and C. R. Peters, eds. 1999. *Handbook of human symbolic evolution.* Oxford: Blackwell.
Oller, D. K., and U. Griebel, eds. 2004. *Evolution of communication systems: A comparative approach.* Cambridge, MA: MIT Press.

Gesture Theory of Language Origin

Corballis, M. C. 2002. *From hand to mouth: The origins of language.* Princeton, NJ: Princeton University Press.

2   The History of Linguistics

Harris, R., and T. J. Taylor. 1989. *Landmarks in linguistic thought: The Western tradition from Socrates to Saussure.* London: Routledge.
Joseph, J. E., N. Love, and T. J. Taylor. 2001. *Landmarks in linguistic thought II: The Western tradition in the twentieth century.* London: Routledge.

Robins, R. H. 1967. *A short history of linguistics*. Bloomington, IN: Indiana University Press.

Sampson, G. 1980. *Schools of linguistics*. Palo Alto, CA: Stanford University Press.

Tomalin, Marcus. 2006. *Linguistics and the formal sciences*: *The origins of generative grammar*. Cambridge: Cambridge University Press.

Waterman, John. T. 1963. *Perspectives in linguistics*. Chicago: The University of Chicago Press.

Ferdinand de Saussure

de Saussure, Ferdinand. 2006. *Writings in general linguistics*. Cambridge: Cambridge University Press.

Sanders, Carol, ed. 2004. *The Cambridge Companion to Saussure*. Cambridge: Cambridge University Press.

Other approaches

Hjemslev, L. 1961. *Prolegomena to a theory of language*. Madison: University of Wisconson Press.

Lamb, Sydney. 2004. *Language and reality*. Ed. Jonathan Webster. London: Continuum.

3   Fields of Linguistics

General Reference Works on Linguistics

Aronoff, M., and J. Rees-Miller, eds. 2001. *The handbook of linguistics*. Oxford: Blackwell.

Brown, K., ed. 2005. *Encyclopedia of language and linguistics*. 2nd ed. Oxford: Elsevier.

Bussmann, H. 1996. *Routledge dictionary of language and linguistics*. London: Routledge.

Chapman, S., and C. Routledge, eds. 2005. *Key thinkers in linguistics and the philosophy of language*. Oxford: Oxford University Press.

Frawley, W. J., ed. 2003. *International encyclopedia of linguistics*. 2nd ed. Oxford: Oxford University Press.

General Introductions to Linguistics

Altman, G. T. M. 1997. *The ascent of Babel: An exploration of language, mind, and understanding*. Oxford: Oxford University Press.

Bauer, Laurie. 2007. *The linguistic student's handbook*. Edinburgh: Edinburgh University Press.

Crowley, Terry. 2007. *Field linguistics: A beginner's guide*. Oxford: Oxford University Press.

Crystal, David. 2004. *The language revolution*. Cambridge: Polity Press.

Fasold, Ralph W., and Jeff Connor-Linton, eds. 2006. *An introduction to language and linguistics*. Cambridge: Cambridge University Press.

Fromkin, V., R. Rodman, and N. Hymans. 2003. *An introduction to language*. 7th ed. Boston: Heinle.

Hall, Christopher J. 2005. *An introduction to language & linguistics: Breaking the language spell*. London: Continuum.

Huddleston, Rodney, and Geoffrey K. Pullum. 2005. *A student's introduction to English grammar*. Cambridge: Cambridge University Press.

Hudson, G. 2000. *Essential introductory linguistics*. Oxford: Blackwell.

Justice, P. W. 2004. *Relevant linguistics: An introduction to the structure and use of English for teachers*. 2nd ed. Stanford, CA: CSLI Publications.

Kroeger, Paul R. 2005. *Analyzing grammar: An introduction*. Cambridge: Cambridge University Press.

Macaulay, Monica. 2006. *Surviving Linguistics: A Guide for Graduate Students*. Somerville, MA: Cascadilla Press.

Moravcsik, Edith A. 2006. *An introduction to syntactic theory*. London: Continuum.

Moravcsik, Edith A. 2006. *An introduction to syntax: Fundamentals of syntactic analysis*. London: Continuum.

Napoli, D. J. 1996. *Linguistics*. Oxford: Oxford University Press.

O'Grady, W., J. Archibald, M. Aronoff, and J. Rees-Miller. 2005. *Contemporary linguistics: An introduction*. 5th ed. Boston: Bedford/St. Martin's.

Payne, Thomas E. 2006. *Exploring language structure: A student's guide*. Cambridge: Cambridge University Press.

Tallerman, Maggie. 2005. *Understanding syntax*. 2nd ed. London: Hodder Arnold

Trask, R. L. 1999. *Language: The basics*. 2nd ed. London: Routledge.

Winkler, Elizabeth Grace. 2007. *Understanding language*. London: Continuum.

Yule, George. 2006. *The study of language*. 3rd ed. Cambridge: Cambridge University Press.

Linguistic Anthropology

Duranti, Alessandro, ed. 2006. *A companion to linguistic anthropology*. Malden, MA: Blackwell Publishing.

Ecolinguistics

Fill, Alwin, and Peter Muhlhausler, eds. 2001. *The Ecolinguistics reader: Language, ecology and environment*. London: Continuum.

Forensic Linguistics

Olsson, John. 2004. *Forensic linguistics: An introduction to language, crime and the law*. London: Continuum.

4   The Generative Enterprise

Introduction to the Chomskyan Parametric Approach

Baker, M. C. 2001. *The atoms of language: The mind's hidden rules of grammar*. New York: Basic Books.

About Noam Chomsky

Antony, L. M., and N. Hornstein, eds. 2003. *Chomsky and his critics*. Oxford: Blackwell.
Chomsky, N. 2002. *New horizons in the study of language and mind*. Cambridge: Cambridge University Press.
Chomsky, N., A. Belletti, and L. Rizzi. 2002. *On nature and language*. Cambridge: Cambridge University Press.
McGilvray, J. 1999. *Chomsky: Language, mind, and politics*. Cambridge: Polity Press.
McGilvray, James, ed. 2005. *The Cambridge Companion to Chomsky*. Cambridge: Cambridge University Press.
Smith, N. 1999. *Chomsky: Ideas and ideals*. Cambridge: Cambridge University Press.

Important Works

Chomsky, N. 1981. *Lectures on government and binding*. Dordrecht: Foris Publications.
Chomsky, N. 1995. *The Minimalist Program*. Cambridge, MA: The MIT Press.
Chomsky, N. 2000. *New horizons in the study of language and mind*. Cambridge: Cambridge University Press.
Chomsky, N. 2006. *Language and Mind*. 3rd ed. Cambridge: Cambridge University Press.

Minimalism

Boeckx, C. 2006. *Linguistic minimalism: Origins, concepts, methods, and aims*. Oxford: Oxford University Press.
Bošković, Željko and Howard Lasnik, eds. 2007. *Minimalist syntax: The essential readings*. Malden, MA: Blackwell Publishing.
Cook, V. J., and Mark Newson. 2007. *Chomsky's Universal Grammar: An introduction*. 3rd ed. Malden, MA: Blackwell Publishing.
Hinzen, Wolfram. 2006. *Mind design and minimal syntax*. Oxford: Clarendon Press.

Lasnik, Howard, and Juan Uriagereka with Cedric Boeckx. 2005. *A Course in minimalist syntax: Foundations and prospects*. Malden, MA: Blackwell Publishing.

Critiques of Minimalism

Culicover, Peter W., and Ray Jackendoff. 2005. *Simpler syntax*. Oxford: Oxford University Press.

Goldberg, Adele E. 2006. *Constructions at work: The nature of generalization in language*. Oxford: Clarendon Press.

Johnson, David, and Shalom Lappin. 1997. A critique of the minimalist program. *Linguistics and Philosophy* 20:273-333.

Lappin, Shalom, David Johnson and Robert D. Levine. 2000. The structure of unscientific revolutions. *Natural Language and Linguistic Theory* 18:665-671. [followed by replies and an answer in *NLLT* 18:837-889]

Seuren, Pieter A.M. 2004. *Chomsky's minimalism*. Oxford: Oxford University Press.

Part II: Grammar

5　　The Parts of Grammar

Anderson, J. M. 1992. *Linguistic representation: Structural analogy and stratification*. Berlin: Mouton de Gruyter.

Bromberger, S., and M. Halle. 1989. Why phonology is different. *Linguistic Inquiry* 20:51-70.

Hulst. H. van der. 2005. Why phonology is the same. In *The organization of grammar* [*Festschrift for Henk van Riemsdijk*], ed. H. Broekhuis & J. Koster. Berlin: Mouton de Gruyter.

Hulst, H. van der. 2006. On the parallel organization of linguistic components. *Lingua* 116:657-688.

6　　The Organization of Grammar

Pinker, S. 1999. *Words and rules: The ingredients of language*. New York: Basic Books.

7　　The Grammar as a Checking Device
8　　Checking Three Dimensions and at Two Levels

Jackendoff, R. 2002. *Foundations of language: Brain, meaning, grammar, evolution*. Oxford: Oxford University Press.

Marantz, A. 2006. Generative linguistics within the cognitive neuroscience of language. In *The role of linguistics in cognitive science*, ed. N. A. Ritter. Special triple issue of *The Linguistic Review* 22/2–4: 429-446.

9   Hierarchical Structure Everywhere

Abler, W. 1989. On the particulate principle of self-diversifying systems. *Journal of Social and Biological Structures* 12:1–13.

Hildebrant, S., and A. Tromba. 1985. *Mathematics and Optimal Form*. New York: Scientific American Books, Inc.

Simon, H. 1996. *The sciences of the artificial*. 3rd ed. Cambridge, MA: MIT Press.

Thompson, D'Arcy. 1942. *On growth and form*. 2nd ed. Cambridge: Cambridge University Press. (First ed. 1917.)

Volk, T. 1995. *Metapatterns across space, time and mind*. New York: Columbia University Press.

Part III: The Modules of Grammar

10   Phonological Structures (Word and Sentence Level)

Anderson, J., and C. Ewen. 1987. *Principles of dependency phonology*. Cambridge: Cambridge University Press.

de Lacy, Paul, ed. 2007. *The Cambridge handbook of phonology*. Cambridge: Cambridge University Press.

Ewen, C., and H. van der Hulst. 2001. *The phonological structure of words: An introduction*. Cambridge: Cambridge University Press.

Goldsmith, J., ed. 1995. *The handbook of phonological theory*. Oxford: Blackwell.

Gussenhoven, C., and H. Jacobs. 2005 *Understanding phonology*. 2nd ed. London: Arnold.

Kaye, J. 1989. *Phonology: A cognitive view*. Hillsdale, NJ: Erlbaum.

McMahon, A. 2002. *An introduction to English phonology*. Oxford: Oxford University Press.

Mompeán, José Antonio, ed. 2006. Cognitive Phonology. *International Journal of English Studies* 6/2.

Odden, D. 2005. *Introducing phonology*. Cambridge: Cambridge University Press.

Pierrehumbert, J., M. Beckmann, and B. Ladd. 2000. Conceptual foundations of phonology as a laboratory science. In *Phonological knowledge: Its nature and status*, ed. N. Burton-Roberts, P. Carr, and G. Docherty, 273-304. Oxford: Oxford University Press.

Taylor, J. 2006. Where do phonemes come from? A view from the bottom. *International Journal of English Studies* 6/2:19-54.

Silverman, Daniel. 2006. *A critical introduction to phonology: Of sound, mind, and body*. London: Continuum.

Phonetics

Ashby, M., and J. Maidment. 2005. *Introducing phonetic science*. Cambridge: Cambridge University Press.

Coleman, J. 2005. *Introducing speech and language processing*. Cambridge: Cambridge University Press.

A Popular Work on the Human Voice

Karpf, Anne. 2006. *The human voice: How this extraordinary instrument reveals essentials clues about who we are*. New York: Bloomsbury.

11   Categorial ("Morphological") Structures (Word Level)

Anderson, Stephen. 2005. *Aspects of the theory of clitics*. Oxford: Clarendon Press.

Aronoff, M., and K. Fudeman. 2005. *What is morphology?* Malden, MA: Blackwell Publishing.

Aronoff, Mark. 1994. *Morphology by itself: Stems and inflectional classes*. Cambridge, MA: The MIT Press.

Bauer, L. 2003. *Introducing linguistic morphology*. 2nd ed. Washington, DC: Georgetown University Press.

Haspelmath, Martin. 2002. *Understanding morphology*. London: Arnold.

Inkelas, Sharon, and Cheryl Zoll. 2005. *Reduplication: Doubling in morphology*. Cambridge: Cambridge University Press.

Lieber, Rochelle. 2004. *Morphology and lexical semantics*. Cambridge: Cambridge University Press.

Marchand, H. 1969. *The categories and types of present-day English word-formation*. Munich: Beck.

Plag, I. 2003. *Word-formation in English*. Cambridge: Cambridge University Press.

Spencer, Andrew, and Arnold M. Zwicky, eds. 2001. *The handbook of morphology*. Malden, MA: Blackwell Publishing.

12   Categorial ("Syntactic") Structures (Sentence Level)

Adger, D. 2003. *Core syntax: A minimalist approach*. Oxford: Oxford University Press.

Cinque, G., and R. S. Kayne, eds. 2005. *The Oxford handbook of comparative syntax*. Oxford: Oxford University Press.

Baker, M. C. 2003. *Lexical categories: Verbs, nouns, and adjectives*. Cambridge: Cambridge University Press.

Haegeman, L. 1994. *An introduction to government & binding theory*. Oxford: Blackwell.

Tallerman, M. 1998. *Understanding syntax*. London: Arnold.

Huddleston, R., and G. K. Pullum. 2005. *A student's introduction to English grammar*. Cambridge: Cambridge University Press.

Inflection

Butt, Miriam. 2006. *Theories of Case*. Cambridge: Cambridge University Press.
Corbett, Greville G. 2006. *Agreement*. Cambridge: Cambridge University Press.
Siewierska, Anna. 2004. *Person*. Cambridge: Cambridge University Press.

Binding

Buring, Daniel. 2005. *Binding Theory*. Cambridge: Cambridge University Press.

Function words

Den Dikken, Marcel, and Christina M. Tortora, eds. 2005. *The function of function words and functional categories*. Berlin and New York: Mouton de Gruyter.

13 Semantic Structures (Word and Sentence Level)

Cruse, Alan. 2004. *Meaning in language: An introduction to semantics and pragmatics*. 2nd ed. Oxford: Oxford University Press.
Goddard, C., and A. Wierzbicka. 1994. *Semantic and lexical universals*. Amsterdam: John Benjamins.
Löbner, S. 2002. *Understanding semantics*. London: Arnold.
Murphy, M. Lynne. 2003. *Semantic relations and the lexicon: Antonymy, synonymy and other paradigms*. Cambridge: Cambridge University Press.
Saeed, J. I. 2003. *Semantics*. 2nd ed. Oxford: Blackwell.

Concepts

Margolis, E., and S. Laurence, eds. 1999. *Concepts: Core readings*. Cambridge, MA: The MIT Press.
Prinz, J. J. 2002. *Furnishing the mind: Concepts and their perceptual basis*. Cambridge, MA: MIT Press.

Metaphors

Kövecses, Zoltán. 2007. *Metaphor in Culture: Universality and Variation*. Paperback ed. Cambridge: Cambridge University Press.
Lakoff, George, and Mark Johnson. 1980. *Metaphors we live by*. Chicago: Chicago University Press. [New afterword, 2003.]
Rakova, Marina. 2003. *The extent of the literal: Metaphor, polysemy and theories of concepts*. Basingstoke, UK and New York: Palgrave Macmillan.

14   The Lexicon

Aitchison, J. 1997. *The language web: The power and problem of words. 1996 BBC Reith lectures*. Cambridge: Cambridge University Press

Aitchison, J. 2003. *Words in the mind: An introduction to the mental lexicon*. 3rd ed. Oxford: Blackwell.

Allan, Keith, and Kate Burridge. 2006. *Forbidden words: Taboo and the censoring of language*. Cambridge: Cambridge University Press.

Burridge, Kate. 2004. *Blooming English: Observations on the roots, cultivation and hybrids of the English language*. Cambridge: Cambridge University Press.

Burridge, Kate. 2005. *Weeds in the garden of words: Further observations on the tangled history of the English language*. Cambridge: Cambridge University Press.

Denning, Keith, Brett Kessler, and William R. Leben. 2007. *English vocabulary elements*. 2nd ed. Oxford: Oxford University Press.

Dixon, R. M. W., Bruce Moore, W. S. Ramson, and Mandy Thomas. 2006. *Australian Aboriginal words in English: Their origin and meaning*. 2nd ed. Oxford: Oxford University Press.

Singleton, D. 2000. *Language and the lexicon: An introduction*. London: Arnold

Stockwell, R., and D. Minkova. 2001. *English words: History and structure*. Oxford: Oxford University Press.

15   The Linguistic Structure of Sign Languages

Fisher, S., and H. van der Hulst. 2003. Sign language structures. In *Handbook of Deaf Studies, Language and Education*, 319–331. Oxford: Oxford University Press.

Stokoe, W. C. 1960/1978. *Sign language structure*. 2nd ed. Silver Spring, MD: Linstok Press.

Sandler, Wendy, and Diane Lillo-Martin. 2006. *Sign language and linguistic universals*. Cambridge: Cambridge University Press.

Wilbur, R. B. 1987. *American Sign Language: Linguistic and applied dimensions*. 2nd ed. Boston: Little, Brown.